HUMAN SECURITY
& *business*

01

BENJAMIN K. LEISINGER
MARC PROBST

Published by rüffer & rub
All rights reserved
Copyright © 2007 by rüffer & rub
www.ruefferundrub.ch

Printed in Italy by Zanardi Group

Edited by Benjamin Leisinger, coordinator of the sympo-
sium "Human Rights Values and International Business
Transactions" and Marc Probst, Political Affairs Division IV,
Federal Department of Foreign Affairs.

"Human Security and Business" is the first volume of a
series of books which takes up themes of the annual
conferences of Political Affairs Division IV (PD IV) and
of other events related to human security. This volume
is based on PD IV's annual conference 2006 "Political Risks
in a Globalized Marketplace: Company Approaches to
Conflict Prevention and Human Rights" as well as on the
symposium "Human Rights Values and International
Business Transactions organized in January 2007 by the
Novartis Foundation for Sustainable Development,
in collaboration with the Law Faculty of the University
of Basel."

ISBN 978-3-907625-39-2

Content

PREFACE
Thomas Greminger

The liberalization of global trade and investment has led to an unprecedented surge in the transnational activities of companies and has had a positive impact on business opportunities. However, the trend of moving operations and investing abroad is also confronting companies with uncertainties and risks, such as inadequate legal security (for example, the lack of a functioning system of property rights), exposure to unpredictable government regulations (for example, concerning health and safety), as well as political instability. In parallel to these increased risks, globalization is also having the effect of refocusing many social expectations from state to private actors, in particular to international companies. This development has arisen as a result of the view shared by many that the unprecedented powers that corporations have now acquired place upon them correspondingly important social responsibilities. Consequently, demands are now being made and pressures exerted on foreign investors to promote environmental, social, as well as human rights issues.

The concept of corporate responsibility covers a wide variety of issues including climate change, environmental protection, HIV prevention, conflict transformation, and human rights. The common denominator of all these aspects is the expectation placed on companies to take into account the needs of all stakeholders in their business operations. For companies, corporate responsibility should be seen as an instrument to help them manage and mitigate their operating risks, as well as address newly awakening social expectations. It is crucial to understand corporate responsibility not as an ideal, which companies of a particular size or those active in a particular sector should subscribe to, but rather as a means to enhance their competitiveness and business performance.

The issue of human security and business is the least developed aspect of corporate responsibility, and the one that harbours the most potential for misunderstandings and confusion. Human security is a key element of Switzerland's foreign policy. The concept of human security goes further than what is traditionally understood by the term territorial security. It puts the emphasis on the protection of individuals from political violence, war and arbitrary acts. Through promoting human rights, humanitarian and migration policy as well as peace policy Switzerland can create human habitats that are free of fear. Human security is also in the interests of companies because the security of individuals is an important factor for ensuring political stability in the broadest sense and, as such, reduces political risks and contributes to consolidating the globalization process.

The Political Affairs Division IV (PD IV), with its staff of about 70, is the center of expertise in the areas of peace policy, human rights policy, humanitarian policy, and migration policy of the Swiss Federal Department of Foreign Affairs. Due to the impact of globalization on human rights, the issue of human security and business has become one of PD IV's priority areas of activity. We aim to support the private sector by developing tools and policies with a view to maximizing the impact of those aspects of companies' behaviour that strengthen human security. To achieve this, it is important to establish a close partnership with the business community.

Every autumn, PD IV organizes a conference on a topic dedicated to one of its focal countries or themes: "Political Risks in a Globalized Marketplace: Company Approaches to Conflict Prevention and Human Rights" was the theme of last year's annual conference, which took place in September 2006. In January 2007, the Novartis Foundation for Sustainable Development, in collaboration with the Law Faculty of the University of Basel, organized a symposium on the subject "Human Rights Values and International Business Transactions".

These two events and the current importance of this issue for politics, business and civil society have led us to the idea of publishing the results of these discussions in the form of this book. Our aim is to make readers more familiar with the current trends and future challenges of globalization. We address this increasingly topical issue from the perspectives of foreign policy, private companies and civil society organisations, and describe new social expectations and how companies are responding to them. The book is however not limited to the results of the PD IV 2006 Annual Conference and the symposium on "Human Rights Values and International Business Transactions". It also presents the opinions of a number of experts who did not participate in these two events as well as various views expressed in discussions conducted at the Global Compact Leaders' Summit, in July 2007 in Geneva, where issues related to corporate responsibility were discussed extensively. PD IV intends to start with "Human Security and Business" a series of books which takes up themes of the annual conferences of PD IV and other events related to human security.

I would like to extend a warm word of thanks to all those who contributed to this book, in particular

+ KIaus Leisinger, President and CEO of the Novartis Foundation for Sustainable Development, and Ingeborg Schwenzer, professor at the Law Faculty of the University of Basel, for co-chairing and financing the symposium on "Human Rights Values and International Business Transactions".
+ Wolfgang Amadeus Bruelhart, Head of Human Rights Policy Section and Natalie Erard of Political Affairs Division IV, for their valuable help in revising and editing the book.

The views expressed in the essays and interviews are those of the authors and need not concur with the position of the Political Division IV of the Federal Department of Foreign Affairs (DFA).

SWISS FOREIGN POLICY AND BUSINESS*

SENTIMENTALISM OR INTEREST?

Micheline Calmy-Rey

Switzerland is campaigning for a world in which everyone can live in peace and security, human rights are duly respected and conflicts are resolved through dialogue. The main aim behind our efforts to promote peace and the observation of human rights – which are key elements of our foreign policy – is to enable human beings to feel safe and secure.

But these key elements cannot be separated from our economic interests. Switzerland is fully aware of this link and in fact makes it the basis on which it defines its foreign policy goals. In our 1993 Foreign Policy Report, and again in the report for 2000, equal importance was attached to the promotion of the economy, development policy, the preservation of natural resources, and peace and human rights policy. Switzerland's foreign policy is based on these five pillars and takes account of the fact that the promotion of development, human rights and peace is the basis for securing sustainable prosperity.

For a long time, however, a short-term, if not somewhat simplistic, perspective linked our commitment to human rights and the promotion of peace with a sentimental idealism, in stark contrast to the supposed realism of economic interests. But of course this was entirely on the wrong track:

Firstly, because human security is also a precondition for stability and security in the broadest sense, and as such reduces political risks. The threats that weigh on individual people endanger their existing values. The security of each individual goes hand in hand with the security of investments.

And secondly, because Switzerland depends on an open and globalised economy. But the globalisation process is still fragile, and it will only be able to firmly establish itself once it is seen to bring human as well as economic security.

This is the reason why I believe that, in the next few years, the interaction between politics and business will intensify and gain in importance within the globalisation process. I also believe that a better understanding of this interaction between business interests and those relating to development, peace and human rights policy will be essential if we are to successfully deal with the challenges we face today and in the future.

I am, of course, aware that economic interests and the other pillars of foreign policy can give rise to difficult choices and trade-offs. But the difficult situations and incoherencies we have experienced in the past – for example, dormant assets or our foreign policy during the era of apartheid in South Africa – have clearly shown us that, over the long term, we can only maximise our gains through strong coherence.

Our foreign policy sets out to convince and encourage players in the international arena to adopt an attitude and observe rules that are in line with our interests. This applies to governments, of course, but to an ever increasing extent it also applies to companies.

Switzerland needs to increase its prosperity. It also needs to create new jobs and find new business partners. But emerging markets, which open up enormous business potentials, are often associated with major economic and political risks. These countries, which are anxious to open their markets, are not yet able to guarantee political stability, and can thus be equated with countries towards which Switzerland offers its support in terms of development, promotion of peace and respect of human rights.

For the past 15 years, for example, Switzerland and China have been engaged in a process of human rights dialogue, and within the framework of this process, questions concerning the relationship between human rights and business have emerged, and these have since become an integral part of the ongoing dialogue. Swiss companies active in China, as well as Chinese companies themselves, require codes of conduct and identical and valid standards for all business players. In this way, companies and governments are able to respond to the demands of society in terms of transparency, responsibility and progress. One of the central issues in China today in the area of implementation of human, economic and social rights concerns the protection of private property as a fundamental human right. In June 2006, the Federal Department of Foreign Affairs and the University of Zurich published the first "Swiss Human Rights Book", which is entirely devoted to this topic. Switzerland is also considering the option of launching a multilateral diplomatic initiative aimed at more precisely defining the concept of the right of property ownership.

Switzerland's foreign policy sets out to promote peace and human rights by aiming at strengthening human security. The concept of human security focuses on the individual, and in this way it deepens the traditional understanding of state security. In order to contribute towards the promotion of human security, we work with instruments in the areas of human rights policy, humanitarian policy and peace policy.

However, the defence and promotion of human rights and conflict transformation are still kept on the sidelines in debates on the ties between foreign policy and economic interests. It appears that they continue to be regarded as tasks that are solely the responsibility of the state, although the private sector also benefits from political stability, which is directly linked with human security. The upheavals that we witnessed in Eastern Europe at the beginning of the 1990s are a good example here. They kindled fears concerning political insecurity, instability and a possible mass exodus of refugees. But our aid to Eastern Europe helped bring about a transformation of these countries, which have meanwhile become important partners and export markets for Swiss companies. This transformation process was in the interests of both the state and the private sector.

The importance the Federal Council attaches to the promotion of peace and human rights means that we take these into account throughout the entire field of political activity. The leitmotif here is "do no harm". When we make decisions that have an impact on our foreign policy – for example, concerning the export of war materials – we are anxious to avoid acting in contradiction to the principles of human rights and the promotion of peace. And this approach could also be adopted by players in the private sector. Pursuing the essential objective shared by all companies, namely

to make a profit, does not necessarily have to have negative consequences on the human rights situation. The private sector needs to
find a suitable balance between the pursuit of profit and the long-
term preservation of conditions that are favourable to investment,
production and business. In other words, the private sector should
also be committed to the promotion of human rights and peace
within the bounds of reason.

Switzerland wants to gain a better grasp of these complementary and reciprocal effects by creating dialogue and learning
platforms at the national and international levels for players from
the private sector, the political arena and civil society.

In this connection I would like to say a few words about
the Global Compact Network of Switzerland, which was founded
in 2006 by a large number of Swiss companies. I welcome this
private sector initiative, which was launched to support the UN
Global Compact that was initiated by UN Secretary-General Kofi
Annan in 1999. Networks that are active at the national level can
play a major role in the progress of the UN Global Compact. The
Swiss network also aims to more effectively integrate small and
medium-sized companies into the UN Global Compact. In Switzerland, we possess the necessary expertise to effectively help small
and medium-sized companies develop their sense of corporate responsibility, and thus safeguard and strengthen their competitive
capacity on the international markets.

Switzerland together with the Sustainability Forum Zurich
entered into a public-private partnership to develop the UN Global Pact learning platform for small and medium-sized companies.
This project is primarily addressed to internationally active small
and medium-sized companies, and focuses on identifying the main
issues relating to corporate responsibility on the part of such companies, initially in the area of human rights. It set out to identify
specific action fields, as well as provide a forum for dialogue and
exchanges of views. The ultimate goal is to develop and implement
good corporate responsibility practice.

As this example show, we are not trying to tell companies what to do, nor are we trying to stipulate the services they should provide as contributions towards the promotion of peace and human rights. Instead, what we are doing is endeavouring to find solutions through dialogue.

I wish to emphasise the fact here that the formulation of restrictive legal provisions relating to the respect of human rights and transformation of conflicts is not an aim in itself: on the contrary, it is necessary for voluntary initiatives and existing instruments to be rendered more effective, since we have to be aware of the fact that voluntary actions and self-regulation have their limits. It is often the case that the companies that take such actions are those that are the most visible and have the broadest public exposure.

I would like to cite the mining industry as an example, or to be more precise, gold or diamond mining, both of which have demonstrated that self-regulation can certainly function very effectively. These companies are often active in conflict regions. At first sight, they do not appear to display much interest in conflict transformation – and here they are of course well within their rights, since conflict management is in fact the responsibility of the state. However, their activities automatically make them a party in the conflict. Some non-governmental human rights organisations that are concerned about the financing of "blood diamonds" have consequently threatened to boycott the companies concerned. One international group that was the target of such threats decided to take steps to safeguard its reputation. Since taking this decision, it has been actively participating in the creation of a certification system to ensure legal trading in diamonds – a move generally referred to as the Kimberley process.

The state can certainly support this type of process between government and private sector. In this case, for example, Switzerland was strongly involved in the implementation of the Kimberley process.

But we can also imagine an inter-governmental process that could be complemented by a process led by the private sector at a later date. I would like to cite the following example here:

In some conflict regions, companies more and more frequently call on the services of private security organisations. But how can we know whether these groups are integral and which legal provisions govern their activities? In order to find answers to such questions, Switzerland launched an initiative together with the International Committee of the Red Cross calling for such organisations and states to respect the provisions of international humanitarian law and the principles of human rights. By means of this inter-governmental initiative, Switzerland wants to reinforce the existing legal principles and submit recommendations to governments. And I can readily imagine a process, initiated by Switzerland for private security companies, aimed at developing standards and good practices for private companies delivering security services in conflict areas and weak states.

Regardless of its effectiveness, self-regulation nonetheless has its limits. In some areas it remains essential for the state to issue directives: for example, corruption of foreign officials and private citizens abroad is a criminal offence in Switzerland. Furthermore, Switzerland supports recommendations developed by institutions such as the Organisation for Economic Co-operation and Development (OECD) or the International Labour Organisation (ILO) which are targeted at enterprises.

Foreign policy and business interests coincide on a number of points – or to put it another way, there is a pronounced coincidence of interests. There is a particularly large number of such points in the area of development and integration policy, and here they are more readily accepted than in the fields of peace and human rights policy. But co-operation in general, and in the area of promotion of peace and human rights in particular, is intensifying, and needs to continue to intensify. What is required is a close partnership between politics, business and civil society.

I see particular potential for synergies in working together to promote our common interests:

+ Switzerland is contributing towards the stabilisation of developing and transition countries, and supports efforts to reduce political and economic risks.
+ Switzerland is endeavouring to raise awareness among business, political and civil society players about the issue of human security and business. It encourages exchanges of know-how and experience between players in these three areas, and sets out to form ties between the various sectors.
+ Switzerland supports existing multilateral initiatives such as the UN Global Compact, and is actively involved in developing such initiatives in a qualitative sense.
+ Switzerland provides support by creating partnerships and financing projects aimed at defining conceptual issues and finding instruments and opportunities for translating fundamental principles into concrete action.

Switzerland is regarded as an independent and neutral country that is committed to the promotion of peace and human rights. To some extent we owe this image and this credibility to the establishment of the International Committee of the Red Cross and the Geneva Conventions. And Swiss companies also benefit from this image.

So let us learn how to make good use of our political and economic weight. Let us learn how to make good use of our influence. And let us present a Switzerland that is able to play a pioneering role in creating a business sector that is aware of the issues relating to human security. Because those who are afraid of change will in the end experience both fear and change at the same time.

02

HUMAN SECURITY AND BUSINESS – A CONTRADICTION IN TERMS?*

Marc Probst

" The private sector and security are linked
in many ways, most obviously because
thriving markets and human security go
hand in hand. Global corporations can
do more than simply endorse the virtues of
the market, however. Their active support
for better governance policies can help
create environments in which both markets
and human security flourish."

Kofi Annan
Former United Nations Secretary-General

1. Introduction

The history of the world has included a number of attempts at "globalisation" in one form or another. And yet what today we know
colloquially as globalisation is not simply "a continuation of the
familiar."[1] The extent to which all areas of life – economic, political and social – are now interconnected, creating opportunities
as well as risks, has taken on a new dimension and is clearly visible in the daily life of everyone. Public interest is above all focused
on the effects of the process of economic globalisation and on the
transnational companies driving this process. But while the critics of globalisation and of the corporations in the driving seat see
the process as the cause of the sufferings in this world – underde-
velopment, conflicts and human rights violations – the defenders
of advancing economic globalisation share the neoliberal[2] assumption that profit maximisation is a company's only responsibility.
Both views are undifferentiated, ideologically inspired and simplistic. The fact is that in today's world there are many problems that
do not stop at national borders: environmental pollution, diseases

and terrorism to name but the most obvious. It is also a fact that 18% of the world's population still live on less than a dollar a day,[3] that 854 million people are chronically undernourished, that atrocious innerstate conflicts are raging in many parts of the world.[4] And it is a fact that the neoliberal logic behind economic globalisation places economic interests above social interests. It is mistaken and short-sighted, however, to make economic globalisation and its champions responsible for all the world's evils. It is indeed true that globalisation must not be measured solely as growth in prosperity. It also needs to be assessed in terms of its ability to promote human rights, stability and the possibility for all people to enjoy human security and a life "free from fear" and "free from want." In this context it is equally important for each individual, as well as the political, economic and civil society institutions, to accept responsibility and to agree on universally accepted principles and standards so as to shape the various processes of globalisation.

2. From territorial security to human security

The past 15 years have brought sweeping changes in the security situation around the world. The end of the East-West conflict greatly reduced global tensions and potential threats, and many proxy wars were brought to an end. Quantitative surveys including the Human Security Report 2005[5] show that the world overall has become a more secure and peaceful place. However at the same time new conflicts, and new kinds of conflict – civil wars, armed separatist movements and violence within societies – as well as terrorist attacks, natural disasters and pandemics, are increasingly being brought to the public's attention. And it is to be feared that climate change too will lead to political tensions. Human rights violations associated with natural disasters and wars over scarce resources already count among the major risks in the countries of the South.

As part of efforts to come to terms with all these various risks and threats, a new and broader definition of security was developed in the 1990s, the so-called "human security" concept. This goes further than the traditional security concept which is limited to the protection of national territory, shifting the focus to the individual. Broadly defined, human security includes poverty, hunger, disease, environmental disaster and physical violence that threaten the security of individuals and, as they spread, global security. The declared aim behind the concept is to make it possible for each individual to enjoy a life that is "free from fear" and "free from want." The United Nations Development Programme's Human Development Report of 1994 listed seven aspects of human security: economic security, security of food supplies as well as health, ecological, personal, social and political security. This broadly defined concept has been narrowed somewhat in the context of Switzerland's foreign policy. Thomas Greminger, Head of the Political Affairs Division IV (PD IV) of the Federal Department of Foreign Affairs points out in his introductory remarks that human security is above all implemented through human rights policy, peace policy and humanitarian policy, the purpose being greater protection from political violence, war and arbitrary acts, particularly for the most vulnerable groups.

Human rights have become increasingly important since the end of the Cold War, and now play a major role in all aspects of human security. In the words of Kofi Annan – there is no development without security, no security without development and neither security nor development without respect for human rights.[6] The consensus in the international community today is that it is imperative to include the protection of basic human rights in the concept of state sovereignty. If a government is not in a position to protect its citizens from the most serious violations of human rights, then it is the responsibility of the United Nations to guarantee this protection.[7] The discussion on the promotion of human security is of course not limited to state actors. The past 15 years have seen the emergence of a lively debate on the role of the business community in the promotion of human rights and peace.

"Today, alongside governments, companies often are viewed as a source or cause of human rights abuse, and at the same time as international actors with the capacity to promote human rights.[8]" Again in the words of Kofi Annan: "Private companies operate in many zones of conflict or conflict-prone countries. Their decisions – on investment and employment, on relations with local communities, on their own security arrangement – can help a country turn its back on conflict, or exacerbate the tensions that fuelled the conflict in the first place."[9]

3. A return to ethics through economic globalisation?

The theories on free trade and the division of labour formulated by such economists as Adam Smith and David Ricardo in the 18th and 19th centuries are still today the determining factors of economic activity and practices. The central credo is that the free market, untrammelled by state interference, will perform in an optimum manner and promote the well being of all. This belief and its promulgation was institutionalised following the Second World War with the founding of the International Monetary Fund, the World Bank and, at a later stage, the World Trade Organization. Right up to the present, transnational companies have worked hand in hand with national governments for the purpose of dismantling barriers to trade and achieving the liberalisation of international trade. The interconnection of national markets has led to the emergence of a world market with competition on a global scale. Expansion abroad has thus become a survival strategy for companies. The transnational corporations export their investments, production and sales to regions where lower costs increase their international competitiveness. This has created competition between locations, which affects the developing countries and emerging economies as well as the industrialised nations. Being dependent on direct foreign investment, the developing countries and emerging economies often have little interest in creating the framework conditions required for the protection and promotion of human rights.

Economic globalisation also has an impact on the home market. Companies are no longer as dependent on the home market as an outlet for their products as they once were. Their attention has shifted to the relative costs associated with the country of origin. In industrialised nations this means that economic interests tend to have greater weight than social matters.

What has long been obvious to those concerned with business ethics is now becoming clear to us all. There are no market-oriented control mechanisms at the global level capable of cushioning the negative impact of globalisation. Institutions that might be able to take on such a role, the World Trade Organization for example, tend to take the view that "liberalisation of the economy is in the interest of people all over the world."[10] Trade questions have a higher priority than health, the environment or human rights standards. And yet Adam Smith himself acknowledged that the theory of a free market economy could only function properly in a society of moral subjects.[11] And Milton Friedman, who is best remembered for his quip that "the business of business is business," nonetheless wrote in the New York Times Magazine in 1970 that the responsibility of companies is to "make as much money as possible while conforming to the basic rules of the society, both those embodied in law and those embodied in ethical custom." And this is precisely the crucial point: the economy is embedded in a national system of laws and in a system of social expectations, which constitute the framework conditions for corporate activities. For a long time the policy of business has been determined by the so-called "shareholder value" which makes the prosperity of shareholders and profit maximisation the essential goal of the company. However, to the extent that companies' ability to act and their influence has grown, so groups of "stakeholders" (i.e. owners, workers, customers, suppliers, trade unions, the local population etc.) increasingly expect these economic actors to refrain from abusing the freedoms entrusted to them and instead to use them in a responsible manner while respecting certain minimum social and ecological standards, both at home and abroad.

The question of the responsibility of business is not a new one. It has already been discussed in relation to the postulate of the new economic order in the 1970s and 1980s, in the United Nations and elsewhere. The UN created its own Commission on Transnational Corporations, which as of 1977 coordinated negotiations on a special Code of Conduct for such companies. Due to certain political developments at the end of 1970s, the negotiations on the Code bogged down. Discussions on the responsibility of business are again receiving attention for the following reasons:

+ In connection with South Africa's policy of Apartheid as well as negative events involving companies in developing countries and emerging economies.
+ Pressure from ethical investors. Socially Responsible Investment (SRI), i.e. ethical funds which moderate the classical financial objectives (income, wealth creation, security, yield, availability) by social, ethical or ecological parameters. These are particularly widespread in the USA and the United Kingdom and are also gaining popularity in Switzerland. Indeed, investments in SRI products in Switzerland in 2006 were worth CHF 17.9 billion.[12] Institutional investors such as pension funds and insurance companies are in the front ranks. And although the impact of disinvestment is far from certain, institutional investors in the USA for example have put pressure on companies doing business in Sudan, and this has resulted in the withdrawal of a number of companies (including Swiss). Philippe Spicher, CEO of Centre Info and President of the SiRi Company, in an article on "the place of human rights in investment practices" speaks of various instruments and techniques that enable investors to integrate human rights in their investment practices. Georg Kell, Executive Director, UN Global Compact, cites research done by Goldmann Sachs which highlights that companies considered leaders in implementing environmental, social and governance policies have outperformed the general stock market by 25% since August 2005.

+ Through increased ethical awareness in companies. Corporate responsibility is above all value management and increasingly "consultants and managers concern themselves with corporate responsibility and sustainability and long for ethical approaches, that go beyond mere fine words."[13] Speaking to us in an interview, Eberhard von Koerber said that most entrepreneurs are aware of their responsibility to society. From the point of view of business ethics, there has to be a limit to profit maximisation. This limit must reflect the concerns of all stakeholders. So business should no longer be entirely based on the principle of profit maximisation. It should also take note of and incorporate ethical principles that have been identified through dialogue with other stakeholders. This is known as the "stakeholder view."

+ In parallel there is a growing conviction that corporate responsibility can bring economic benefits, whereas the non-observance of social and ecological concerns can have serious legal consequences, as well as on a company's reputation as Fritz Brugger, Senior Consultant and Thomas Streiff, Partner, Brugger and Partners, point out in their article.

The responsibility of companies is usually discussed under the label of "Corporate Responsibility" or "Corporate Social Responsibility," defined by the EU Commission in the following way: "a concept whereby companies integrate social and environmental concerns in their business operations and in their interactions with their stakeholders on a voluntary basis."[14] As a subdivision of Corporate Responsibility, Corporate Governance sums up the ways and means of successfully managing a company with a sense of responsibility and ethical commitment.

4. Human security and business

There are currently over 72 countries in which foreign companies operate that are categorised as somewhat, very or extremely lacking in security. They fall into the following categories: weak governance zones, authoritarian states, situations in which the local community exhibits particular cultural or religious sensitivity, or in which the local community is dependent on water or land resources.[15] On the one hand, in all of the above-mentioned contexts, companies through their activities become actors in the society; have an influence on their employees and on the community in which they operate, and often also on the local and national authorities; face risks including legal uncertainty, but also the expectations of the population or international civil society. On the other hand, the populations in these states often live in difficult conditions, with no freedom of opinion or worse. The weaker the state monopoly of violence is the greater is the risk of human rights violations and conflict. In extreme cases the state monopoly of violence collapses and armed groups fill the vacuum. Violence at levels below the threshold of war together with serious human rights violations becomes the everyday reality for the populations concerned.

Foreign investment gives companies influence on the context in which they operate and thus on human security. There is a trade-off between investment and human rights violations or conflicts. Companies can cause or prolong conflicts and human rights violations:

+ In its final report the UN Panel of Experts on the Illegal Exploitation of Natural Resources and Other Forms of Wealth of DR Congo identified 85 companies which directly profited from the war economy and thus helped to maintain the conflict.[16]
+ Companies from the extractive sector in particular, which make use of private security firms, are regularly accused of being involved in human rights violations in that the private security firms use violence to put down demonstrations or participate in torturing the leaders.
+ Various firms have had to agree not to recruit or to continue employing persons belonging to certain ethnic groups. In the USA, for example, accusations of this sort have already resulted in companies having to pay millions of dollars in fines. In Af-

rican countries discriminatory policies against certain employees have already led to a number of strikes and the destruction of infrastructure.

And vice versa: situations involving human rights violations and conflict have an influence on investments, for example when foreign companies are targeted by groups of insurgents.

Companies, especially those operating in developing countries and emerging economies, must decide how they wish to deal with human rights and conflict-related risks, i.e. whether they wish to promote or obstruct human security. Should they profit from the situation in a country? Or on the contrary, should they act in a human rights and conflict-sensitive way? Peter Buomberger, Group Head Government and Industry Affairs, Zurich Financial Services, argues that enterprises can contribute to an improved investment climate by operating in accordance with international human rights standards. Eberhard von Koerber who chairs an international Investment and Asset Management company, Eberhard von Koerber AG, in Zurich, refers to a positive example from South Africa in the era of Apartheid, in which a Western company made the opening of a factory contingent on non-whites being treated in conditions of equality with their white colleagues.

Human rights and conflict-related risks are just as much a concern for small-to-medium-sized enterprises (SMEs). To begin with, because smaller projects are increasingly monitored by civil society organisations. Ratings concerning toys and human rights published recently in the Swiss press by Swiss civil society organisations was severely critical of companies, including SMEs, for disregarding social contract standards. It was also pointed out that many SMEs in the chain of suppliers to the bigger companies are expected to "tow the line". In an article on this subject, Thomas Streiff and Fritz Brugger explore the interface between SMEs and human rights, describing the problem areas and taking a pragmatic look at the challenges and how these can be converted into opportunities.

Human rights can serve as guiding principles for drafting corporate responsibility policies. But it is important for companies that they are fully aware of the human rights and conflict-related risks to understand that their well-meaning efforts can be counterproductive unless guided by comprehensive knowledge of the local circumstances:

+ A mining company that paid compensation to the local community closest to the place of production as part of its corporate responsibility programme only created rivalry within the society.
+ A telecommunications company buys minerals from an intermediary, who is in turn supplied by a warlord. The latter uses the money to purchase weapons.[17]

5. Human rights and business: a red flag?

The current human rights discussion on the question of the responsibility of companies for human rights has divided opinions along two main lines: the obligation of the state for the protection of human rights and approaches according to which companies should have direct human rights obligations.

Article 56 of the Charter of the United Nations requires all member states, individually and together, to work with the Organisation to achieve its objectives (which include the implementation of human rights). A state that adheres to the UN – which at present counts 192 members out of a possible 193 states – recognises, politically at least, the universal validity of human rights as being necessary for the creation of stability and public welfare.[18]

Human rights is a concept which holds that the individual is entitled to make legal claims on the state for the protection of fundamental aspects of the human person and human dignity. The ultimate source of human rights is the International Bill of Human Rights of the United Nations. This includes the Universal Declaration of Human Rights (UDHR), the International Covenant on Economic, Social and Cultural Rights (66 signatories, 156 parties) and the International Covenant on Civil and Political Rights (67 signatories, 160 parties).[19] Since 1948, the corpus of human rights legislation has been augmented by various human rights conventions including those of regional organisations, such as the European Convention on Human Rights. According to the traditional interpretation of international law, states have three-fold human rights obligations:

+ Each state must respect and apply human rights and refrain from violating these rights, for example by renouncing the use of interrogation methods that cause serious suffering to persons held in detention.
+ States must protect human rights against third parties' infringement; the obligations of the state with regard to human rights include direct responsibility for punishing human rights violations by private actors, including companies, and for measures to prevent such violations. In some of the more recent human rights conventions, such as the Convention on the Protection of the Rights and Dignity of Persons with Disabilities, this is expressly stated. The UN committees to which the states must report on their observance of the various conventions increasingly pay attention to this obligation to protect human rights.
+ Every state must guarantee the complete implementation of rights for those in which they are not yet fully realised.

Although states are above all under an obligation to ensure the protection of human rights, most states including those of the industrialised world do not act on it, or do so only partially. John Ruggie, Special Representative of the UN Secretary-General on Human Rights and Transnational Corporations as well as other businesses, notes in his final report,[20] "the state duty to protect against non-state abuses is part of the international human rights regime's very foundation. The duty requires states to play a key role in regulating and adjudicating abuse by business enterprises or risk breaching their international obligations", and again: "not all state structures as a whole appear to have internalised the full meaning of the state duty to protect, and its implications with regard to preventing and punishing abuses by non-state actors, including business. Nor do states seem to be taking full advantage of the many legal and policy tools at their disposal to meet their treaty obligations."

The second point of focus in the debate on business and human rights concerns the question whether or not companies have direct human rights obligations.

The Universal Declaration on Human Rights (UDHR) holds that each individual and all organs of society are under an obligation to promote the rights and freedoms set down in the Declaration and to ensure that these are recognised. Business enterprises are thus included, although the UDHR is not an instrument that is binding in international law. The Human Rights Commission's Subcommission on the Promotion and Protection of Human Rights addressed this question in the 1990s. In 2003 it published a document entitled "Draft Norms on the Responsibilities of Transnational Corporations and Other Business Enterprises with regard to Human Rights". These norms are a compendium of human rights standards of particular relevance to companies. While they confirm that the main responsibility for human rights lies with the state, there are nonetheless important areas in which companies have special obligations: non-discrimination; the right to security, employment rights, the promotion of economic, social and cultural rights, and the right to development in accordance with company capacities. The Office of the UN High Commissioner for Human Rights found the Draft Norms useful, but denied them any binding legal force. In reaction to this, UN Secretary-General Kofi Annan appointed Professor John Ruggie as his Special Representative in 2005. Ruggie published his final report, "Mapping International Standards of Responsibility and Accountability for Corporate Acts", in the spring of 2007. His report is published in this book on page 232. Up to now, companies have had no direct human rights obligations – either in international law or in customary law.[21] This leaves a significant gap in the protection of human rights, especially since not all states have signed the relevant human rights instruments or are either not able or not willing to implement them.

However, John Ruggie points out in his final report that developments can be discerned that are beginning to fill the legal vacuum. Ruggie argues that individual punishability for war crimes, genocide and crimes against humanity is increasingly being adopted in national law, and in some instances it even applies to legal persons. There are some cases, though only in a few jurisdictions, where direct legal enforcement is possible in national courts. The most celebrated example is the US Alien Tort Claims Act (civil law). This law dating from 1789 enables private plaintiffs to bring US and foreign private enterprises before a US court for violations of human rights. In 2001, the Presbyterian Church of Sudan accused the Canadian oil company Talisman Energy and the state of Sudan of collaborating in human rights violations. The church argued that these violations amounted to genocide. The judge ruled that the company could be tried for serious human rights violations. In times of conflict, companies are also subject to international humanitarian law, which must be respected by all conflicting parties regardless of whether they are state or non-state actors. This means that companies could theoretically be made responsible for violations of international humanitarian law if they are directly involved in conflicts, for example in the form of security forces that have been explicitly employed for this purpose.[22] An interesting approach is adopted by Ingeborg Schwenzer, Professor of Private Law at the University of Basel and Benjamin Leisinger, former Research and Teaching Assistant at the University of Basel, in their article. On the basis of the "Convention on Contracts for the International Sale of Goods" (CISG, ratified by 67 States) they examine the question: What can a buyer do if it realizes that the products it has purchased were produced under child labour? What are the seller's possibilities if it learns about serious human rights violations by one of its buyers, where one of its products is involved? They also examine the situation when the recourse to public law is not possible.

The introduction of instruments that would impose binding human rights obligations on companies has been blocked not least by the resistance of western industrial countries which, as has been shown, consider economic interests to be more important than social ones. This blockage has prompted the launch of various initiatives to encourage companies to comply with human rights and other social standards. Among the most important of these are the following three:

+ In 1972 the International Labour Organization (ILO) drafted the Tripartite Declaration on Principles concerning Multinational Enterprises and Social Policy. To this day it has remained the only code of ethics on the social responsibility of transnational corporations adopted by an international organisation. The declaration is addressed directly to the governments of ILO member states, to participating employer and employee associations and to transnational corporations operating in their areas. The declaration is not as yet binding in international law. Its 59 paragraphs state principles in the fields of employment, training, working and living conditions and labour relations with which governments, employer and employee associations should voluntarily comply.
+ The OECD "Guidelines for Multinational Enterprises" were adopted for the first time by the governments of the OECD member states in 1976 as an annex to the "Declaration on International Investment and Multinational Enterprises." These guidelines are non-binding recommendations to transnational companies but they are also intended as an orientation for small and medium-sized companies. They are a joint recommendation by all of today's 30 OECD member states as well as by Argentina, Brazil, Chile, Estonia, Israel, Lithuania and Slovakia. The revised version of 2000 expressly contains a general

exhortation to respect human rights. The commentary stresses that it is the task of states to protect human rights and basic freedoms. However, it also recognises that in areas where corporate behaviour and human rights overlap, transnational corporations have a role to play in human rights. The idea of human rights protection is also mentioned in various places in the guidelines.

✦ At the World Economic Forum in Davos in 1999, the then UN Secretary-General Kofi Annan launched the UN Global Compact. The Global Compact is a worldwide, voluntary compact that supports companies in efforts to structure and to implement their corporate responsibility according to ten principles covering human rights, labour norms, protection of the environment and the fight against corruption. The Global Compact addresses all leading social actors, including governments, civil society and academic institutions. This initiative has now been signed by over 3000 companies throughout the world, including 25 Swiss companies, ranging from major corporations such as ABB and Novartis, to small and medium-sized companies such as Air Zermatt or MSM Fininco.

In addition, numerous other private sector-specific, country-specific and international initiatives on human rights were also developed. These initiatives are based on the principle of voluntary self-regulation and in most cases have no, or only weak, monitoring and accountability mechanisms. Many are very general in their formulation, and in some instances they overlap. A veritable jungle of initiatives has developed, which is very confusing, particularly for SMEs.

For a long time companies argued that human rights and even peace promotion were political issues that were the sole responsibility of states. Although there are still companies that benefit from human rights violations, an increasing number of companies is now actively addressing these issues and working for the promotion of human rights and of peace. It is true that human rights bind states first and foremost, but human rights are also the values that are most widely accepted throughout the world: "The human rights standards are the only set of standards on the treatment of people that are globally recognized and accepted."[23] Philippe Spicher also argues that human rights are part of the "business agenda," and he cites various examples to show which human rights are particularly taken into account by companies. Danièle Gosteli, coordinator of Business and Human Rights Switzerland, confirms this view, but also points to the various challenges that remain. The above- mentioned John Ruggie conducted a survey on respect for human rights among the companies in the Fortune Top 500. His survey found that a large number of the companies surveyed take into account human rights aspects in their corporate social responsibility policies, in particular the right to non-discrimination, health and safety standards as well as the prohibition of child and forced labour and the right to privacy. However, only few companies have an explicit human rights policy. Such a policy is essential in order to fully evaluate the attendant risks and opportunities.

6. Global Compact as a frame of reference

The first two Global Compact principles on human rights provide guidelines on dealing with human rights questions. Klaus Leisinger, President and CEO of the Novartis Foundation for Sustainable Development, shows in his article how Novartis addresses the human rights issue and also describes what in my view is the "state of the art." The first UN Global Compact principle states that companies are required to support and to respect the protection of human rights within their sphere of influence. One difficulty often mentioned by companies is the definition of what a company's sphere of influence is and what human rights are "relevant to the company." In principle, all human rights set out in the Universal Declaration of Human Rights and in the core conventions are important for economic actors. The following rights are particularly relevant to the activities of companies: the right to non-discrimination and equality, minority rights, the rights of indigenous peoples, labour rights, the right to privacy, the right to health and to an adequate standard of living, rights concerning racial and gender discrimination.[24]

A large number of human rights standards can therefore be applied to economic actors, depending on their sphere of influence. A company's sphere of influence is divided into three areas: the situation at the workplace or within the company and in subsidiaries of the parent company (direct investments); the situation outside the workplace (for example relations with suppliers and customers); and the situation in the society in which the company operates.

The second UN Global Compact principle says that companies should ensure "that they are not complicit in human rights abuses." This principle concerns co-involvement of companies in human rights violations. A distinction is drawn here, as it is described in the article of Fritz Brugger and Thomas Streiff, between three different categories:

+ Direct complicity occurs when companies directly support human rights violations.
+ When a company directly benefits from human rights violations by others, then it is co-responsible .
+ Finally a company can be complicit through silence, when for example it fails to inform the relevant authorities of human rights violations.

In order to prioritise the various human rights, companies may find the following distinctions helpful as explained in Klaus Leisinger's article:

+ non-negotiable and binding norms, including compliance with national legislation;
+ norms with which they are morally expected to comply;
+ norms with which they can comply and in doing so they demonstrate that they are "good citizens."

It is crucial that in the framework of their risk management companies ensure that they do not violate fundamental human rights. First and foremost, companies must comply with national law. Particularly in countries with great legal uncertainty, it is necessary to analyse whether in the given context human rights are sufficiently protected and how good the implementation is. It is also important to examine the effects of the company's activities on human rights and the potential impact of legal loop-holes on the company. Measures that go beyond this are also desirable and could create comparative competitive advantages. A Swiss company in the wood industry, for example, withdrew from projects because they violated fundamental rights of indigenous peoples. The company highlighted this measure in its communication, and as a result it has not only enhanced its reputation but is also now regarded as a partner of preference by local bodies. Nestlé Waters, as Carlo Donati, CEO Nestlé Waters, explains, has a clear interest in water sustainability. In the dialogue with their addressee groups, they discuss the direction in which Nestlé's activities to improve the world's access to clean water should go. This article illustrates what proactive commitment can mean and also shows the nature of implementation after management has taken a value-based decision. Following a value-based decision by the company management in favour of human rights, the decision has to be implemented within the company, has to be communicated internally and externally and must be regularly reviewed. It seems to be essential to internally define principles, procedures and mechanisms that make it possible to identify individual as well as corporate responsibility. Katharina Pistor, Professor of Law, Columbia University, examines whether formal legal framework conditions of corporate governance for companies produce incentives to tackle human rights issues. Ultimately it remains a confrontation between the rights of owners and the claims of persons whose human rights are violated by companies.

When implementing their human rights activities, there are a number of reference sources and experiences to which companies can turn. For example, fourteen companies, including ABB and Novartis, have formed the Business Leaders' Initiative on Human Rights. Its aim is "to help lead and develop the corporate response to human rights."[25] Civil society organisations such as Amnesty International have been concerned for years with the relation between business and human rights and have acquired relevant country expertise. A variety of instruments to analyse the relationship between companies and human rights has also been developed. Mads Holst Jensen, advisor to the Danish Human Rights Institute for Human Rights and Business maps out the entire field of human rights and business and makes the reader appreciate how this field is imbedded into the Chinese business context. Key aims of his article are to promote a common language of Business and Human Rights and to develop an approach combining principles and practices in addressing and enhancing companies' human rights performance in China. For this purpose he uses the Human Rights Compliance Assessment Tool, which enables companies to identify potential human rights violations caused by their corporate activity. The International Business Leaders' Forum and the international Finance Corporation, in close collaboration with the UN Global Compact, have also developed a Human Rights Impact Assessment Tool which supports companies in their efforts to examine the effects of their projects on human rights. Human rights in conflict zones are essential and can foster or prolong conflicts. Moreover, companies in such zones are confronted with further challenges. The methodology of Conflict Sensitive Business Practice developed by the British non-governmental organisation International Alert guides companies through all the stages of a production cycle, explains the risks and also how they can be tackled. Salil Tripathi, Senior Policy Advisor, International Alert, explains this methodology in his article.

7. Human security and business: a common approach for common concerns?

Global economic networks can improve the integration of developing and threshold countries into the world economy and hence into world trade and growth. They can thus contribute directly to the reduction of poverty. Developing countries with stable political frameworks, says Eberhard von Koerber, attract more foreign direct investments than countries with high levels of corruption, for example. Capital is necessary for economic and human development. Numerous research studies have shown that the strengthening of human rights reinforces the rules of law and contributes to a stable political and economic environment. In the ideal case, economic activities promote human security and create the conditions for successful business activity.

However, it has also been shown that corporate activities can have a negative impact on human rights and on the stability of a country. There is no doubt that states should protect human rights and peace – the pillars of human security. But as governments are often simply not in a position to do so, or are not interested in doing so, companies also need to assume some responsibility by not violating human rights, not stoking up conflict and, ideally, exerting a positive influence on human security. Such behaviour should not only be based on an ethical imperative but also on enlightened self-interest:

+ Companies exert influence on the economic policies of states and also benefit from human rights such as property rights. In return, it is reasonable to expect that companies should to some extent advocate measures that include human rights promotion.
+ The world economy reacts sensitively to conflicts and to human rights violations. Even conflicts in remote parts of the world have global effects, and even the inhabitants of Switzerland feel these effects. The world economy reacts sensitively to upheavals and to threats to trade links, transport connections

and economic stability. Higher prices for energy or tighter security regulations at airports and borders remind us daily of these facts.

+ As Micheline Calmy-Rey, President of the Confederation and Head of the Federal Department of Foreign Affairs (DFA), states in her article, Switzerland depends on globalisation as the engine of its economy. Swiss exports to developing and threshold countries total CHF 35 billion, while its imports from these countries amount to CHF 17 billion. This export surplus enables Switzerland, for example, to finance the bulk of its imports from the European Union. Swiss companies employed 1.88 million people abroad in 2002, one in four from developing or threshold countries.[26] In 2006, Swiss companies invested CHF 67.5 billion abroad, of which 25% went to developing and threshold countries.

41

+ A stable environment is an essential condition for business activity. Human rights and peace policy help to create stability. Poverty, under-development and discrimination on the other hand create a breeding ground for violent conflicts.

The areas of activity of political actors who seek to promote human security and of companies are different. But the goals, at least the primary goals of both actors, are the same – stability and security as the prerequisites of economic success and of human security. To achieve these goals, it is necessary to assume responsibility and to look for new forms of cooperation on the basis of human rights.

Instead of concluding remarks, I would like to outline some possible future areas of action:

+ Given the nature of today's world order and of the existing problems, a multi-layered cooperation approach between politics and civil society and above all between politics and business must be developed. Economic actors must realise that they have an influence on contemporary political events and thus have a responsibility for the creation of stability. Political actors in turn need to start accepting greater responsibility and to acknowledge that foreign trade policy is not neutral and that they therefore need to find the correct balance between economic, social and ecological interests.

+ Ultimately, states are responsible for the promotion of human rights and for conflict resolution. As John Ruggie stated in his concluding report, states are not adequately performing their duty to protect and are not exhausting all the possibilities of protecting human rights. It is now up to the states to make up for lost time in this respect. For example, states could strengthen their exchange on how human rights principles can be translated into economic policy; on how business and human rights can and should be promoted. The mechanisms in the UN system should be made better use of to ensure that states can perform their duty to protect more effectively and to involve economic actors in reporting on the implementation of human rights treaties.

+ Critical problems of content, as well as implementation issues, need to be clarified. It is still not widely known what the extent of company influence is and when it is legitimate to talk of complicity. The same holds for the question of how human rights can be implemented in practice – particularly in supply chains – and how implementation can be monitored. Or how companies can avoid competitive disadvantages when, for example, they disinvest and are then replaced by unscrupulous companies from the South.

+ The private sector, besides maximising profits, can make a major contribution to improving human security. Although the "business case" for complying with human rights and for contributing to peace promotion has been made, the connection between ethical behaviour and financial performance needs to be established. Although this field has not yet been studied in sufficient depth, studies show that there is no negative correlation between company responsibility and economic performance.[27] The choice should be clear when confronted with the question: shall we make profits or shall we make profits and create additional social benefits?

+ The debate on company responsibility in general often reaches deadlock when the question of voluntary versus binding mechanisms arises. It is necessary to put this mode of thinking behind us. The crucial point is the need to negotiate minimum guidelines with which economic actors should comply. The question to be decided is not whether these standards should be binding or voluntary but rather how many actors comply with them and how their implementation can best be monitored. Here, too, the onus is also on states to, for example, compile national lists of best practices together with companies and on this basis to develop internationally accepted standards. Human Rights, as universally accepted values, could serve as guiding principles.

03

CORPORATE RESPONSIBILITY FOR HUMAN RIGHTS

Klaus M. Leisinger

"The recognition of the inherent dignity and of the equal and inalienable rights of all members of the human family is the foundation of freedom, justice and peace in the world."

Preamble Universal Declaration of Human Rights

1. Accepting a new conceptual challenge

Business and human rights is today a central theme on the international corporate responsibility agenda – and the year 2008, marking the 60th anniversary of the Universal Declaration of Human Rights, as well as the Beijing Olympics, will see another rise in its importance. Two processes in particular have contributed to this: ongoing discourse on the practical consequences of the two United Nations Global Compact principles specific to human rights, and the work of a sub-commission of the Human Rights Commission, under the chairmanship of American law professor David Weissbrodt. The resulting set of *Draft Norms on the Responsibilities of Transnational Corporations and Other Business Enterprises* was considered to contain "useful elements and ideas," but was not accepted by the Human Rights Commission as having legal standing.

To overcome the deadlock of irreconcilable positions among different stakeholders, former UN Secretary-General Kofi Annan, on the request of the UN Commission on Human Rights, appointed a *Special Representative on the Issue of Human Rights and Transnational Corporations and Other Businesses,* John Ruggie. He was asked to submit a report in 2007 identifying corporate responsibilities with regard to human rights and elaborating the role of the state in regulating and adjudicating business on such issues, clarifying ambiguous concepts such as "complicity" and "sphere of influence," developing materials and methodologies for undertaking human rights impact assessments of business activities, and compiling a compendium of best practices.

This turned out to be significantly more complex than originally assumed. In his first Draft Interim Report, Ruggie noted that "some companies have made themselves and even their entire industries targets by committing serious harm in relation to human rights, labor standards, environmental protection, and other social concerns."[1] In his last report to the Human Rights Council, the Special Representative deals with the most important human rights and business-related issues of the day. The following points are, in my opinion, the most significant from a business point of view:[2]

+ Nation states are the primary duty bearers: "In sum, the state duty to protect against nonstate abuses is part of the international human rights regime's very foundation. The duty requires states to play a key role in regulating and adjudicating abuse by business enterprises to risk breaching their international obligations" (para 18, p.7). And, "where national legal systems already provide for criminal punishment of companies the international standards for individuals may be extended, thereby, to corporate entities" (para 24, p.8f).

+ The Ruggie report notes in (para 44, p.14) that "... it does not seem that the international human rights instruments discussed here currently impose direct legal responsibilities on corporations. Even so, corporations are under growing scrutiny by the international human rights mechanisms. And while states have been unwilling to adopt binding international human rights standards for corporations, together with business and civil society they have drawn on some of these instruments in establishing soft law standards [such as the OECD Guidelines for Multinational Enterprises or the ILO Tripartite Declaration of Principles Concerning Multinational Enterprises and Social Policy; KML] and initiatives [e.g. the Kimberly Process

Certification Scheme or the Extractive Industries Transparency Initiative; KML]."

+ With regard to "self-regulation," the report acknowledges that business enterprises are starting to respond to social expectations, but deplores the current lack of accountability provisions (para 75, p. 21), especially for supply chain assurance (para 80, p. 22). It advocates "... for businesses with large physical and societal footprints ... assessments of what their human rights impact will be." Overall, the report perceives positively that "self-regulation by business through company codes and collective initiatives, often undertaken in collaboration with civil society," is resulting in "innovation and policy diffusion." The biggest outstanding challenge is to bring such efforts to a scale whereby they become "truly systemic interventions" (para 85, p. 24): "For that to occur, states need to more proactively structure business incentives and disincentives, while accountability practices must be more deeply embedded within market mechanisms themselves" (ibid).

+ Finally: "The extensive research and consultations conducted for this mandate demonstrate that no single silver bullet can resolve the business and human rights challenge" (para 88, p.24) – instead the "courts of public opinion" will be the place where trials on perceived or actual corporate human rights violations will be conducted.

What does all this mean for a company *competing with integrity* – integrity being defined here as not accepting collateral human-rights-related costs in its pursuit of profits? The fact is that 8 out of 10 people in an opinion poll conducted among 21,000 respondents in 20 industrial countries and emerging markets assign to large companies at least part of the duty for reducing the number of human rights abuses in the world.[3]

In view of the complexity of the debate, a few fundamental preliminary remarks are necessary.

1.1 Bearers of rights need corresponding bearers of obligations

Since all human beings are born free and equal in dignity and rights, everyone – simply by virtue of being human – is entitled to all the rights and freedoms enshrined in the Universal Declaration of Human Rights. This entitlement applies without discrimination, whether by race, skin color, sex, language, religion, political or other views, national or social origin, property, birth, or any other criteria. The almost universal recognition of the idea that all people have inalienable rights that are not conferred or granted by the state, a party, or an organization but that are non-negotiable principles is one of the greatest achievements of civilization.

However, it is also implicit in the very first article of the Declaration of Human Rights that freedoms and rights may not be exercised and realized without corresponding responsibilities and obligations: human beings are not only born free and equal in dignity and rights but are also endowed with reason and conscience and should act towards one another in a spirit of brotherhood. Rights and responsibilities are to be seen as a package, and whenever we talk of rights, it ought to be clear upon whom the relevant obligations fall. Otherwise the discourse remains what Max Weber described as "sterile excitation … romanticism of the intellectually interesting, running into emptiness devoid of all sense of objective responsibility."[4] A notable approach to the assignment of responsibilities in line with human rights is the Universal Declaration of Human Responsibilities proposed by the InterAction Council under the chairmanship of former German Chancellor Helmut Schmidt.[5]

It is the nation state and its institutions that bear primary responsibility for ensuring that human rights are respected, protected, and fulfilled: not only must they refrain from subjecting citizens to tyranny and inhumane treatment; they also have a number of legal obligations towards them. The fact that these obligations are not met in the real world is illustrated by the annual reports of Amnesty International – even in the 21st century many countries show terrible human rights deficits.[6] Enlightened observers of the human-rights-related state of affairs agree that tolerance and openness to other cultures have their limits in those instances where human rights abuses are whitewashed with (mis-understood) ethical relativism. Governments bear at least three distinct human-rights-related duties:

+ to create a clear and reliable legal framework and hence a level playing field for the respect and support of human rights;
+ to enforce existing law; and
+ to sanction violations consistently and coherently.

These duties cannot be delegated to any other organ of society. The reference to the state and its institutions as primary bearers of responsibility does, however, not mean that other actors have no obligations. The preamble to the Universal Declaration of Human Rights of the UN General Assembly in 1948 proclaims that "every individual and *every organ of society,* keeping this Declaration constantly in mind, *shall strive by teaching and education to promote respect for these rights and freedoms and by progressive measures, national and international, to secure their universal and effective recognition and observance"* [emphasis KML]. For the former president of the American Society of International Law and University Professor emeritus at Columbia Law School, Louis Henkin, the case is clear: "Every individual includes juridical persons ... and every organ of society excludes no one, no company, no market, no cyberspace. The Universal Declaration applies to all of them."[7] The Million Dollar question remains: "What exactly does *applying to all of them* mean when it comes to, e. g. economic, social and cultural rights?"

Increasingly, human rights groups adopt Henkin's point of view as the basis for numerous far-reaching demands on companies. Many such groups hold a vision of the world in which transnational corporations fall under general suspicion and are tarred with the same brush: namely, that they are driven solely by greed for profits and care little about human rights. Some go so far as to present companies that operate on the international stage as "major violators of human rights" and as the principal rogues in a *chronique scandaleuse* showing nothing but contempt for humanity.[8] Most often, such generalized accusations are leveled on the back of worst-case examples from the extractive sector, which – regardless of the specifics of individual cases – present unique human rights issues that usually do not apply to other sectors (such as textiles, leather processing, the construction and electricity generating sector, or pharmaceuticals).

Accusations based on such crude generalizations can quickly and readily be disproved through serious empirical analysis. The challenge – both intellectually and politically – lies instead in working out a meaningful and broadly accepted package of corporate human rights responsibilities and implementing these in the day-to-day business of different sectors through appropriate management processes.

1.2 Different generations of human rights
While it is not called into question that all human rights together represent an integral, indivisible whole, it is helpful to distinguish between different "generations" of human rights when assigning human rights obligations to companies.

The first generation: rights of defense against state tyranny
Civil and political rights (such as the protection of life and freedom from bodily harm, non-discrimination, personal freedom, and legal and political rights) form the first-generation rights. They are "defensive" rights that are intended to protect individuals from infringements by the state – and they typically require little in the way of financial resources beyond good governance and accountable public servants. It is therefore to be expected of even the poorest countries that the prohibition of torture, slavery and even genocide be fully implemented, without any need for a transitional period. Where this is not done, political officials place their coun-

try outside the community of civilized nations. Today, governments or government-supported actors are unequivocally responsible for the overwhelming majority of violations of human rights – particularly the most basic rights, such as the right to life and freedom from bodily harm.[9]

The overriding corporate obligation with regard to the first generation of human rights is to respect and support these within their sphere of influence and make sure the company is not complicit or – even worse – benefiting from violations by third parties.

The second generation: rights of entitlement to a life of dignity

Economic, social, and cultural rights (such as the right to an appropriate standard of living that guarantees health and well-being for a family, including food, clothing, accommodation and medical care) form the second generation. These are "positive" rights that require resources to be fulfilled – resources, for example, to ensure non-discriminatory access to basic medical care and to guarantee a living standard that allows all people to fulfill these rights. Sometimes, of course, they merely require refraining from interference with the enjoyment of such rights.

Since poor countries cannot immediately guarantee these rights in view of a shortage of resources, it is expected that governments make measurable progress in tandem with the increasing availability of resources – or, in the words of the International Covenant on Economic, Social and Cultural Rights; "to take steps, individually and through international assistance and co-operation, especially economic and technical, to the maximum of its available resources, with a view *to achieving progressively the full realization of the rights* recognized in the present by all appropriate means, including particularly the adoption of legislative measures" [emphasis KML].

In view of the sad reality that about 2.5 billion people face a daily struggle for survival on US$ 2 a day or less, that more than 10 million children die – annually – before they reach their fifth birthday, and that 500,000 women succumb to preventable illnesses during pregnancy and birth complications, it is obvious that not only do the state and international community have a *legal* duty to do all in their power to promote human development, but also that all fair-minded members of civil society have a moral obligation to support such endeavors.[10]

Corporate contributions to respect, promote, protect and fulfill human rights of this generation are realized predominantly through doing business based on good management principles as well as through corporate philanthropy.

The third generation: rights to development in peace and justice

The third generation of human rights encompasses collective rights, such as the right to peace, to development, or to a social and international order in which the rights and freedoms proclaimed in the Universal Declaration can be fully realized. This generation of rights remains the most debated and is least covered by legal or political instruments.

The most important corporate contribution to these rights is successful and responsible entrepreneurial engagement as an important driver of economic growth. Economic growth increases choices, widens opportunities and makes all other development efforts easier to achieve.[11] By creating employment and income, providing technical and managerial skills as well as social benefits, and bringing innovative solutions to economic, social and environmental problems, corporate activities contribute to the fulfillment of third generation rights.

2. Corporate human rights management is values management

A business enterprise is a societal (sub-)system with a specific mission and purpose which is committed to achieving specific results. Where corporate purpose is not focused solely on the next quarterly financial result but is also concerned with attaining the highest possible social and ecological quality in the pursuit of its economic interests, the managers of that company have to engage in "values management," namely the use of "company-specific instruments designed to define the moral constitution of a team or organization and its guiding values and to live them in all day-to-day practices."[12] A proper values management system embraces all the process variables that a company has at its disposal to achieve its aims.

With regard to corporate human rights compliance, this means first of all applying the "principle of materiality," i.e. identifying, analyzing and prioritizing what the company considers to be the most significant issues. As with all normative requirements, for practical relevance a distinction should be drawn in the context of human rights between:

+ non-negotiable **"must" norms** – these demand compliance with relevant national laws and regulations in all cases as an *ethical minimum;*
+ **"ought to" norms** – these are not stipulated by law but are *morally expected* of a company competing with integrity,[13] (for instance, living up to reasonable social or environmental standards even where local regulations would allow a "race to the bottom"); and
+ **"can" norms** – these encompass additional responsibilities not covered by the first two dimensions. Acknowledgment of "can" norms is *desirable* from a human development point of view and the respective corporate deliverables (e.g. corporate philanthropy programs, *pro bono* research, community programs, and other not-for-profit endeavors[14]) may be equated with excellence in corporate citizenship.

Responsibility for the implementation of these norms in corporate activities may be direct or indirect in nature. Drawing on the materiality distinctions highlighted above, corporate policies can be formulated on what to do and what not to do (articulated as codes of conduct and corporate guidelines) to enact the company's values in day-to-day business operations. Beyond their prescriptive nature, these "moral guidelines" also have the function of providing employees with a positive reference framework they can invoke, when confronted in their work environment with unreasonable demands that violate the spirit of the principles and guidelines.

Using numerous methods and instruments – among them corporate communications programs, agreements on individual business objectives and performance targets, performance dialogues and appraisals, human rights compliance assessments and compliance monitoring, ombuds-institutions and auditing – the implementation phase encompasses all other components of the management processes used to achieve financial, technical and other objectives.

By acting in this informed and structured way and by being able to justify its portfolio of corporate responsibility-related activities in a coherent and consistent manner, a company avoids the pitfall of making random concessions to the most vociferous demands and finding itself at the mercy of external interests and constantly escalating demands from, among others, non-governmental organizations (NGOs).

2.1 The human rights principles of the UN Global Compact as a reference framework

There is no doubt that responsible corporate activities can make a substantial contribution to the achievement of development policy goals and social objectives. The UN Global Compact initiative, based on the conviction that weaving universal values into the fabric of global markets and corporate practices would help advance broad societal goals while securing open markets, is therefore of great significance.[15] The underlying idea is that international companies, in particular, should commit themselves not only to observe and exceed certain *minima moralia* in terms of employment conditions, environmental protection and the fight against corruption, but also to comply in their sphere of influence with two important principles:

+ to support and respect the protection of international human rights; and

+ to ensure that they do not become complicit in the human rights abuses of others.

Straightforward as this may sound, the complexity of translating this into action should not be underestimated. On the one hand, ambiguous terms are used which acquire different meanings for different stakeholders (such as "sphere of influence" or "complicity," clarification of which is part of the terms of reference of John Ruggie). On the other hand, given the broad array of normative preferences and institutional self-interests, there is huge scope for interpretation, especially with regard to the positive statutory obligations that result for companies from economic, social, and cultural human rights. A company therefore has to engage in a values management process specific to human rights to decide which second-generation rights and obligations are relevant and the extent to which they can assume responsibility for these. For companies with integrity, this is about far more than the legalistic obligation to comply with relevant laws and regulations – one reason being the sometimes inadequate quality of national law in less developed countries.

2.2 The decision-making process for corporate commitment to human rights

As with all decisions on complex issues, in the case of human rights it is necessary to do one's "homework" first in terms of both fact-based and value-based knowledge. This involves identifying the stakeholders essential to the company and evaluating their concerns. It is also useful to enter into dialogue with competent human rights institutions and to take part in "learning forums" such as those offered by the UN Global Compact and the Novartis Foundation for Sustainable Development.[16] These inspire ideas that go beyond one's "own backyard" and help ensure that, as far as possible, all relevant aspects of a complex issue have been identified.

The "midwife function" of internal and external dialogue

Socrates pointed out that "truth" lies in all people, they simply need help in seeing it. In view of the huge knowledge potential within companies and their ability to mobilize resources to buy in knowledge that is lacking, there is little doubt that the "truth" about company-specific human rights obligations is also present in every company – they simply need help in seeing it. The points of intersection between human rights and corporate responsibilities are, however, "chaotic and contested": on the one hand, there are those who regard companies (especially multinationals) as the "source of all evil"; on the other, there are those who have a touching faith in the ability of companies, economic growth, and the laws of the market to solve all human rights problems.[17] Clearly, reality is more complex than these extreme views allow for and, as a result, the expectations directed at companies remain unclear.[18]

A useful starting point includes the materials produced by competent institutions such as Amnesty International UK Business Group, the Business & Human Rights Resource Centre, or the Business Leaders Initiative on Human Rights.[19] Debates with constructive lateral thinkers outside the corporate "silo" can help identify risks that normally lie beyond the boundaries of corporate perception. Although by far not all the demands tabled during such discussions comprise "corporate obligations," anyone who wants to be successful in product markets over the long term must be familiar with the most important "opinion markets." Posing the following critical questions can lead to new insights and increased corporate social competence:

+ What are the different human-rights-related risks of our business operations and in what order of priority should we tackle them?
+ Are there significant differences between our internal corporate point of view and those of relevant external stakeholders?
+ On the basis of what special circumstances (such as market failures or failing states[20]) do we recognize particular demands for

the fulfillment of economic or social human rights (such as the offer of life-saving medicines at special conditions), and what concrete deliverables result from this?

+ Are there priority arrangements in place for overcoming conflicts between human rights considerations and meeting profit targets?

+ Which actors of civil society (NGOs, media, churches, etc.) do we want to include in our internal analysis to ensure that the information (fact- and value-based knowledge) on which we base our decisions is appropriate to the complexity of the issue under debate?

+ Where do we draw the limits of our responsibility for the respect, support, and fulfillment of human rights – in other words, how do we define our *sphere of influence?*

+ What do we understand by *complicity?*

Distinguishing between "must", "ought to" and "can"-norms also assists companies to negotiate the continuum between what constitutes *good management practice* and *corporate responsibility excellence* in their sector.

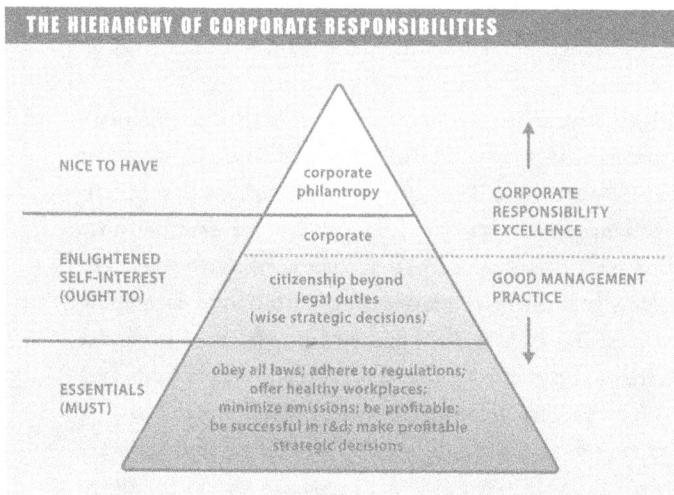

THE HIERARCHY OF CORPORATE RESPONSIBILITIES

NICE TO HAVE

corporate philantropy

CORPORATE RESPONSIBILITY EXCELLENCE

corporate

ENLIGHTENED SELF-INTEREST (OUGHT TO)

citizenship beyond legal duties (wise strategic decisions)

GOOD MANAGEMENT PRACTICE

ESSENTIALS (MUST)

obey all laws; adhere to regulations; offer healthy workplaces; minimize emissions; be profitable; be successful in r&d; make profitable strategic decisions

All first-generation human rights responsibilities are an integral part of the "must" dimension, hence an essential ingredient of good management practice. Companies competing with integrity will not place first generation rights in the negotiation basket with economic goods. On the contrary, where these rights are concerned, a company must do everything in its power to ensure there are no violations within its sphere of influence and that it does not benefit from human rights abuses by other parties. The tacit obligation for companies is to amass as much relevant knowledge in this area as is reasonably possible.

The normal business operations of a company form the main corporate contribution to the preservation of *second-generation* human rights. It is the basic social function of companies to produce products and services in a legal way and to sell these through markets. To this end, they hire employees of adult age who work of their own volition in exchange for pay as defined in legally binding contracts or collective bargaining agreements. In addition, companies pay contributions to the social security system. In this way, they enable their employees to secure their own economic human rights. Companies purchase goods and services at market prices and thereby engender economic linkage effects. Last but not least, companies make a financial contribution to the community through taxes and duty. This enables the state to fulfill its functions.

All activities subject to legality are part of the "must" dimension. Activities that go beyond what is legally required fall under the "ought to" dimension. Most are moral obligations that constitute good management practice. This includes, for example, a remuneration system which ensures that basic needs can be met even for those people at the lowest levels of qualification in developing countries (a "living wage"[21]), affirmative action for greater gender equality, training beyond a person's immediate needs (improvement of "employability"), corporate pension funds and so on.

Delivering on *moral* obligations over and above what is required by law lies within the realm of corporate responsibility excellence – that is, the acceptance of ambitious challenges that belong to the upper part of the "ought to" and "can" dimensions in the hierarchy of corporate responsibilities. Companies seeing themselves as good corporate citizens may choose to provide such additional services of their own volition, for example, by offering products under special circumstances at special conditions (such as differential pricing of medicines for poverty-related and tropical diseases, or product donation programs), financing philanthropic foundations, undertaking *pro bono* research, making donations and contributing, on a case-by-case basis, to the fulfillment of economic, social and cultural rights.[22]

It is as yet too early to apply the "must", "ought to" and "can" grid to third generation human rights. Essential questions – such as who is entitled and who is under obligation, on the basis of what criteria and to what extent? – remain for the time being unanswered. These are therefore treated by companies as aspirations, albeit ones whose fulfillment is in the interest both of the international community and of companies themselves. The UN Global Compact, which serves as a platform for clarification efforts and provides with its 10 principles a reference framework, is on record as stating that among its objectives is to help meet the UN millennium goals through "fair globalization".

Rational justification of normative maxims of behavior is an essential step in values management, but it will not guarantee their implementation. For this reason, appropriate management processes and standard operating procedures must be put in place.

Implementation through management processes

While it is true that progressive processes cannot be set in motion without value-based management decisions, such decisions are only the first step. Principles of action and behavior resulting from these decisions, as well as corporate guidelines for dealing with human rights, have to be formulated and communicated both inside and outside the company. Moreover these often have to be rehearsed, by using e-learning modules for example, or case studies.

Leading by example and visible commitment at managerial level, as well as an attractive launch campaign addressing imperative and prohibited modes of behavior, are important initial steps, as are the appointment of someone at top management level with responsibility for human rights issues, the development of measurable benchmarks, and the setting of concrete, bonus-relevant goals and corresponding performance appraisals. Finally, compliance with self-imposed commitments must be monitored in just the same way as compliance with legal requirements.[23] A useful support for internal learning and cognitive processes in this regard is the Human Rights Compliance Assessment tool developed by the Danish Institute for Human Rights.[24]

There are currently many different approaches to measuring and reporting on corporate human rights performance.[25] Hopefully the new set of Global Reporting Initiative indicators will provide a widely accepted basis such that corporate performance becomes comparable between companies and over time. Since both the legal

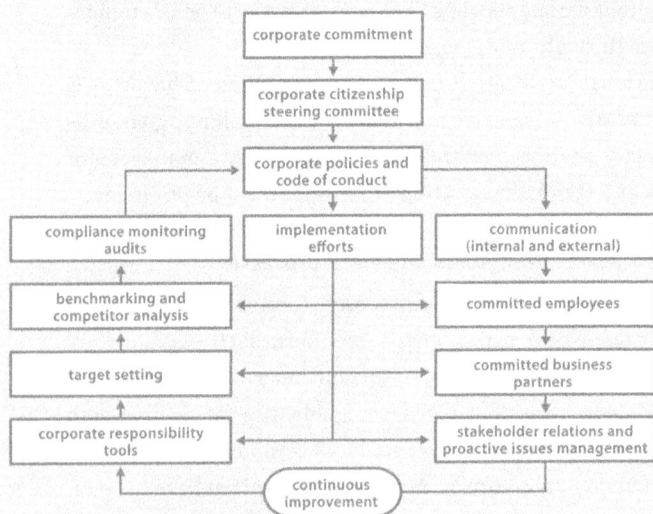

CORPORATE HUMAN RIGHTS MANAGEMENT CYCLE

state of the art and the sense of what constitutes legitimate action are evolving concepts, corporate guidelines and recommendations for action derived from these guidelines must be periodically reviewed and adjusted, where necessary. Companies willing to make a difference but unsure how to proceed can draw on the steadily expanding stable of good practice.[26]

Not all challenges can be satisfactorily met in the long term by means of "standard operating procedures", however. To deal with unexpected or structurally new challenges, a corporate culture has to be cultivated in which moral insights mature into convictions founded on an inherent motivation to achieve excellence. Adherence to compliance monitoring procedures alone will not deliver this. Especially in the context of human rights issues, sensitivity and keen intuition are required to recognize ambivalent situations and assess them critically in the light of existing guidelines. Help desks, clearinghouses, and ombuds-institutions can provide further assistance.

When designing appropriate management processes and standard operating procedures, it is important to perceive corporate human rights engagement not as a "project" that is complete once the objective has been achieved, but as an open-ended process that, once launched, may fundamentally alter basic corporate practices. Companies – especially large multinationals – are increasingly confronting questions of responsibility which lie well beyond the conservatively-defined, "normal", day-to-day business routine. Examples include claims related to the economic, social, and cultural human rights realm, such as the "right to health" demands being placed upon the pharmaceutical industry.[27] Against a background of persistent mass poverty and its associated diseases, successful companies will increasingly face new societal expectations which effectively amount to the substitution of private sector patronage for the obligations of the state and the international community.

One of the great future challenges for values management will be to adopt a credible approach in striking the right balance between human rights responsibility extremes: on the one hand, a basic refusal to accede to external demands, citing the obligations of the primary bearer of responsibility (the state); and, on the other, blanket acceptance of the obligations advocated by some pressure groups. Both "fundamentalisms" would lead in the long term to competitive disadvantages detrimental to business as well as society. In this context, it is useful to recall Peter Drucker's insight many years ago: successful companies are those that focus on responsibility rather than power, on long-term success and societal reputation rather than piling short-term results one on top of the other.[28]

Credible verification

Although the verification of corporate responsibility achievements is an integral part of the management process, it is examined separately here due to its enormous political sensitivity. Credible corporate activity calls for independent jurors. But who can be considered an independent juror for human rights? Most companies prefer verification processes similar to those used in other business areas – financial auditors or consultants such as PricewaterhouseCoopers or KPMG, for example. Such firms have the professional skills and tools to assess human rights performance, but they do not enjoy the same credibility in this area as, say, Amnesty International or Human Rights Watch. Moreover, while institutions such as these do not, necessarily recognize the findings of commercial auditor firms, no human rights defense group is yet able or willing to provide verification services. This is commonly explained through a fear of "capture" and becoming "involved" and thereby – at least in the perception of critical human rights stakeholders – losing their objectivity and jeopardizing their most important asset, their credibility.

Innovative solutions are therefore called for. This could entail, for example, multi-stakeholder projects in which several actors with specific competences, impeccable reputation and practical experience collaborate to reach sustainable and credible solutions. Finally, a human-rights-specific benchmark, or "Richter scale" (like that used to measure earthquakes) would help give the broader public a better idea of how to weigh and put into perspective reports on corporate human rights abuses.[29]

3. Emerging core concepts and remaining dilemmas

The human rights set out in the Universal Declaration encompass different categories of entitlements raising a broad array of conceptual issues for companies to consider. As outlined above, remarkable first steps have been taken to help companies deal with practical issues and dilemmas that arise in the context of corporate human rights commitment – but dealing with these issues means committing to an ongoing political process. Three of the most important recurring questions are discussed here briefly. What is a fair definition of a company's *sphere of influence?* How should a company competing with integrity define *complicity?* And, last but not least, what *corporate deliverables* can be reasonably expected *in the context of economic, social and cultural human rights?*

3.1 What is a company's sphere of influence?

The Declaration of Human Rights and its subsequent covenants represent the greatest normative consensus of the international community. Any respectable company must therefore ensure that its legitimate pursuit of profits does not lead to "collateral human rights damage." Companies of integrity will, in their own interest, provide for transparency wherever they can exert a direct influence – but where do the boundaries of this influence lie? Here, opinions are polarized, with corporate actors tending to define the sphere of influence as tightly as possible and human rights activists perpetually seeking to expand it.

As a rough guide, political, contractual, economic, or geographic *proximity* to human rights abuses are important criteria for determining the sphere of influence. But where *exactly* a company's "sphere of influence" begins and ends will always remain a subject of controversy. The emerging consensus will lie, of course, somewhere in the middle. It is wider than what lies within the factory gate (i.e. the realm where a company is fully able to enforce its corporate rules and regulations) – and it will undoubtedly stop short of including the Nation state to which the company pays tax.

Bigger and ongoing business partnerships, such as those with major suppliers, are likely to fall within the corporate sphere of influence – those involving small volumes of interaction and one-time-contracts are less relevant. No respectable company today can hide behind a supplier with low standards: it is not the "small", local supplier in the poor country who will be criticized for their misdemeanors, but the "big" multinational that is seen to be benefiting from unacceptable practices. Gone, too, are the days when companies could get away with poor standards by saying "we are only obeying the law". Corporate "influence" is inextricably linked with "size" and "power" in the wider sense – hence the bigger and more strategically significant a company becomes, the larger its attributed sphere of influence is likely to be.

Ultimately, sphere of influence questions must be answered by

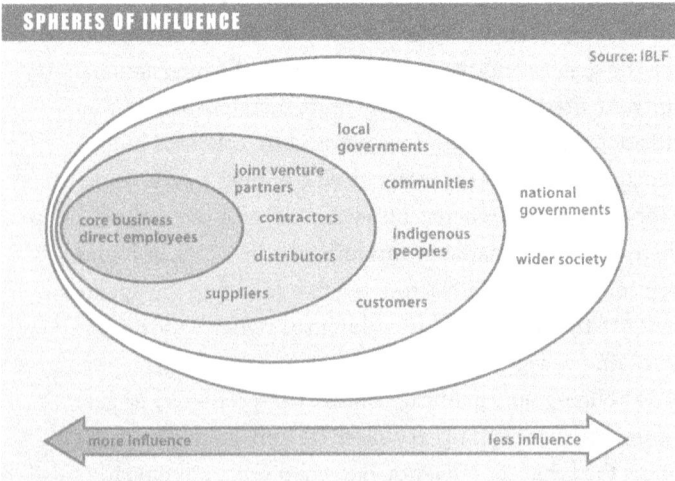

SPHERES OF INFLUENCE

Source: IBLF

local governments

joint venture partners

communities

national governments

core business direct employees

contractors

indigenous peoples

distributors

wider society

suppliers

customers

more influence   less influence

the company itself, albeit with external input. For a better understanding of corporate sphere of influence, the UN Global Compact recommends "mapping the stakeholder groups affected by your business operations" and concludes "a key stakeholder group that will normally lie at the centre of any company's sphere of influence will be employees. Other groups, such as business partners, suppliers, local communities, and customers will follow. The final group will usually be government and the wider society."[30]

Nicolas Howen from the International Commission of Jurists recommends that companies "look for the warning signs. The closer you are to victims, the more you have a responsibility to watch out for the impact of your actions. The closer you are to those who commit the violations, the greater the danger. And the more systematic the nature and scale of the violations, the more dangerous they are." He continues: "Do not be limited by the law. The law is a vital test of accountability and will give clarity [as] to what is acceptable and unacceptable behavior. But we're all forced to swim in a much rougher and more profound sea of morality and public policy, and that's how it should be."[31]

In view of the pluralism of societal interests, any corporate definition of its sphere of influence can be criticized as too restrictive – but a company has to be able to live with such dissent. Not all stakeholder demands constitute a moral corporate obligation.

3.2 What is complicity?

Mapping one's sphere of influence is not the only challenge facing companies: "complicity," too, tends to be afflicted with what Paul Watchman once called "definitional anarchy". "In the common law world alone," Watchman writes, "offences of complicity come in a kaleidoscope of different shapes and titles: aiding, abetting, counseling, procuring, inciting, facilitating, conspiring, assisting, encouraging, authorizing, tolerating, acting as accessory, acting as accessory after the fact, failure to control, relieving, comforting, handling ... the list is endless and mind-boggling."[32]

Against this background, in what instance does a company become complicit in human rights abuses in the course of its normal business activities? What kind of proximity to abuses by the state, by terrorists, by individuals, or by other companies can justify the allegation of complicity in rights violations? These questions are answered in many ways by different stakeholders – again, it is basic corporate values that will determine the kind of definition arrived at by a company.[33]

John Ruggie's latest report acknowledges the plurality of understanding when it comes to corporate complicity (para 31, p.10) but sees potential for the fairly clear standard for *individual* criminal aiding and abetting liability (*knowingly providing practical assistance, encouragement or moral support that has substantial effect on the commission of the crime*) to be extended to corporations (ibid).

The UN High Commission for Human Rights points out in this regard that a company is guilty of complicity if it "authorizes, tolerates or knowingly ignores human rights abuses committed by an entity associated with it, or if the company knowingly provides practical assistance or encouragement that has a substantial effect on the perpetration of human rights abuse".[34] The Global Compact Website adds that "the participation of a company need not actually cause the abuse. Rather the company's assistance or encouragement has to be to a degree that, without such participation, the abuse most probably would not have occurred to the same extent or in the same way".

Corporate responsibilities in this regard have, as yet, not been laid down in international law – different national views and instruments of law (such as the Alien Tort Act in the United States) apply different standards. Ultimate judgment as to the legitimacy of corporate acts committed or omitted is reached in the court of public opinion. This should prompt companies to make best use of the expertise of their legal counsels and corporate lawyers, but decisions on complicity matters should not be made on legal grounds alone.[35]

The definition offered by the UN High Commission for Human

Rights suffers from the same "interpretational schizophrenia" as the two principles of the Global Compact: at first glance, the definition seems self-evident – however, since different civil society actors interpret ambiguous terms in different ways, a company will need to decide precisely what is to be understood by "encouragement", and how "knowingly" and "substantial" are to be construed. In the light of these complexities, management of the complicity issue should be holistic rather than legalistic. Sensitivity to human rights is vital, as is a precautionary approach: third parties whose integrity is not beyond reasonable doubt will not make sound business partners for the complicity-aware company.

Direct responsibilities (such as the prohibition of forced or child labor) are more readily identifiable than indirect ones (such as improvements in human rights practices of a host country) which straddle institutionally separate spheres of influence. Yet both can affect the human rights track record of a company to a similar extent.

Last but not least, first-generation rights normally present fewer problems of implementation than second-generation rights – not to mention third generation, although exceptions to this can be found within the extractive sector (oil, gold, or diamonds). Since the geographical presence of a company in this sector depends on the local availability of raw materials, human rights commitments have limited room for maneuver in countries with strong natural reserves but structural governance deficits (such as despotic dictatorships or lawless areas in civil war zones). Under such conditions, a company that does not wish to operate in close proximity to human rights abuses has little choice but to withdraw from the country – a decision that is not necessarily the best solution, as constructive engagement has in the past led to significant change for the better.[36] And there are a number of additional arguments:

+ Although the presence of a company can imply indirect (if unintentional) support for a government that permits or commits human rights violations, presence should not be judged unconditionally as negative. Enlightened presence can lead to processes being initiated that bring about concrete improvements in safeguarding human rights.[37] Anyone, individual or company, that leaves a country abandons any possibility of exerting such influence.

+ Demand for sanctions or the withdrawal of companies committed to compliance with local laws even though their compatibility with human rights is questionable, may fail to take into account the consequences of withdrawal for those who there-by become unemployed. While this argument can undoubtedly be exploited by a company as an excuse for inactivity, it is also of human rights relevance to take into account the potential damage such a withdrawal would entail. Legitimate commitment to the defense of human rights should focus on the interests of the people one is seeking to protect. To say that "things must get worse before they can get better" is cynical at best. Complete withdrawal in most cases does not improve the basic political situation, yet leads to considerable material sacrifices being made by individual companies. There is, moreover, no guarantee that the situation will not be made worse still by the arrival of successor companies from countries for which human-rights-specific demands are not an issue.

+ Focusing criticism on companies has another undesirable consequence, namely that the *actual* culprit – the state, as primary duty bearer for political responsibility – escapes public scrutiny. Without fundamental improvement in the governance of a state, however, anything else are just patch repairs.

Apparent complicity in human rights violations triggers worst associations in the mind of the public, hence it is in the corporate self-interest to avoid the perception – let alone the reality – of complicity. There is a "business case" to clarify grey areas and, if in doubt, err on the side of safety: use due diligence to identify and eliminate reputational risk.

3.3 What corporate activities can be reasonably

expected to appropriately address economic, social and cultural human rights issues?

As mentioned earlier, companies mainly contribute to the safe-guarding and fulfillment of second-generation human rights in the course of their usual business activities. But today's human rights champions demand substantially more – and the expectations of society in some cases far exceed what managers regard as business duty. A survey carried out in Germany shows, among other things, that a large majority of people expect pharmaceutical companies, for example, to distribute medicines free of charge – or at massively reduced prices – if patients cannot afford them because they lack the necessary purchasing power.[38] John Ruggie mentioned in his Interim Report that major pharmaceutical companies are "widely perceived to abuse their power" and quotes as examples "overpricing and patents of AIDS treatment drugs in Africa."[39]

Most managers of pharmaceutical companies would be astonished to hear that patent rights are equated with abuse of power – they would probably quote Article 17 of the Universal Declaration of Human Rights, which states that "everybody has the right to own property" and "no one shall be arbitrarily deprived of his property". Some would also raise the argument that, as primary bearers of responsibility, governments have a duty to ensure that their resources are used to satisfy basic needs – and that the international community should assist those countries whose lack of resources renders them vulnerable in spite of good governance. Yet even leading business schools debate whether there is a "morally right" price for drugs in the developing world.[40]

Issues like access to medicines under conditions of market failure necessitate a differentiation between what constitutes "legal" entitlement and the legitimate handling of what is an extraordinary social catastrophe. In the light of persistent mass poverty and the human suffering that goes with it, and as a reaction to what in many cases are evident shortcomings in engagement by the primary bearers of responsibility, concerned people are turning to the private sector for help. Companies – especially profitable ones – have to cope with the fact that societal expectations do not necessarily equate to a fair societal distribution of responsibility.

Establishing a credible corporate standpoint on this issue is achieved through informed decisions based on "homework" and dialogue with stakeholders, as described earlier. There will never be complete agreement in society on the issues under discussion here. But neither uncompromising rejection nor uniform acceptance of societal demands can be a substitute for measured corporate as- sessment of what constitutes a reasonable degree of human rights engagement. All companies must avoid direct or indirect involvement with human rights abuses – and large profitable companies in the upper section of the "corporate responsibility pyramid" can and should do more to exceed the minimum standard than small to medium-size enterprises or those with fewer resources.

Companies striving for leadership in corporate responsibility must be prepared to do more in this regard – and not only to provide resources but also to offer potential innovation and knowledge, as well as management processes, in the search for new or improved solutions. Avoiding human rights problems is one thing. Affirmative action for the safeguarding of human rights is another – and a far more positive and constructive form of engagement.

4. The business case for corporate human rights engagement

Individuals and corporations in breach of the most important consensus of the international community place themselves outside the corridor of legitimate activities. For companies of integrity, there can be no rational justification for sacrificing other people's human rights to achieve corporate profits. This applies first and foremost to those human rights obligations enshrined in law. Nation states should ensure – if necessary, with international support – that domestic laws relating to human rights are compatible with what most governments have ascribed to by explicitly recognizing the International Bill of Human Rights.[41] Where this is not the case, moral corporate obligations come into play.

There are a number of good reasons for assuming corporate responsibility to respect and uphold human rights in cases where national law either is not state-of-the-art or is only a "paper tiger":

+ Companies that critically reflect on the quality of standards relating to human rights, that gauge the pulse of society's expectations through dialogue with stakeholders, and that are prepared to be judged by criteria of legitimacy and not merely those of legality reduce their legal, financial, and reputational risks.[42] Any increased costs incurred as a result can be viewed as an "insurance premium" against such risks occurring.
+ Companies that reduce the potential for friction with society on human rights issues by taking a proactive approach tend to be seen as "part of the solution," rather than "part of the problem". This reinforces a company's societal "license to operate" and buffers it against calls for boycotts or "naming and shaming" campaigns.[43]
+ Companies with a reputation for integrity tend to have better motivated employees because they look on their company with pride and identify with its objectives; such companies are also more attractive to *highly qualified talent* – and both tend to lead to increased *productivity*.
+ Companies whose performance is exemplary in terms of human rights tend to be preferred by ethical investment funds and ethically sensitive customers (other performance criteria being equal). This ethical differentiation can lead to advantages in the valuation of the company and in the competitive environment of established markets (especially with products that are subject to high competitive pressures).
+ Sustainable responsible corporate performance creates greater reliability and thus better opportunities for collaboration between potential partners (business partners, joint ventures, and mergers and acquisitions).
+ Finally, shouldering responsibility that is credible by virtue of

the fact that it is verifiable is the best argument against political demands for additional regulation: freedom, including corporate freedom, is always tied to responsibility for the common good – and here human rights have absolute priority.

Companies are increasingly being assigned moral responsibility. While the scale and complexity of society's expectations often makes it difficult to satisfy all stakeholders, human-rights-related expectations should be dealt with in a constructive and positive way. Enlightened companies will take a "rights-aware approach" – that is, be willing to accept that stakeholders have universally accepted human rights and to take appropriate action to respect these.

Many of the deliverables that result from a "rights-based approach" can be seen as part of good management practice – making management a "force for good".[44] A significant multiplying effect could be achieved, however, if civil society actors (NGOs, media, political parties) made more distinctions between companies based on their corporate human rights commitment. Today, exemplary companies (in social and ecological terms, as well as in efforts to combat corruption) are often tossed into the same discussion basket as the worst-case corporate laggards. By differentiating leaders from those that choose not to take an enlightened approach towards human rights, moral reputation capital could be earned, rewarding their additional efforts. This, in turn, would increase the discretionary freedom of management to do more, resulting, possibly, in a new realm of corporate competition founded on human rights excellence. This is undoubtedly in the interest of anyone concerned about human rights.

As former UN Secretary-General Kofi Annan stated: "Wherever we lift one soul from a life of poverty, we are defending human rights."[45] Economic deprivation is a core feature of most definitions of poverty and no social phenomenon is as comprehensive – or as relentless – in its assault on human rights as poverty. Economic development is the single most important element to alleviate it. The private sector contributes to poverty alleviation by driving economic growth, job creation and helping to raise poor people's incomes. Encouraging corporate activity and unleashing entrepreneurship is therefore crucially important.[46]

Responding to the many facets of poverty in the pursuit of economic growth need not violate human rights. On the contrary, sustainable responses to poverty alleviation involve securing[47] and enlarging freedom,[48] increasing choices, and enabling empowerment. The promotion of human development and the fulfillment of human rights share, in many ways, a common motivation and reflect a fundamental commitment to promoting the freedom, well-being, and dignity of individuals in all societies.[49] Good companies become part of the solution by filling these aspirations with living content.

04

NOWADAYS THERE IS NO LACK OF AWARENESS AMONG MOST BUSINESS LEADERS OF THEIR RESPONSIBILITY TOWARDS SOCIETY

Interview with Eberhard von Koerber

You are a businessman yourself, a member of numerous supervisory and advisory bodies and as vice president of the Club of Rome you are involved closely in concerns of a social political, societal and cultural nature. How do you see the attitude of business towards social and ecological issues?

There are two issues that must not be mingled – one is philanthropy, the other is responsibility.

Philanthropy is a widespread, long-standing entrepreneurial tradition in Europe as well as in the United States. Educational projects like the Orchestra Academy of the Berlin Philharmonic and countless other social, sporting and cultural events would not exist without the dedicated support of the business sector.

Responsibility for the broader effects of business activities in a globalised world is a different dimension of entrepreneurial activity. It has taken some time for many business leaders to realise that there is a corporate responsibility not only towards shareholders, supervisory boards and employees – but also towards society and the environment as a whole.

The willingness to deal with the issue of broader social responsibility has increased steadily in recent years. In 2006 a study by the Swiss Ethos Foundation showed that 67% of Switzerland's largest companies listed on the stock exchange already publish a detailed or partial report on how they deal with their social and ecological responsibility.

Nowadays there is no lack of awareness among most business leaders of their responsibility towards society. However, quite often there is an urgent need for ideas, best practice and hands-on guidelines on how to actually implement corporate responsibility.

In your view, how should businesses deal with societal expectations such as in the sphere of human rights (using an example as an illustration)? Should/can the same standards apply to large businesses as to small and medium-sized businesses?

Let me give you a very interesting example: During my time as managing director of BMW South Africa in the seventies and eighties during apartheid, we qualified and promoted non-white employees, even to management positions, gave them equal pay for equal work and let them use the same canteen in contravention of the existing laws. This was tolerated by the apartheid state administration after I had negotiated with the government of South Africa. I explained to them that we would build a new BMW plant in South Africa only if non-whites in our company were treated equally. The government accepted this on the condition that we would not talk about this issue to the South African media – which I accepted. What is the conclusion? As an attractive foreign investor, big or small, you can always negotiate certain concessions with local governments and unions because you invest, transfer critical skills and knowledge and create new employment.

Openness for employees from all parts of local society and equal opportunities can become an important driving force for change and development. In countries with widespread corruption and inefficient governance, global companies can help develop local economic elites that can become drivers and catalysts for change and development in their society. In China's Pearl River Delta alone, there are 11 million local people working for foreign companies. In a few years, some of these workers will become business leaders. We now have the chance to shape their ideas on how responsible business should be done.

It should also be self-evident that global companies, small or large, shape human working conditions and minimum standards for safety, social security and environment in all their facilities.

Surveys show that young workers increasingly want to join businesses which are committed to "ethical" values. Have you had similar experiences?
In a recent edition, the German business monthly "Manager Magazin" reported on the retailer Lidl's current difficulties in recruiting skilled management. Lidl's lack of corporate culture would seriously hamper the company's growth in several European markets. "Manager Magazin" reported that the reason for Lidl's recruit-

ment problems was the company's hire-and-fire policy and the bad overall treatment of employees on all levels of the company's hierarchy.

On the other hand, companies that invest heavily in their employee's qualification and have a good overall reputation for being socially and environmentally responsible find it easy to attract highly skilled employees.

It is very important for business leaders to understand that commitment to ethical values and social responsibility is not an end in itself but a vital precondition for the long-term success of their companies.

How do you assess such existing instruments as the UN Global Compact or the OECD Guidelines for Multinational Enerprises which should show businesses how to initiate responsible corporate conduct?
Guiding principles like the ones fixed in the UN Global Compact might serve as a rough orientation.

However, such principles are not enforceable and do not release companies from their commitment to actually integrate corporate responsibility into their daily work life. It should be clear that this cannot be done by assigning a budget for corporate social responsibility to the corporate communications or marketing department or by just joining the UN Global Compact.

Institutions like the Wittenberg-Centre for Global Ethics (www.wcge.org) help global companies to develop long-term guidelines to implement responsible behaviour specifically for their industry and scope of activities. A growing number of companies are recognising the importance of responsibility on a global scale. Accordingly, the Wittenberg Centre is supported by BASF, Deutsche Bank, RWE, Dow Chemical, Vattenfall, Commerzbank, Daimler and many others.

Enterprises will integrate human rights sustainably in the business process only when social expectations are reflected more strongly in market mechanisms. You yourself are the chairman of the largest infrastructure fund for investment in Africa and the Middle East. What role can and should financial markets play in promoting human rights issues?

Financial markets can promote free economies. Free economies can promote open societies.

Developing countries with a stable political framework attract far more foreign direct investment than instable countries prone to corruption. Such investments, above all infrastructure investments in electricity, water and transport are the key to further economic and human development. Overcoming unemployment and poverty is the first and most important step to human development and security.

According to recent World Bank figures, private investment in developing countries peaked in 2006 with 647 bn US$. This is 25 times as much as the development aid granted by the G8 countries in the same time. Global financial markets can provide both equity and debt capital to promote development and equal opportunities. It should be thoroughly understood by politicians and development experts: It is the private sector which makes the difference as it provides the capital and the skills and monitors the implementation in its companies.

Is a new order necessary to overcome present and future social and ecological problems; more policy and less economy taking us to a market economy which is more in the service of life?

The question should not be about one or the other but about more of both.

It has become clear that through foreign trade and the membership in WTO, national governments all over the world have lost considerable influence and power to regulate and develop their economies. As a quantitative example, the annual revenue of General Electric is larger than the Swiss national budget.

Efficient international institutions are needed to monitor global capital flows and business standards. In a world of global business activities there is still no international court for white collar crime to deal with cartels and corruption on a truly global scale. International organisations like the UN, ILO, WTO, IMF or World Bank and their leaders are still not using their full potential to encourage, promote and monitor human development and human security worldwide as it is or should be effected by global business.

05

WALKING THE TALK: HOW TO CREATE BUSINESS VALUE WHILE DELIVERING STAKEHOLDER VALUE

Interview with Peter Buomberger

You are working as a senior manager with an insurance company and you are very dedicated to political, social and cultural questions. In a general view, how do you perceive companies' attitudes to social and ecological demands? How did this attitude change in the last 5 years?

Along with unprecedented opportunities for wealth creation made possible by the liberalization and integration of markets worldwide, companies are also confronted with mounting competitive pressures and a host of new challenges. Increasing stakeholder demands for business to be part of the solution to social and environmental challenges has induced companies to take a more open and considerate attitude to their role in society. In general, business has become more responsive to a wider group of stakeholders, and issues which were once perceived to be marginal have moved to the mainstream.

What companies have come to realize is that a disciplined approach to the integration of social and environmental considerations into business operations and core strategic decision-making is not only beneficial for society but is also a rapidly growing source of business advantage. Proactive management of a company's social and environmental impact helps to build the confidence and trust of society essential to delivering innovation. Social and environmental demands can also create valuable market opportunities by highlighting unmet social needs and new consumer preferences.

Corporate social and environmental responsibility has therefore become integral to the way many businesses operate. Companies make the greatest impact on society and have the greatest potential to contribute to positive change, business growth, and long-term profitability through their core competencies. As a result, they are increasingly moving beyond traditional philanthropy and aligning their social and environmental efforts with core business interests and strategies.

How should firms in their day-to-day business deal with human rights (are you able to illustrate your opinion on the basis of a case study)? Where are the limits of companies' responsibilities in this regard and shall there be the same benchmarks for small and medium enterprises? How does Zurich Financial Services deal with corporate responsibility and with human rights issues in particular? How is an insurance company concerned by such issues?

Human rights violations destabilize the investment climate and jeopardize employee safety, company assets, project viability, and corporate reputation. However, business can contribute to an open environment less prone to human rights violations by operating in a manner which is transparent and consistent with international human rights and labor standards. Defining clear boundaries of the role and responsibilities of business with regard to human rights is no easy task, but internationally recognized standards offer an objective and coherent minimum benchmark against which all businesses should measure their conduct.

Zurich's approach to corporate responsibility is to embed a sense of commitment into the corporate culture and to engage in long-term, sustainable initiatives linked to its core competence. As Zurich implemented its global change management, operational improvement, and internal branding efforts that fueled our turnaround, a constant theme was our role as leaders in our markets and in society more generally. This focus is reflected in Zurich *Basics,* our group's core principles and values, which rests upon the four cornerstones of corporate citizenship, corporate governance, compliance, and ethically-sound decision-making. Together with Zurich's General Compliance Rules for Employees, Zurich *Basics* constitutes our Group's global code of conduct. Our employees have a duty to comply with the law but above all to pursue high standards of integrity and to avoid activities which would compromise the values of the company or of society.

Beyond the primary obligation to respect human rights, business should have an interest in extending its role to contribute to the promotion of human rights. Providing affordable access to financial services is a promising means of reducing the vulnerability of populations to exploitation by empowering them to provide a secure future. Earlier this year, Zurich entered into a partnership with the Swiss Agency for Development and Cooperation and the International Labour Organization for joint implementation of a cross-regional microinsurance initiative. The initiative's primary aim is to expand insurance coverage to disadvantaged segments of the population in emerging countries, thereby promoting basic risk management principles and helping to reduce poverty.

We recognize that there is a significant, unmet need for insurance among disadvantaged segments of the population in emerging markets, and Zurich has been one of the early movers among the major insurance companies in providing insurance coverage to low-income customers through innovative products in Latin America. The new microinsurance initiative, however, represents the first concerted effort across different regions within the Group, focused on the underprivileged population segment. The microinsurance initiative foresees the implementation of a series of projects in up to four countries during the first three years. A pilot project has been launched in South Africa in 2007, and additional projects will be considered in Asia and Latin America. Through our new cross-regional approach to microinsurance, we will explore new business models which can allow us to help more people protect their livelihood and their dignity by offering affordable insurance solutions.

Where Zurich is unable to solely lend its expertise to help alleviate exposure to and impact of risk, hazards, and disasters on lives, it partners with organizations aligned with its values. For example, we served as a catalyst to creating the Corporate Support Group of the International Committee of the Red Cross. Together with six other Swiss-based companies, we have raised over 20 million CHF to enhance the capacity of the ICRC to provide effective humanitarian protection and assistance and to promote humanitarian principles. Collaborative exercises and opportunities to share knowledge and skills foster continuous improvement in crisis management and reinforce our commom efforts.

How do you assess such existing instruments as the UN Global Com-
pact, the OECD Guidelines for Multinational Enterprises, and the
work of John Ruggie? How involved is Zurich Financial Services in
these processes? How useful are such instruments in daily business
operations?
In the face of multiple and intersecting pressures placed on business, these initiatives provide useful frameworks for determining
what human rights, labor, and environmental standards are linked
to business. They make important contributions to advancing high
standards of corporate conduct by raising awareness and laying
the groundwork for enhanced cooperation.

Convening bodies, such as the UN Global Compact, enable
companies from around the world to engage and, through sharing
best practices, find effective ways to support the principles in practice. They also make it easier for public and private organizations
to come together to realize common goals. In this context, business, together with other key stakeholders, can increasingly help
shape the international agenda and policy development on global
economic and social issues to support a more stable, inclusive system. The voluntary nature of the joint initiatives has encouraged
companies to participate and to integrate the principles into their
operational culture, complementing the necessary action by governments.

The Global Compact and the OECD Guidelines provide two
complementary models for helping companies make a broad commitment to appropriate standards of conduct and to better assess
their risks. They are of particular value for companies operating
globally in disparate social and legal environments, clarifying the
relevant norms by interpreting the meaning and application of international instruments and domestic laws.

Voluntary, multistakeholder initiatives and the work of
John Ruggie have advanced the process of creating globally recognized standards for business. The challenge is for business to implement these standards in practice on a global basis and to establish credible systems of public accountability. Concurrently,

a top-down and bottom-up approach should be taken to identify human rights norms throughout a company's operations and to integrate human rights principles into decision-making processes.

Firms will integrate human rights in their business process in an enduring way when social expectations are reflected in market mechanisms. Which roles should and could insurance companies, as well as financial institutions/markets and investors play to advance human rights issues?
By extending access to financial products and services to disadvantaged segments of the population, insurance companies and financial institutions can play a significant role in advancing human rights. Microcredit and microinsurance schemes are instrumental in combating poverty and economic insecurity and empower people to protect themselves against infringement of their rights.

By integrating human-rights-related issues into sovereign or project credit risk assessments, and adopting the Equator Principles for sustainable project finance, financial institutions can protect the viability of transactions as well as human rights. Considering the connection which often exists between human rights abuses and money laundering, financial institutions could be implicated in facilitating or funding such operations. The adoption of "Know your customer" rules therefore not only makes good business sense but also a good business case.

Business can be actively involved in addressing the issue of human rights by including non-financial criteria in business and investment decision-making. In countries beset by conflict or weak governance, however, companies and investors can play a more helpful role by engaging as opposed to divesting, providing they act in alignment with fundamental principles of human rights.

According to surveys, young people increasingly want to work in companies which are dedicated to human rights and other "ethical values." Is this true in your perception, and how does your company deal with these expectations?

Yes, growing numbers of graduates do seem to be taking ethical issues into account as they search for jobs. A big part of Zurich's restructuring over the past five years was a renewed focus on people, with the understanding that people find motivation in knowing that they are working for a company that acts with integrity and that cares about their community as much as they do. Our employees are very passionate about engaging in their communities, and we support them through relationships with civic and charitable organizations, numerous opportunities to volunteer and fundraise, and matched giving schemes.

Now we also see, and this is supported by third-party research, that the significance of corporate responsibility activity differs based on historical cultural attitudes and geographies. That said, we are committed globally, so no matter where Zurich is hiring we are highlighting our commitment to ethical values and principles and to playing a positive role in society. In turn, we are approached by people interested in working in areas such as microinsurance which underscore our commitment.

Do we need new regulatory policies to cope with future social and ecological challenges? Do we need again more "politics" on the way to a more social market economy?

In the case of clear-cut market failure, new regulatory policies may indeed be required. For example, the case could be made for regulation aimed at internalizing the social cost of production and consumption to combat global environmental challenges like climate change. Reducing excessive greenhouse gas emissions requires the participation of all large corporations, and adaptations to the consequences of past emissions will likely require changes in corporate practice. Binding regulation provides fair conditions whereby all competitors face the same obligations and ensuing opportunity costs and may prove to be the best means of tackling certain global ecological challenges.

With respect to many societal challenges, industry self-regulation or multistakeholder processes involving the voluntary adoption of higher standards of corporate conduct often provide more efficient solutions than state regulation. Particularly in emerging countries, where the capacity to enforce state regulations is quite low, self-regulation also works to the benefit of laborers.

06

PROMOTING HUMAN RIGHTS AND BUSINESS IN CHINA
Mads Holst Jensen

1. In search of a common language

The concept of CSR (Corporate Social Responsibility) was invented in the West nearly two decades before China began acceleration to its present speed of integration into the global value chains. By the mid 1980s, when Shenzhen was still a fishing village, attention on CSR emanated from academic circles in Northern America to a wider audience in the Western countries. Developing their CSR understanding and performance over the following decade, Western companies gained ownership for the concept and formalized it into policies and codes of conduct to monitor their suppliers in the developing countries.

By the mid 1990s, the CSR wave hit China, "the workshop of the world", and its introduction can be seen as a process. Initially, CSR was conceived of almost entirely as demands placed on Chinese companies by Western business associates. This conception has certainly survived to the present day, but from the early 21st century on we have seen a rapid increase in CSR projects based on multi-stakeholder engagement and partnerships that aim at step-by-step progress to pave the way from Chinese realities to CSR ideals. Increasing Chinese ownership of CSR is the basic thrust of this process and it yields promising results. However, the essence of CSR should remain intact throughout the process and therefore we need a common language to guide it.

The first and second principles of the UN Global Compact manifestly establish the key role of human rights for business. Human rights laws have proved their practical and theoretical worth and combining reliability and flexibility they offer an adequate framework for a common language for standards that stay the same in essence despite fluctuations in business practices and contexts.

2. Meeting the Chinese half way

Promoting a common language for human rights and business cannot rely on one-way communication. That would imply the risk that many of those for whom the language is intended do not understand it to begin with and would never feel confident in using it. While Chinese civilization has a long, proud history, the Chinese also have a long history of welcoming ideas from abroad. But like other peoples proud of their civilization, the Chinese are inclined to receive foreign ideas as add-ons to the existing order. Hence the conventional Chinese saying, "take Chinese learning as the essence and Western learning for its utility" (zhongti xiyong). To some extent, this saying epitomizes the Chinese reception of CSR. CSR, as conveyed in codes of conduct, is commonly regarded as a foreign idea. On repeated occasions, CSR has been subject to strong sentiments and sweeping rumours. Pointing to the rising costs of compliance, some suspect that CSR represents a "hidden trade barrier" devised by the West, while others claim that compliance and certification automatically bring orders from Western buyers. Despite disagreements on whether CSR is a blessing or a curse, however, most Chinese acknowledge that the concept has come to stay. This leads to the process of translating CSR into the Chinese context and part of the process consists in comparing the concept to what is considered essentially Chinese.

The Chinese tradition of business ethics is often highlighted as a predecessor of CSR. For instance, a review of a conference on CSR that was held in Beijing in 1994 remarked:

"The basic norms of business ethics were founded in the eras of The Spring and Autumn and The Warring States and have developed in scope ever since. From the founding of The People's Republic of China, the concept of Serve the People has not only become the common belief of all citizens, it has also been the unwavering precept of the companies." (Liu 1995: 26–27)

Critics may remark that this argument implies sheer generalizations about CSR as well as the Chinese past, but still, Chinese business ethics scholars have developed and expounded it for more than a decade now. Representatives of Chinese business also share the notion that CSR does correspond to Chinese realities, past and present. For instance, a prominent Chinese business leader made the following observation at a Global Compact meeting in Beijing in 2004:

"This is the time when Chinese and United Nations concepts of development are closer than ever before. The UN Global Compact is not something new to China, because being socially responsible has long been the history of the Chinese business community. It is a framework to help Chinese businesses to become global citizens." (UN press release 2004)

However, the fact that there are overlaps between Western CSR and Chinese preconceptions does not imply full assimilation of the former into the latter. In effect, this would lead to a reverse kind of one-way communication in which the essence of CSR is getting lost in translation, so to speak. Instead, it is important that Western and Chinese actors may meet half-way to create a common language for CSR. "This is the time when Chinese and United Nations concepts of development are closer than ever before," as conveyed by the Chinese business leader, and while showing respect for Chinese preconceptions, it should be stressed that respect for international standards is a precondition for Chinese companies' sustainable integration into global markets. This leads to the introduction of human rights.

3. Introducing the concept of human rights in China

In 1991 the Chinese government officially declared its endorsement of human rights. China has ratified the following five core conventions: Convention against Torture and Other Cruel, Inhuman or Degrading Treatment or Punishment (CAT), Convention on the Elimination of All Forms of Discrimination against Women (CEDAW), Convention on the Elimination of All Forms of Racial Discrimination (CERD), Covenant on Economic, Social and Cultural Rights (CESCR), and Convention on the Rights of the Child (CRC). Moreover, China has signed the Covenant on Civil and Political Rights (CCPR). China has not ratified the optional protocols or the Convention on the Protection of the Rights of All Migrant Workers and Members of Their Families (CMW). The Chinese Constitution of 1982 (last revised in 2004) includes a full bill of rights. The latest revision added an article stating that "The State respects and protects human rights." Human rights now constitute an issue of recurring official and public debate and more than ever before China demonstrates genuine commitment in international human rights activities and dialogues.

However, the concept is still charged with controversy and dilemmas for many Chinese, from top-level to the grassroots, who are reluctant to be associated unconditionally with it. But alternative concepts imply alternative connotations and the risk of losing the universality, indivisibility and consistency elaborated for so long under the heading of human rights. Therefore, we should not discard the concept of human rights but strive instead to introduce the concept appropriately into the Chinese context.

President Hu Jintao and Premier Wen Jiabao are signalling commitment to promote common prosperity and equity under the concept of "Harmonious Society" and in this context they come close to expressing endorsement of human rights. For instance, Hu Jintao has highlighted "universal respect for personal rights as the core norm of the Harmonious Society" (Xinhuanet, 2005).

The declaration of "The 2005 GoTone-Nanchang International Forum of Constructing Harmonious Society and Corporate Social Responsibility" of 15 October 2005, which is commonly recognized to be among the very first CSR forums organized at the government level in China, shows that Chinese and internationally recognized conceptions are comparable. This declaration puts the comparison in straight-forward terms by asserting that:

"[...] those basic conceptions in terms of human rights, employee, environment, anti-corruption, etc. in the Global Compact sponsored by UN Secretary-General Kofi Annan are basically the same as those endorsed by the human-entered strategies of the Chinese government, and that we support enterprises to join Global Compact." (GoTone-Nanchang, 2005)

4. Outlining Chinese companies' human rights responsibilities

Venturing into Chinese tradition we find that Mencius, the famous Confucian thinker, expounded the virtue of righteousness denoting the responsibility of knowing and acting according to what is right, and he stressed that showing concern for the welfare of others is in fact what constitutes the image of the Virtuous Man (junzi) to be emulated by the people. In fact, both Chinese and Western advocates of values-based leadership in CSR management refer to this element of Chinese tradition explicating what might be called the role model responsibility of the leader. The preamble to the "Universal Declaration of Human Rights" as well as Chinese sources indicate that companies do bear their part of the responsibility in respecting human rights. Thus, Hu Jintao stresses "professional ethics" as a constituent element of the Harmonious Society (Xinhuanet, 2005) and the abovementioned "GoTone-Nanchang Forum Declaration" states that social responsibility performance is just as important as technology, price and quality for Chinese companies wishing to compete on global markets.

Moreover, the "China Social Compliance 9000 for Textile & Apparel Industry" (CSC9000T) also stresses companies' responsibilities. Issued in June 2005 by their China National Textile and Apparel Council, this management standard is commonly acknowledged as setting the tone for future developments in Asia and is demonstrating a commitment by the Chinese companies to take ownership for CSR. The preface of the CSC9000T states:

"Promoting and achieving social responsibility will help the China textile and apparel industry integrate well into the global supply chain, create a fair market, and meet the requirements of the global market. The implementation of a social responsibility management system will enhance business enterprises' core competitiveness, protect the legal rights and interests of all employees, and benefit all parties involved."

The normative framework of CSC9000T includes a comprehensive list of human rights treaties and conventions, as well as ILO conventions.

Critics doubt whether CSC9000T will contribute to real improvements with regard to core labour rights, because it is being developed and monitored by a close alliance between an employer organization and All-China Federation of Trade Unions (ACFTU), the official government-sponsored union federation, which in effect leaves no bargaining power to independent trade unions (ICFTU 2006: 4). The critics will not be appeased when seeing that a representative of the China National Textile and Apparel Council highlights the following feature of CSC9000T to illustrate its China-specific essence: "some topics such as Freedom of Association are addressed in ways that are more prudent for the Chinese operating environment" (Sun 2006: 22) and when finding that ILO Conventions nos. 87 and 98 on freedom of association and collective bargaining are not included in the normative framework of CSC9000T.

Certainly, these thorny issues should be addressed insistently, however, the fact remains that CSC9000T represents an explicit and rather comprehensive endorsement by one of the most influential Chinese employer organizations of the relevance of human rights to Chinese business.

The above examples show that recognition of human rights and business is emerging in Chinese government agencies and the business community. But still, human rights advocacy is vulnerable to changes in the political climate and companies addressing their human rights responsibilities are not up to an easy task. Therefore, the business case for human rights deserves special attention.

5. The business case for human rights in China

After more than a decade of demands on compliance to diverging codes of conduct by varying Western business associates, Chinese companies are beginning to express the wish to take a more proactive stance anticipating the demands, rather than having to react to them on an "ad hoc" basis. Moreover, Chinese companies in the coastal provinces are beginning to feel a vested interest in learning about ways to attract and keep employees. Performing as accelerating engines for the economic boom, these companies have had the upper hand setting the conditions when recruiting from a seemingly inexhaustible low-skill labour force. In recent years, however- er, these companies are being struck by labour shortage as workers are seeking elsewhere in search of better conditions. To use a phrase in common use, the companies have come to appreciate the "why" of CSR and are now searching for the "how" of CSR. Seen in this light, the business case for human rights can be based on the following argument:

CSR policies and codes of conduct vary between companies and they may even change over time. But the human rights standards – a key essence of CSR – are universal in space and time. In order to reduce their vulnerability vis-à-vis fluctuations in CSR policies and codes of conduct companies must therefore acquire an understanding of the human rights standards that relate to business and continually assess their compliance with these standards in their management and strategic processes. This is the way for companies to attain a proactive stance with regard to CSR and reap the combined benefits of anticipating the demands and seizing the opportunities in the global markets in a sustainable manner.

Citing a term derived from Chinese management theory, it can be observed that the "stakeholder model illustrates the art of Managing the Relationship of Efficiency and Equity (chuli xiaolü yu gongping guanxi) as it offers an answer to the difficult question of how business strategy may come to terms with ethical responsibility." The model comprises three aspects:

+ **The descriptive aspect** – indicating that the company is in fact imbedded in a network of stakeholders, who affect the surviv-

al of the company.
+ **The strategic aspect** – indicating that stakeholder management is an instrument recommending attitudes, structures,
and practices that can enhance the prosperity of the company.
+ **The normative aspect** – indicating that the interests of all
stakeholders are of intrinsic value. In other words, stakeholders have rights that management has a responsibility to respect
in an appropriate manner.

Through the application of the stakeholder model the synergy effect of responsibilities and opportunities for companies addressing human rights issues in their management strategies can be
illustrated. This puts the business case for human rights in perspective, highlighting possible benefits for a company committed to the stakeholder model, such as better reputation and image, more constructive dialogue with pressure groups, higher trust
by investors, more open national and global markets, higher employee loyalty and motivation, and lower employee turnover rates.

6. Defining the sphere of company responsibility

The concept of sphere of company responsibility offers an understanding of the international standards guiding the human rights
approach in business in concrete, operational terms.

It is important – not least in the Chinese context – to distinguish between the human rights responsibilities of governments and companies, respectively. While stressing that "companies should consider all rights when assessing the effect of their
operations," it should be asserted that generally speaking, companies only bear immediate responsibility with regard to the rights
of entitlement to a life of dignity in economic, social, and cultural terms and further distinctions may show how these rights can
be divided into three areas: Employment practices, community impact, and supply chain management (details on these areas follow
below). The concept of human rights tends to bring connotations

to torture, death penalty etc. and understandably, companies are reluctant to be linked with such controversial issues. This is not least the case with companies operating in China. Indicating the distinctions summarized above may anticipate this reluctance.

Moreover, Chinese companies should be introduced to the key concepts of human rights and business. "The reach of company responsibility" may serve as a heading for this introduction, divided into three sections. The first section points out the reasons why companies should develop a clear and operational definition of their reach of responsibility, as well as the three key concepts relevant in this regard: Due diligence, the precautionary principle, and risk management. Two subsequent sections describe the reach of company responsibility in more detail. "One of these sections may concern 'the nature of company responsibility'." Here, the distinction between defensive and positive rights is introduced, as well as the further distinction into four modes of duty, that is, to respect, to protect, to promote and to fulfil. This section ends with an explication of three categories of actions relating to company responsibility: essential actions, expected actions, and desirable actions.

The third and final section in an introduction to the key concepts of human rights and business may concern "the scope of company responsibility", offering rather detailed explanations of the two key concepts of sphere of influence and complicity. Concluding the part on the reach of company responsibility, this section remarks that companies should pay special attention to the risks related to investment in zones of current or potential conflict. It may quote the "Voluntary Principles on Security and Human Rights" to guide companies in balancing the needs for safety while respecting human rights and fundamental freedoms and it recommends the "Global Compact Business Guide for Conflict Management and Risk Management" as a tool to developing strategies for assessment of the impact of investment in conflict zones.

The general introduction of human rights and business should be accompanied by a tool offering practical guidance to Chinese companies on how to translate human rights principles into business practices in the Chinese context. The "China-specific Human Rights Compliance Assessment Quick Check" (China-specific HRCA Quick Check) is such a tool.

7. Translating human rights principles into business practices in China

The Danish Institute for Human Rights developed the "Human Rights Compliance Assessment" (HRCA) through a 6 year research process involving representatives from over 100 companies, human-rights-related organizations, and international specialists/researchers. The HRCA is the most comprehensive and reliable tool for helping companies deal with human rights issues relevant for their particular operations. The HRCA database comprises over 350 questions and 1000 corresponding human rights indicators, based on the principles contained in over 80 international human rights treaties and the ILO conventions.

The "HRCA Quick Check" is a condensed version of the "HRCA" and it concerns some of the most essential human rights issues, particularly relevant to companies, divided into the areas:

+ **Employment Practices** – concerning the rights of individuals employed by the company, or seeking employment with the company.
+ **Community Impact** – concerning the rights of individuals residing in societies, which are affected by company operations or products.
+ **Supply Chain Management** – concerning the rights of individuals affected by business partners.

Each area summarizes relevant human rights standards under a number of headings. Each heading guides the company through a process of self-assessment in three stages.

+ **General question** – conveying the issue in the form of a question enquiring about compliance in general terms.

+ **Narrative description** – describing the key aspects of the issue illustrated by examples.
+ **Indicators** – conveying the issue in the form of a number of questions concerning specific, concrete aspects of the company's policies, procedures and performances.

The "HRCA Quick Check" was launched in China at the Global Compact Summit in Shanghai in December 2005.

Development of the "China-specific HRCA Quick Check" is an ongoing process that is already well under way. The DIHR launched the tool at the Global Compact Summit in Shanghai in December 2005 and a Chinese translation is now available at the Website of Human Rights and Business Project, Danish Institute for Human Rights: http://www.humanrightsbusiness.org/020_project_publications.htm. Currently, it is undergoing a comprehensive consultation process aimed at ensuring that it will fit the Chinese context and appeal appropriately to a Chinese audience.

8. Conclusion

Promoting human rights and business in China does at times seem like fighting an uphill battle with two fronts. One front results from the fact that addressing human rights issues is not always uncontroversial in China. While China's human rights record bears a significant share of the responsibility, we should not forget that Western governments and organizations sometimes fail to address the issues in a constructive manner. The fact remains, however, that human rights now constitute an issue of recurring official and public debate and that China demonstrates genuine commitment to international human rights activities and dialogues. The body of human rights laws does, indeed, offer Chinese managers an adequate framework for companies developing and implementing a sustainable management strategy.

This relates to the other front resulting from the fact that concern for responsibility and sustainability in a broader perspective all too rarely matches up with concern for short term survival in an environment of relentless competition. This problem is part of the reality for all companies around the world and it becomes no less real in China, often playing a key role in "a race to the bottom" with other countries of similar status in the global value chains. At the same time, China's integration and gradual ascent in these value chains result in the emerging acknowledgement of the fact that compliance with international standards is the most viable way forward.

07

BEST INTENTIONS CANNOT GO FAR ENOUGH*
Salil Tripathi

———

The film "Blood Diamond" released this year, raises issues which may seem dated – conflict in Sierra Leone which was the prime focus of the campaign to stop trade in rough diamonds sourced from rebel-held areas in conflict zones. And yet the film raises important issues concerning the role of business, the law, societal expectations, and what companies can do.

Let us stay with Sierra Leone for a moment. That country had one of the most brutal civil wars in the 1990s. That conflict, as we now know, was funded primarily through revenues from natural resources – diamonds, in this case. The Revolutionary United Front was in control of large swathes of territory in Sierra Leone and it sold the rough diamonds extracted from those fields in international markets. The international trading community had no reason to classify diamonds by their origin. But that changed, thanks to sustained pressure from global civil society, UN sanctions, and the active interest of some governments. UN experts' panels established that the revenue the armed group received provided it with resources to continue the conflict, which led to attacks on civilians, widespread human rights abuses, and violations of international humanitarian law. Sanctions followed, and a certification scheme – first for Angola and Sierra Leone, and later for all rough diamonds – came into being after more than two years of negotiations involving the industry, governments, and the civil society. That scheme, Kimberley Process Certification Scheme, has brought considerable order to the trade, and its strength derives from its being partly mandatory.

Then again, staying in West Africa, let us look at the Niger Delta, which has been exceptionally violent since November last year. There have been several instances of mass killings, involving militias and security forces, and abduction of expatriate oil industry workers has increased. The cycle of violence begins with the deprivation experienced by communities in the Niger Delta, which host oil companies, suffer the costs and consequences (of leaking pipelines, gas flaring, and pollution), and see benefits going to the capital. The state is virtually absent in the Niger Delta – you don't easily find schools, primary health care clinics, or post offices. But you do find well-armed security forces, protecting the oil industry's infrastructure. Driven by a sense of good intentions, philanthropy, corporate social responsibility, the need to enhance reputation, or out of a sense of self-interest, most companies in the Niger Delta have large social investment programmes. But rather than benefiting the communities, many programmes have ended up dividing them, since benefits reach only some communities. Some projects don't work; companies promise more than they can deliver. When expectations are raised and not met, the communities are frustrated, leading to demonstrations and more violence targeting the companies. With widespread unemployment, communities seek jobs from companies, but being a capital-intensive industry requiring skilled labour, the oil industry has few direct jobs to offer the communities. Communities don't like jobs with contractors, who typically offer fewer benefits than the company does. When these frustrations reach boiling point, communities protest against the companies, and security forces respond, often with disproportionate force against the communities.

Add to this equation the easy availability of small arms, the peculiarly Nigerian phenomenon of bunkering (in which armed groups steal oil from pipelines and sell it in international markets), and the cycle of violence, violations, conflict, and repression continues. Partly to address these concerns, the international community came up with the Voluntary Principles for Security and Human Rights which included four governments (UK, US, Norway and the Netherlands), 16 companies, and seven international NGOs, including International Alert. These principles call upon companies to analyse the political and human rights risks in their area of operations, and govern the conduct of security forces, to ensure that in protecting the assets and staff of the companies, the forces operate within a framework that protects fundamental freedoms. Another, similar initiative was launched by the UK government, the Extractive Industry Transparency Initiative which seeks to ensure greater transparency in revenue sharing and management in countries where extractive industries operate.

To avoid the kind of problems that have beset Nigeria, the international community has increasingly explored the idea of getting things right at the beginning. One such example is the Chad-Cameroon pipeline, where the World Bank has devised an escrow account, in which future oil revenues from the pipeline will be deposited. Money from that account can be drawn only for legitimate development expenditure, such as health and education. However, the accumulated balances have risen, given the current increase in oil prices, and the government of Chad has drawn money for other purposes, which has led to the World Bank to stop further lending.

The conflict in Sudan is another interesting example of how companies can and do assist a government fighting a war. Sudanese officials have been on record saying that their ability to continue the war in southern Sudan was strengthened by the easy availability of resources due to the oil boom. There is a marked correlation between increased oil production, increased revenue to the state, and increased expenditure on defence. In Sudan, the oil industry is closely involved, and in some cases implicated with the conflict.

In the Democratic Republic of Congo, UN experts' panels have identified ways in which companies are exploiting resources which are contributing to a climate of corruption and conflict. The DRC is a major diamond producing nation, but the Kimberley Process cannot address the issues there because the KPCS is designed to address illicit activities by rebel forces, not state security forces. And in Mbuji Mayi, artisanal miners found stealing diamonds from a ring-fenced mine have been shot. Nobody is condoning theft, but the use of force is clearly disproportionate. However, under Kimberley Process, these rough diamonds are not covered because the violation occurred on a state-owned site, involving state security forces.

But let us not assume that this is a uniquely African problem. In Latin America, in Colombia, for years, rebel forces of FARC and ELN have regularly attacked the oil industry infrastructure in the regions of Caño Limón and Casanare. Communities that live by the oil industry are in constant danger of human rights abuses committed by the state forces or by the armed opposition groups. The war shows no sign of ending, and the communities remain caught in this conundrum.

In Asia, in Indonesia, communities living around mining companies and oil companies, in disparate parts such as Aceh and West Papua have also had to deal with human rights abuses, sometimes committed by the armed opposition groups, and at other times, by state forces. In each case, a company is present; while its presence alone does not constitute complicity, it raises fundamental questions about the role of business in weak governance zones, and responsibilities of companies operating in sub-optimal environments.

The industry has responded by creating voluntary initiatives meant to ensure that their own conduct within their sphere of influence does not lead to abuses. These initiatives include the Voluntary Principles, the Extractive Industries Transparency Initiative, the Kimberley Process, and the Global Compact. Collectively, these initiatives have helped create a climate in which companies begin addressing their responsibilities and devising operational policies to achieve meaningful change in behaviour. But the reality on the ground is often so violent and complicated, that these best intentions simply cannot go far enough.

Indeed, we cannot always depend on good intentions and individual initiatives for the protection of human rights, or for the elimination of conflict. What companies need is guidance at the ground level so that they can develop their procedures. Over the last few years, several tools have become available.

In December 2005, at the Shanghai meeting of the Global Compact Learning Forum, the Business Leaders' Initiative on Human Rights presented a publication on management processes that can help a company mainstream human rights concerns in its operational policies. Called the Guide for Integrating Human Rights into Business Management, the publication divided activities and scenarios into three categories – essential, expected, and desirable.

The Danish Institute for Human Rights has a comprehensive, detailed tool available, which collects international and regional laws, treaties, and appropriate domestic legislation, and provides a methodology to test the company's policies with existing international law to assess the firm's compliance.

The International Finance Corp., together with the International Business Leaders' Forum, the Global Compact, and several leading NGOs, is in the process of putting together a Human Rights Impact Assessment tool which is described as a tool to facilitate a company's ability to anticipate human rights risks and ways of mitigating them so that a company can respond proactively by developing appropriate processes.

Finally, let me turn to the tool we have developed at International Alert. It is called the Conflict Sensitive Business Practices (CSBP) tool and the iteration I will talk about is the Guidelines for Extractive Industries.

Why extractive industries? For the very reasons John Ruggie, the special representative of the UN Secretary-General on business and human rights, has described in his interim report presented to the Human Rights Council, which included an analysis of 65 NGO reports compiling credible allegations of human rights implicating companies. His study found that these violations tended to occur preponderantly in low income countries with a high degree of corruption, suffering from weak governance, and where the extractive industry tended to dominate. In such a climate, where resources are available and grievances are not addressed, conflict frequently results, causing deaths and misery, leading to human rights abuses and violations of international humanitarian law. International humanitarian law in this regard is particularly important because, unlike human rights law, it applies to non-state actors at all times, and unlike human rights law, it applies all the time and is therefore non-derogable.

Companies operating in such an environment need a robust tool to ensure that they are not complicit in human rights abuses, do not contribute to violations of international humanitarian law, and operate in a manner that is sensitive to the surroundings.

There has been considerable discussion around what constitutes complicity: while a broad-ranging, all-encompassing definition is not yet in place, it is sufficient to state, that if a company is in close proximity with a violation, a violator or a victim; if it is assisting, aiding, abetting, encouraging, supporting, or providing means to an entity that commits human rights abuses; if it knows, or should have known that such abuses were taking place; if it derives benefit from the abuses; if the abuses have gone on for some time; and if the company has taken no corrective action, or shown any due diligence to sever its links with the abuses; then it runs an extremely high risk of exposure to charges of complicity.

The CSBP tool that International Alert (IA) has developed provides a framework that helps companies raise the right questions, and to operate in a manner that does not contribute to conflict. It should be stressed that when we talk of conflict impact, we mean two-way impact; where companies are affected by conflict as well as where companies, their policies, and conduct, have an impact on conflict.

The CSBP was developed after extensive consultations with companies, academics, governments, and civil society. It was three years in the making, and it was funded by the Swiss Department of Foreign Affairs, the UK Department for International Development, Foreign Affairs Canada, and Swedish SIDA. It was based on field trips to Azerbaijan, Colombia and Indonesia. Many experts were also consulted, and a steering committee, comprising extractive industry companies and consultancies, guided the process. The full text of the report can be downloaded from International Alert's website (www.international-alert.org/). It is being piloted at the moment at two projects in Colombia.

The report comprises a screening tool, which includes conflict risk impact assessment at the macro level and at the project level. It also underscores project level risks, including land use, revenue sharing, security force management, stakeholder consultation, and relationship with the community. Finally, there are flash points, including stakeholder engagement, resettlement, compensation, indigenous peoples, social investments, dealing with armed groups, security arrangements, human rights, and corruption and transparency.

For a company to act properly, it needs more than individual goodwill, or corporate good intentions. It needs a framework. Well-meaning principles and codes of conduct address specific crises, but cannot prevent or end conflict. Tools exist which may help companies to mainstream their values and principles, as well as their moral responsibilities under human rights law and obligations under international humanitarian law, into operational practices. Are they sufficient in ensuring that the company will never abuse human rights or contribute to conflict?

It is not possible to think of such guarantees; a tool is, in the end, a tool; it depends on what use the user makes of it. But are such tools necessary? The way companies can improve their performance is through a well-designed framework, and that's what the tools set out to do: to provide such a framework. What the companies do with the tools is, in the end, in their own hands.

08

WATER, RIGHTS AND RESPONSIBILITIES

THE REACH AND LIMITS OF CORPORATE ENGAGEMENT

Carlo Donati

John F. Kennedy said "Anyone who can solve the problems of water will be worthy of 2 Nobel Prizes – one for peace and one for science."

This is even more true today than it was over 40 years ago when President Kennedy said it.

And Nobel Prize winning biochemist Albert Szent-Gyorgi said, "Water is life's mother and medium. There is no life without water."

The UN's World Water Commission for the 21st Century stated seven years ago:

"Every human being, now and in the future, should have access to safe water for drinking, adequate sanitation and enough food and energy at reasonable cost. Providing adequate water to meet these basic needs must be done in an equitable manner that works in harmony with nature."

But what do we need to do to meet that basic need and right? And what is the role of a company like Nestlé in the process?

Before getting to specific actions and solutions, we should understand the context and extent of the water issue.

First, water availability around the world has a link to the broader – and very topical – issue of climate change.

Sir Nicholas Stern, Head of the UK Government Economic Service, clearly made the connection in his April 2006 report, "Responding to the Challenge of Climate Change."

"Climate change will affect the basic elements of life for people around the world – access to water, food production, health, and the environment. Hundreds of millions of people could suffer hunger, water shortages and coastal flooding as the world warms.

Warming will have many severe impacts, often mediated through water:

+ Melting glaciers will initially increase flood risk and then strongly reduce water supplies, eventually threatening one-sixth of the world's population, predominantly in the Indian sub-continent, parts of China, and the Andes in South America.

+ Declining crop yields, especially in Africa, could leave hundreds of millions without the ability to produce or purchase sufficient food.

+ In higher latitudes, cold-related deaths will decrease. But climate change will increase worldwide deaths from malnutrition and heat stress.

+ Developed countries in lower latitudes will be more vulnerable – for example, water availability and crop yields in southern Europe are expected to decline by 20% with a 2°C increase in global temperatures. Regions where water is already scarce will face serious difficulties and growing costs."

And this is without taking into account the effects of population growth. According to Dr. Ismael Serageldin, who was formerly the Vice-President of the World Bank, the Founding Chair of the Global Water Partnership, a founding governor of the World Water Council, as well as the chairman of the World Commission for Water in the 21st Century:

"Assume 3 billion more people on the planet, mostly in the developing countries.

Note that currently it takes on average a litre of water to produce a calorie of food. The average human being therefore requires some 2700 litres of water per day through food. It takes 2000 to 5000 tons of water to produce a ton of rice, and about 1200 tons of water to produce a ton of wheat.

Assume further that the contribution of water to all food production is 40%. Assume further that all irrigation systems achieve water use efficiency of 70% at the basic level, a remarkable achievement if it were to happen. *Approximately 17% more water is still required in irrigation to meet the food production demand!*

Altering any of those assumptions means that the forecast for water needs will *increase by about 50% or more*. However, irrigation is not likely to get more water. The urban populations of the developing world are going to *treble* in the next 30 years. Industry is going to increase, and pollution is not going to decrease."

A bleak prospect so far, and there is further warning – but also hope – in the words of the United Nations Development Programme:

"Water plays a pivotal role for sustainable development, including poverty reduction. Given the importance of water to poverty alleviation, human and ecosystem health, the management of water resources becomes of central importance. Currently, over 1 billion people lack access to water and over 2.4 billion lack access to basic sanitation.

This water crisis is largely our own making. It has resulted *not* from the natural limitations of the water supply or lack of financing and appropriate technologies, even though these are important factors, but rather from profound failures in water governance."

The UNDP has further commented that water management will be a critical factor in whether we can realistically expect any one of the eight Millennium Development Goals to be achieved.

Although population growth, increased food production, rising standards of living, urbanization, pollution by households, agriculture and industry, and just plain wastage, are putting unsustainable demands on our water resources, if water is essentially not so much in short supply as mismanaged, perhaps it is also within our collective reach to remedy the situation?

As an aside, we need to be mindful of the impact of other "unforeseen" factors in water availability. For instance, the growing demand of agricultural crops to produce ethanol to replace gasoline in our cars. It's estimated that it takes 1400 gallons of water to produce enough corn for one gallon of ethanol. We are treating these gallons of water as if there were no environmental cost, when, in fact, much of this water is being taken from fossil aquifers whose water was deposited during the last ice age, and is not being replaced.

In the United States, the Ogalala Aquifer, covering 8 major states, is being rapidly depleted, with less than 10% of the water being replaced on an annual basis, and in the southern areas, closer to 1%.

In India, farmers are now drilling 200 to 300 feet into the ground to access water, where only a few years ago, it was less than 100 feet. And there is now a competition for water and a race as to who can drill further down. The same thing is happening in China – and this cannot be sustained.

What we must realize – and realize now – is that we're caught in the twin jaws of, on the one hand, a rapidly escalating demand for water, and on the other hand water disappearing forever from our non-renewable fossil aquifers. We can replace oil with other sources of energy, but there is no replacement for water. And without water, there is no life.

That is the bad news.

The good news is that we have it within our power to solve the problem. There are very practical things that we can do within our reach which can reverse this life-destroying trend.

30% of water in municipal water systems is lost through leakage. If we simply did a better job of attaching pipes to each other, we could go a long way to fix the problem.

Vast amounts of water are lost through open irrigation and water transport channels. For instance, we bring vast amounts of water from northern California to support life in southern California, a large percentage of which evaporates on its way to Los Angeles.

We want to make sure that even the poorest people have access to clean water, but that cannot happen if the users of water don't pay its true cost. Water today is treated more like a free, disposable resource. If we were to price it correctly, it would have an immediate, large, and positive impact on water conservation.

As the UNDP and others point out, effective water governance can have a major impact on preserving and extending access to clean water. Governments have a major job to do in this regard.

70% of our water is extracted by agriculture, and it is clear that agricultural policy needs to change. For instance, rice is the world's most popular grain, but it requires about twice as much water as wheat, and ten times a much as lettuce. Yet rice and wheat are both supported by price guarantees by some governments, giving little incentive to grow anything else or to use less water.

Certainly there are cultural factors to consider around the importance of rice in the diet, but better agricultural policies can greatly reduce water usage. We don't need to stop irrigating, but we need to irrigate in a way that doesn't waste water on such a massive scale.

Meat requires even more water to produce than either rice or wheat, and meat consumption is rising with affluence in countries across Asia. What we eat – our own personal diet – affects the world's water problem.

So it is clear that we all – including industry, agriculture, and households – need to change our ways, if we are to sustain and improve life on this planet.

And the food industry, at least as much as any other, has a real interest in making a positive contribution to solving the water crisis.

There is in fact much the food industry can do to enhance water management for the benefit of all. In this article we will principally focus on what Nestlé is bringing to bear on the issue and what actions we are taking to impact the water crisis, in our own way, through water management. While we won't comment on other industries or indeed on other companies in our industry, many of these measures could be applied elsewhere.

Clearly, Nestlé is a business. This means it must meet the demands of its shareholders and other stakeholders to create long-term, sustainable growth. We square the needs of society with our corporate needs through the concept of creating shared value, as outlined in our 2006 report, "The Nestlé Concept of Corporate Social Responsibility." In the words of Chairman and CEO, Peter Brabeck-Letmathe, who said "It is my firm belief that, in order for a business to create value for its shareholders over the long term, it must also bring value to society."

So even though Nestlé is essentially a relatively low carbon-footprint enterprise, notwithstanding its size, it has a clear interest in water sustainability. Furthermore, we understand that making sure our own house is in order – through implementing best-in-class water management in our own business; then by sharing our knowledge with others and finally by contributing to the broader debate on water – is the most effective, practical way we can make a tangible impact.

Nestlé considers the water issue of sufficient importance to have published a report on water management, which has recently been distributed to its shareholders and discussed in public fora around the world. It has undertaken this exercise for three reasons.

First, as the world's largest food and beverage company, we rely on access to clean water in order to operate, to produce quality products for our consumers.

Second, we would like to document both the actions we have taken in our own food manufacturing operations, where we have direct control, and also the efforts we have made to improve access to clean water in indirect ways beyond our own direct business activities.

Third, we want to obtain stakeholder input and explore what future directions we intend to pursue in order to contribute to improvements in the world's access to clean water. As a company we utilise a very small fraction of the world's water. But by working with others, we believe we can have a positive impact.

There are four main areas in which Nestlé acts to improve water management, and by extension positively impact access to water:

+ Leveraging areas where we have direct control, i.e. over our own manufacturing operations.
+ Managing water for consumers and sensitizing consumers about water issues.
+ Encouraging farmers to promote good water management and bringing clean water to communities.
+ Scaling up and engaging, offering Nestlé experience in the global water management arena.

1. Leveraging areas of direct control

This is where Nestlé can have the most direct impact on water management – regarding the 20% of water used by industry. We take our water management role very seriously.

Nestlé requires continuous improvement of water efficiency and reduction of waste in all its operations. Each year Nestlé raises the bar in terms not only of the amount but also the quality of the water discharged from its plants. We make further enhancements to tried and tested policies and processes so that we can improve further. For example, we expect to achieve ISO 14001 certification worldwide by 2010 for our factories.

It is a Nestlé objective to lower the ratio of water used per kilo of product by at least 3% per year. While Nestlé production volume almost doubled in the past decade, the amount of water used was reduced by 29%.

Perhaps our most long standing impact in water management is in the area of waste water treatment. Nestlé aims to ensure that water leaves its plants as clean as it was when it entered. Today, Nestlé operates 160 treatment plants worldwide; either because in-house treatment is more efficient or, mainly in developing countries, because local infrastructure does not exist or does not meet Nestlé's stringent environmental standards.

We realised back in the 1920s that clean water availability is just as much about what you put back into the environment, as it is about what you take out in the first place. Our first waste water treatment plant was built in 1930; and frequently when we establish ourselves in developing countries in particular, we are the first to develop treatment plants. In fact, local authorities frequently ask us to open our plants to other businesses and even government departments, to share our knowledge with them as they scale up their own efforts.

The basis for all water management activities is the "Nestlé Water Policy – Water Resource Guidelines for Sustainable Management," which serves as a reference and standard for all managers. This is translated into concrete action at the factory level through the Nestlé Environmental Management System (NEMS) that defines and monitors strict criteria for compliance for all its factories.

2. Managing water for consumers and sensitizing consumers about water issues

This is where Nestlé impacts the 10% of water used by consumers. It's worth remembering first of all that the footprint of Nestlé's Bottled Waters business is very small: just 0.0009% of available fresh water.

As the world leader in bottled water, Nestlé is aware that many take a keen interest in our actions in respect of bottled water. For us this means not only at the extraction stage but in terms of packaging and transportation as well.

Our approach begins once again with a comprehensive management system; a dedicated Water Resources Department is in charge of this task which includes the identification and selection of a water resource, installation and maintenance of equipment and material necessary to protect and monitor it, and the on-going monitoring of the source. The monitoring includes hydrogeological assessments of the sites, frequent testing of the source water quality and regular review of environmental conditions and parameters such as water levels in production boreholes, spring flow and rain fall data.

Some would say, what's the point of bottled water; isn't it better to invest in reliable tapwater systems that are in the end cheaper for consumers, especially those in developing countries? Nestlé's believes bottled water can never compete in the marketplace with tap water, which is a fraction of the cost. But to provide clean tap water requires both political will and good water governance. Bottled water essentially competes with other bottled drinks, particularly soft drinks. And those who need access to clean drinking water the most – those living on one dollar a day, are not likely to buy bottled water.

But Nestlé Waters' interface with consumers has in fact significant long term advantages in impacting the water management issue. Through the Water Education for Teachers (WET) non-profit organization, launched in the United States in 1984 and first sponsored by Nestlé Waters in 1992, Nestlé is helping to provide education resources to teachers in 22 countries. The goal is to facilitate and promote awareness, appreciation, knowledge and stewardship of water resources. This is a worldwide programme to encourage future generations to use water responsibly that has reached 400,000 teachers and millions of schoolchildren around the world. **119**

3. Encouraging farmers to promote good water management and bringing clean water to communities

Agriculture accounts for using around 70% of the world's fresh water resources. Nestlé doesn't own any farmland, but it is here, more than anywhere else, that our needs converge with those of society in the field of water availability and water management, now and in the future. It is also here that we are often able to channel our community investments most effectively, in respect of making clean water available.

To maintain consumer confidence in the high quality of its products, Nestlé must be assured a long-term supply of safe and high-quality agricultural raw materials. Increasing water scarcity in many regions of the world threatens this supply and may also create social and economic risks for farmers and communities. Nestlé addresses this risk proactively by turning the attention of its 850 agronomists to the water problem.

More recently, Nestlé has made water a central contribution area of its Sustainable Agriculture Initiative Nestlé (SAIN), which was launched in 2002 to optimize the supply chain "from farm to factory." We're already making some exciting inroads in this area through our more than 850 agricultural extension workers, who interface with more than 400,000 farmers around the world, principally in respect of milk, coffee and cocoa; but also through our partnerships with intergovernmental agencies, other companies and NGOs.

And we're introducing water management aspects in our milk districts. One of the best examples of that is in Pakistan, where we're working with UNDP to empower 5000 female livestock workers, who are sharing water management best practice as part of the animal husbandry techniques they're introducing in dairy farms across the country, using Nestlé-developed techniques as a model.

Nestlé engages directly in clean water projects, including by helping to overcome barriers to local communities' access to safe and clean water and by providing safe drinking water in response to humanitarian disasters – nearly two million litres for Hurricane Katrina, the Tsunami and the Pakistan earthquake.

In our milk districts in India we have a comprehensive programme of providing clean water wells in our milk district villages. We select communities where full engagement by the local government can be relied upon; and where we can site the wells in the schools. This then gives children a safe and clean supply of water; water education is included in their schooling as part of the agreement; and they are enthused and empowered to take good care of that resource for future generations. At the present time, 71 drinking water facilities have been completed, reaching around 25,000 school children.

4. Scaling up and engaging: Offering Nestlé experience in the global water management arena

Nestlé engages with a wide variety of people and organizations to improve the state of water management throughout the world. Focus is on projects to improve local water management: to establish better standards of water resource management: to improve education about water conservation; and to participate in the debate on the impacts of agricultural and other policies on water resources. Regarding our own operations, Nestlé is focusing our own forward-looking water management efforts around water-stressed regions. To begin with, we are compiling our own proprietary water stress index and evaluating the relative performance of Nestlé factories located in 13 water-stressed countries where we found that additional water-use efficiency is possible. These factories will receive special focus, to assist local factory management to further understand the challenges, to prompt local stress assessments that generate new water-saving projects, and assure that local management is informed about and involved in community activities related to water.

To increase further access to water for communities, Nestlé is now using the techniques tested in India in its new partnership with the International Federation of Red Cross and Red Crescent Societies – making water and sanitation a key element in our 3 million Swiss Franc partnership with the IFRC over the coming years. Key areas for investment have already been identified, for example in Mozambique, where the first wells to bring much-needed clean water to 15,000 villagers were inaugurated in November 2006. Recently, the IFRC has used the Nestlé-developed model to secure substantial additional funding from the European Union to scale up this project elsewhere in Africa.

On a more global scale, Nestlé's Chairman and CEO has long been involved with the World Economic Forum's Water Initiative, which essentially seeks to engage its members in promotion of best practice water use technologies, techniques and strategies; participation in multi-stakeholder water resource management strategies within watersheds or specific regions; and participation in broader national and multinational water policy and governance dialogues.

And while preparing the "Nestle Water Management Report," we engaged Accountability International to identify, clarify and synthezize the views of key stakeholders on water issues. This is just the start of a broader commitment to share experience and feedback on water; but Accountability found those key stakeholders ready to engage with us on water issues. They are looking for Nestlé to address water issues beyond our direct operational impact and to take a lead in the international debate on related subjects.

These conclusions are very encouraging for Nestlé; most people have an opinion about the role of private corporations in water, whether positive or negative. Still, we find that many may not be aware of the less visible ways that water matters to a corporation, that water is an issue not only for water distribution and bottled water companies but for all companies. Also, many may not think of business as a credible voice on water. Clearly, corporations have work to do in sharing more of what they are accomplishing, in showing that there is expertise and experience that can be placed in service of others.

In short, everyone has a role to play in water management.

As for Nestlé, we will continue contributing our experience and what we have learned from others to the debate on water management. We believe we have a lot to contribute, and we know we have a lot to learn.

Nestlé can summarize its commitments on water in the following way – an approach launched at the World Water Forum in Mexico in March 2006.

Nestlé will:
W ork to continue reducing the amount of water used per kilo of food and beverage produced.
A ssure that our activities respect local water resources.
T ake care that water discharged into the environment is clean.
E ngage with agricultural suppliers to promote water conservation among farmers.
R each out to others to collaborate on water conservation and access, with a particular focus on women and children.

Though it operates all over the world, Nestlé is a company with its roots in Swiss pragmatism. Hence the practical, action-oriented approaches outlined in this article. For Nestlé, our actions in respect of water management are a practical way of impacting the broader water issue, itself a symptom of environmental macro-issues such as climate change.

It is in terms of practical, action-oriented solutions that Nestlé as a food company is contributing to the water issue. This practical, action-oriented approach is our commitment to making the most substantial, positive impact we can, at the same time as we share our experiences with other stakeholders and learn from them.

To quote again our Chairman and CEO, Peter Brabeck-Let-mathe, "No one partner can do it all, but together we can influence, alter, protect, and preserve the vital resource of water for future generations."

The Nestlé Water Management Report, and additional information on Nestlé's contribution to water management can be found at www.water.nestle.com

09

ETHICAL VALUES AND INTER-NATIONAL SALES CONTRACTS

Ingeborg Schwenzer & Benjamin Leisinger

1. Introduction

1.1 Business and ethics?

Before turning to the subject-matter of this article, it is appropriate to explain what business or contract law has to do with ethics and how this issue becomes relevant in modern international sales contracts.

Years ago, business and ethics were as far apart as to be viewed as some kind of contradiction. According to leading economists – such as the "The Bank of Sweden Prize in Economic Sciences in Memory of Alfred Nobel" winner Milton Friedman – "the business of business is business."[1] Companies' only social responsibility was thought to be to use their resources to make profits for their shareholders.[2] The corporation, as such, was simply used as a means to an end.[3] Human rights were seen as belonging to the realm of government concerns, not of companies, and human rights violations as internal political issues, with which companies should not, on principle, interfere.[4]

It is, therefore, no wonder that the age of industrialization is known as one of the darkest chapters in history regarding human rights and the protection of the environment. In 1788, for example, children made up two-thirds of the workforce on powered equipment in 143 water mills in England and Scotland.[5] Only slowly did governments start to realize that such behavior was unsustainable and react with the enactment of legislation. Thus, first and foremost it was – and still is today – the duty of *states* and the *community of states* to legislate and then enforce such regulations in order to prevent unethical behavior. But is that tool still efficient today? In an age of globalization and, most importantly, of so-called "failing states" – states in which the government is unwilling or unable to react in this regard –, such legislation has, in fact, lost its power to guarantee minimum ethical standards. "Effective enforcement remains the crucial missing piece of the regulatory puzzle."[6] This is one of the reasons why globalization is sometimes called "the race to the bottom."[7] But, failing action by the states, who is then responsible and powerful?

During recent years, publicly listed firms, especially those acting on a global level, have started to realize that ethical behavior can, in fact, have a positive impact and, conversely, unethical behavior a negative impact on their business. A recent study by Claude Fussler concluded that responsible excellence pays.[8] According to his study, 76 companies publicly committed to social corporate responsibility made it to the Dow Jones Sustainability Index[9] (DJSI World Index) and outperformed the Morgan Stanley Capital Index (MSCI) by 3.7% over the analyzed three-year period between June 2001 and June 2004. It has been statistically shown that corporate reputation does indeed translate into financial value.[10] The problem is that measuring the return-on-investment with regard to ethical behavior is little more than guesswork. "Investment is easier to quantify than increased opportunities from an enhanced reputation."[11] Given the different factors that also play a role in such studies and that influence the outcome and the performance, it is perhaps more convincing to take the opposite approach and show that unethical behavior does not pay: "If you think compliance with ethical criteria is expensive try non-compliance"[12]. Shell, for example, faced a tremendous loss of reputation in 1995 when the story was spread that it had tried to sink a platform – the "Brent Spar" – that was allegedly still contaminated with oil. In 1984, Union Carbide Corporation was ordered by the Indian Supreme Court to pay US$ 470 million because of the release of methyl isocyanate that caused the death of 15,000 people and disabled another 170,000.[13] Another example is Bridgestone: in November 2005, the International Labor Rights Fund filed an Alien Tort Claims Act case against Bridgestone before a US District Court in California based on alleged forced labor on the Firestone plantation in Harbel, Liberia. According to the claim,[14] tappers on that plantation are required to tap more than 650 trees a day. This means that, in addition to other mandatory tasks, including cleaning the taps, applying pesticides and fertilizers to the trees, and carrying 75-pound buckets of latex to collection points up to a mile away – all for US$ 3.19 a day –, they have an eight hour day in which to tend to 650 trees twice. Even if these allegations turn out to be untrue, the financial consequences of such lawsuits can be – and usually are – considerable. In today's connected world, not in the least due to the "world wide web," unethical behavior by one company – or even that of a supplier or an associated company – in one country can have world-wide financial consequences.

Another reason for the growing awareness of ethical standards is that, in the long term, unethical behavior can have negative internal effects: talented and quality-focused employees – the most valuable "human resource" of a company – leave the company because they are unable to reconcile its activities with their own conscience.[15] Furthermore, a company with a bad reputation will not be able to obtain and retain the best graduates.[16] There are also additional external consequences: if consumers have the choice between two different, but equally expensive products, the circumstances under which such products are manufactured influence the decision to buy.[17] In the case of Shell, consumers even started to boycott the company. According to a study in 1995, 78% of U.S. consumers would avoid retailers if they knew they were dealing in sweatshop goods.[18]

In addition to this, there is also a more subtle benefit from ethical behavior: the rule of law is promoted. This can have positive effects on the development of legal systems in which contracts are enforced fairly, bribery and corruption are less prevalent, and all business entities have equal access to legal process and equal protection under the law.[19] In such circumstances, a smoother and more profitable operation of business is thereby simultaneously promoted.[20]

Another reason why ethical behavior pays – especially from a shareholder's perspective – is that a considerable amount of money is invested based on social responsibility.[21] In 2005, 375 so-called SRI – socially responsible investment – funds existed in Europe.[22] According to a study by the European Social Investment Forum (Eurosif), socially responsible investment amongst European institutional investors in 2003 was as high as € 336 billion.[23] As early as 1999, socially responsible investment in the United States amounted to as much as US$ 2.16 trillion,[24] growing to US$ 2.29 trillion in 2005.[25]

1.2 States – the primary duty holders

As already mentioned above, it is, first and foremost, the task of public lawmaking bodies, established by states or the community of states, to deal with the attainment of ethical standards. They have to define which standards are to be applied to the respective labor market and concerning the environment. With regard to sales contracts, it is primarily up to the governments in the country where the incriminating behavior takes place to take appropriate action. However, these governments all too often fail in implementing and enforcing human rights, labor or environmental standards.

In the second place, it is arguably also the task of the community of states to react to unethical behavior and to force the failing states to comply, for example, by means of embargoes and other trade sanctions. However, in many cases, the necessary majority cannot be obtained or applied sanctions are not sufficiently efficient, e.g. in the case of the oil-for-food program in Iraq. As all these traditional means have proven inadequate to achieve the intended goals, recent years have seen several initiatives implemented to shift the task from governments to private enterprises.

1.3 "Non-voluntary" initiatives

On an international level, so-called "non-voluntary" initiatives are taking shape with regard to corporations. One important example is the "Norms on the Responsibilities of Transnational Corporations and Other Business Enterprises with Regard to Human Rights" which have been approved by the United Nations Sub-Commission on the Promotion and Protection of Human Rights in its Resolution 2003/16.[26] The Norms, in Article 1, quite traditionally note that "[s]tates have the primary responsibility to promote, secure the fulfillment of, respect, ensure respect and protect human rights recognized in international as well as national law [...]." However, the norms also hold that "[w]ithin their sphere of activity and influence, transnational corporations and other business enterprises have the obligation to promote [...] and protect human rights [...]." This initiative is "non-voluntary" because it places an "obligation" on corporations and not a mere voluntary commitment. Article 15, for example, states that each transnational corporation or other business enterprise shall apply and incorporate these Norms in their contracts. According to the Commentary[27] on this article, enterprises "shall ensure that they only do business with (including purchasing from and selling to) contractors, subcontractors, suppliers [...] or natural or other legal persons that follow these or substantially similar Norms." The Norms are not a treaty. Nor are they mandatorily applicable to any state or company.[28] However, "the legal authority of the Norms derives principally from their sources in treaties and customary international law, as a restatement of international legal principles applicable to companies."[29]

1.4 The OECD Guidelines for Multinational Enterprises

An initiative that is also worth mentioning here is the OECD Guidelines for Multinational Enterprises, which form part of the OECD Declaration on International Investment and Multinational Enterprises.[30] These rules set out recommendations made by governments to multinational enterprises. The governments are committed to promoting the Guidelines. The recommendations cover, among other things, human rights, labor standards, environmental standards, anti-corruption and bribery, and consumer protection. In order to implement the Guidelines, National Contact Points (NCP) have been established in participating countries. Their purpose is to "contribute to the resolution of issues that arise relating to implementation of the Guidelines in specific instances. The NCP will offer a forum for discussion and assist the business community, employee organizations and other parties concerned to deal with the issues raised in an efficient and timely manner and in accordance with applicable law."[31] With the agreement of the parties involved, access to consensual and non-adversarial means, such as conciliation or mediation, is also facilitated.

The scope of the Guidelines was extended in 2000 to the supply chain. According to paragraph 10 of the General Policies of the Guidelines, businesses should "[e]ncourage, where practicable, business partners, including suppliers and subcontractors, to apply principles of corporate conduct compatible with the Guidelines." This weak formulation was heavily criticized by NGOs.[32] Unfortunately, the OECD Committee on International Investment and Multinational Enterprises (CIME) additionally applies a so-called "investment nexus." This requirement leads to the consequence that cases not concerning investment, but only trade, are rejected.[33] CIME held that the Guidelines have been developed in the specific context of international investment by multinational enterprises.[34]

The combination of the voluntary nature of the guidelines and the narrow application unfortunately restrain the OECD Guidelines' power as an efficient tool to combat the violation of ethical standards.

1.5 Private initiatives

As actions by governments and the community of states often, for example, due to their vagueness, lack the necessary power to bind, or take a considerable amount of time to actually come into force – in failing states, it is unlikely that the necessary regulations will come into existence at all –, and since ethical behavior is becoming increasingly more important to businesses, companies have started to take care of the problem themselves through founding private initiatives. As Mary Robinson has put it, "business leaders don't have to wait – indeed, increasingly they can't afford to wait – for governments to pass and enforce legislation before they pursue 'good practices' in support of international human rights, labor and environmental standards [...]."[35]

Know your business partners

Businesses spend a considerable amount of money on so-called "ethics audits" before they actually begin cooperation with another company, such as a supplier. Some companies – for example, Puma[36] – even publish a list of all their suppliers to guarantee transparency. The Global Reporting Initiative[37] is one such measure undertaken in regard of guaranteeing transparency.

Additionally, standard norms have been created, such as the ISO 14000 family from the International Standardization Organization, which deal with – predominantly environmental – ethics in business and have been implemented by some 760,900 organizations in 154 countries.[38] Another example is SA 8000 from Social Accountability International (SAI), which operates as a business tool for defining and verifying compliance with key human rights norms.[39] There are several organizations that are accredited to do SA 8000 certification, which ensures the application of an independent and objective standard.[40] A further example, familiar to most consumers, is the label on food products stating that the food was produced in an ecologically friendly manner.

United Nations Global Compact

On an international level, the UN Global Compact has to be specially highlighted as one of the most successful private initiatives. At Klaus Schwab's World Economic Forum in January 1999 in Davos, Kofi Annan addressed the business community and asked them to join an international initiative.[41] This initiative consists today of ten principles – covering human rights, labor, environment and anti-corruption –, and has a total of 2774 participants, many of whom have more than 50,000 suppliers.[42]

The UN Global Compact begins with a general part, Principles 1 and 2, which state that businesses should, within their sphere of influence, support and respect the protection of internationally-proclaimed human rights and make sure they are not complicit in human rights abuses. As the ethical commitment is, on the one hand, limited to the companies' sphere of influence and, on the other hand, extended to complicity, these terms need further clarification. The concept of "sphere of influence" is not defined in detail.[43] It is, however, safe to say that "sphere of influence" can be understood as the companies' responsibility for their own *employees*, their *next tier suppliers and direct business partners*. Conversely, complicity usually refers to corporate involvement in governmental action.[44] However, the exact meaning of this expression is a highly sensitive question which is yet to be adequately answered.[45]

The second group of principles, Principles 3 to 6, deals with labor standards. Issues addressed here are the freedom of association and the effective recognition of the right to collective bargaining, forced and compulsory labor, child labor,[46] and discrimination in respect of employment and occupation. A corporation's commitment to freedom of association – to take up this example –, however, does not mean that workforces must be organized or that companies must invite unions in, but simply that employers should not interfere with an employee's decision to associate, nor should they discriminate against the employee or a representative of the employee.[47]

The third part of the Global Compact, Principles 7 to 9, addresses environmental issues. Principle 7, for example, states that businesses should support a "precautionary approach" to environmental issues. This principle refers to the Rio Declaration, which – in its principle 15 – states that "where there are threats of serious or irreversible damage, lack of full scientific certainty shall not be used as a reason for postponing cost-effective measures to prevent environmental degradation."[48] The last part of the Global Compact, which was added at a later point in time – on 24 June 2004, during the UN Global Compact Leaders Summit –, deals with corruption. Principle 10 states that businesses should work against corruption in all its forms, including extortion and bribery. This principle enjoyed great support and "sent a strong worldwide signal that the private sector shares responsibility for the challenges of eliminating corruption"[49] while also "demonstrat[ing] a new willingness in the business community to play its part in the fight against corruption."[50]

The UN Global Compact initiative is voluntary and imposes no sanctions if its members fail to comply with the standards. However, as there are reporting obligations associated with membership to the initiative, the behavior of the members becomes transparent. According to a study by McKinsey, 15% of the Global Compact participants did, indeed, change suppliers or other business partners due to concerns over human rights, environmental or labor standards.[51]

Initiatives in special trade branches

Apart from such initiatives on a global level, there are private initiatives in specific trade sectors. One example is the "Electronic Industry Code of Conduct."[52] This code incorporates norms, such as setting a maximum number of working hours at 60 per week, and prescribing human treatment or nondiscrimination in supplier contracts, as, according to the introduction of this code, the participants are under an obligation to, at least, require their *next tier suppliers* to acknowledge and implement the code.[53] Another example is the code of conduct implemented by Yum!. Yum! which comprises All American Food, KFC, Long John Silvers, Pizza Hut and Taco Bell and, thereby, represents nearly 34,000 restaurants in more than 100 countries and territories.[54]

1.6 Problematic cases

If one looks at the aforementioned initiatives, it may be surprising to learn that alarming events still occur in the world – especially in developing countries. Each year, several thousand children are forced to work on cocoa plantations in the Ivory Coast, who have been previously sold into slavery from one of the neighboring countries.[55] In Indian cottonseed production, approximately 400,000 – mostly female – children are employed as "bonded laborers" and have to work between 9 and 11 hours a day for an average wage of US$ 11 per month.[56] Another example regarding environmental issues is tuna: up until recent times, an estimated 300,000 dolphins were killed each year because of old fishing methods.[57] This number has now decreased considerably. How-ever, the fishing-related death of dolphins still poses a problem.[58] Another critical subject is pesticides. By simply adding a few chem-ical components, dangerous chemical weapons can be – and are – produced.[59] Similar problems arise in connection with all so-called "dual-use goods."

What can a buyer do if it realizes that the products it has purchased were produced under such conditions? What are the seller's possibilities if it learns about serious human rights viola-tions by one of its buyers, where one of its products is involved?

Some questions can be answered by referring to the appli-cable public law. With regard to private law matters, these need to be resolved by applying the law governing the contract. In an in-ternational context, this is likely to be the Convention on Con-tracts for the International Sale of Goods – CISG. This convention has been ratified by 70 countries[60] and, according to its Article 1, is applicable to contracts of sale of goods between parties whose places of business are in different states when the States are Con-tracting States or when the rules of private international law lead to the application of the law of a Contracting State. If the CISG is indeed applicable, it is crucial to determine whether ethical stand-ards have become part of the contract in the first place and, if so, what remedies the aggrieved party may resort to.

2. Consequences of public law regulations
2.1 Illegality
If, in a given case, there are indeed public law regulations that con-demn certain behavior, is it up to state law to define the legal con-sequences of a violation of such a prohibition. Although it might be conceivable, albeit in rather rare cases, that a state declares a sales contract to be void if the goods in question have been manu-factured by a means in violation of human rights – such as child la-bor –, this would not fall under the CISG. According to Article 4(a) CISG, the validity[61] of the contract is not governed by the Con-

vention. Thus, the applicable law to the question of validity would have to be determined by private international law.

2.2 Prohibition of import or export

In cases in which the community of states or – as the case may be – even a single state announces an embargo, thus prohibiting either the import or export of goods from or to a state in which the enforcement of basic human rights is not ensured, questions of exemption from liability to perform contractual obligations may arise. State interventions preventing contractual performance, such as quotas, export or import embargoes or trade bans are – generally – outside the parties' sphere of control.[62] This leads to the following consequences: imagine a case where the community of states or a specific state prohibits the import of goods from a country where basic standards of human rights are constantly violated. A buyer who has a contract with a seller in such a state might be excused from paying damages for its failure to take over the goods and to pay the purchase price, in accordance with Article 79(1) CISG. Conversely, where export into a certain country is prohibited, a seller with a contract with a buyer in that country might be excused from paying damages for non-delivery.

The consequences in these cases might be questionable if the import or export ban was foreseeable – for example, because of the bad human rights record of the other state – at the time of the conclusion of the contract. The wording of Article 79(1) CISG provides for exemption only in cases where the supervening event was not foreseeable. However, it is doubtful whether the drafters of the CISG took these situations – situations where trade bans are installed because of unethical behavior of other states – into account at all.[63] The typical case in which the requirement of non-foreseeability seems to be appropriate – and actually could prevent the breaching party from relying on Article 79 CISG – is where the interests of the country, in which the party seeking to rely on the exemption has its place of business, are intended to be protected by the trade ban. In most cases, such interests are of an economic nature and states want to protect their own markets. In this case, it can well be argued that the party in question has to bear the risk[64] of actions taken by its *own* government and, consequently, is not exempted from liability. The case that we are discussing here, however, is different. It does *not* fall within a party's sphere of risk if its *own* government implements a trade ban due to the behavior of a *foreign* state or party. The other party – directly or indirectly profiting from poor standards, for example, because of low wages – should bear the risk of trade bans due to its *own*, or its *own* government's, conduct or mistakes. Thus, this latter party may not argue that the breaching party could reasonably be expected to have taken the impediment into account at the time of the conclusion of the contract. This result is in accordance with Article 7(1) CISG and the ideas underlying Article 80 CISG.

3. Incorporation of ethical standards in sales contracts

In most cases, however, there will be no relevant regulations of public law. The first question that then arises is whether and how basic ethical standards become a part of the contract.

3.1 Express terms

The first way to incorporate ethical standards into sales contracts is to stipulate that the seller, for example, has to abide by specific standards concerning human rights, labor conditions or the environment. By so doing, such norms become part of the contract and may be enforced, or their violation sanctioned, in the same way as with any other terms. It is highly advisable that the interested party insists on incorporating such express terms into the contract, in order to circumvent any later disputes in this respect and in order to "tailor"[65] individual clauses to address specific human rights issues.

Novartis, one of the leading pharmaceutical companies, for example, includes the following clause in its contracts: "Novartis gives preference to third parties who share Novartis' societal and environmental values, as set forth in the Novartis Policy on Corporate Citizenship, Third Party Code: http://www.novartis.com/corporate_citizenship/en/10_2004_third_party_code.shtml. Accordingly, Seller represents and warrants this agreement will be performed in material compliance with all applicable laws and regulations, including, without limitation, laws and regulation relating to health, safety and the environment, fair labour practices and unlawful discrimination."[137]

3.2 Other means of incorporation

Problems may arise where such express terms regarding ethical values are absent. Very often, particularly small and medium-sized companies do not have the bargaining power to insist on incorporating such express terms concerning ethical values into their contracts.[66] Here, however, contract interpretation and supplementation may well lead to similar results to those reached with express incorporation.

According to Article 9(1) CISG, the parties are bound by any usage to which they have agreed and by any practice which they have established between themselves. Thus, two situations have to be distinguished: the first one is where the parties have repeatedly[67] agreed on express terms setting up certain ethical standards; in such a case, a justified expectation might arise that the parties will continue to proceed accordingly in the future.[68] Thus, although an express term is lacking, the contract may be supplemented in accordance with the previous conduct of the parties. The second situation is the one where the parties have individually agreed to a certain usage. This may be presumed where both parties participate in one of the above-mentioned private initiatives, such as the UN Global Compact. Under these conditions, it is irrelevant whether the agreed usage could also fall under Article 9(2) CISG as an international trade usage. If both parties have agreed to certain standards on a broader scale, they must, consequently, be deemed to have, at least implicitly, agreed to such a usage in their individual contracts.

If neither of the foregoing situations is at hand, ethical standards might still become part of the contract via Article 9(2) CISG. This presupposes that they can be regarded as an international trade usage of which the parties knew or ought to have known and which in international trade is widely known to, and regularly observed by, parties to contracts of the type involved in the particular trade concerned. In this regard, first and primary consideration should be given to usages and practices that have been established in certain trade branches, such as the "Electronic Industry Code of Conduct" already mentioned above.[69] Such codes could even be used for evidentiary purposes in legal proceedings.[70] If there are no usages or practices prevalent in the specific sector, special regard can be given to general private initiatives, such as the UN Global Compact. Although its provisions are rather broad and unspecified, there can be no doubt, that – at the very least – minimum ethical standards are to be safeguarded. These include prohibition of child labor and forced and compulsory labor, as well as a minimum of humane labor conditions. Thus, via Article 9(2) CISG, these minimum ethical standards may form, as implied terms, part of every international sales contract.

4. Consequences of the failure to comply with ethical standards

It is commonplace nowadays for corporations to take precautions to ensure that their contractual partners adhere to the required ethical standards. Usually, ethics audits as well as ecological audits are conducted *before* the corporations actually enter into a contract with a new business partner. This, however, cannot prevent ethical values from being violated in individual cases of performance. In such cases, the remedies available to the obligee, be it as a buyer or as a seller, are questionable.

4.1 Buyer's remedies

The first question in cases where goods are or have been produced in violation of the ethical values requirement of the contract is whether this fact constitutes a non-conformity of the goods according to Article 35 CISG.

Non-conformity of the goods, Art. 35 CISG

The problem in this context is that, in most cases, the violation of ethical standards does not negatively influence the physical features of the goods. No third party would be able to ascertain the violation of ethical standards upon a mere examination of the goods. Still, the very way of producing the goods influences their value on the market.[71] Many buyers are willing to pay a higher price for goods produced under circumstances that safeguard ethical standards. This is an established fact with regard to goods produced by observing specific biological and organic standards.[72] However, the same holds true for other goods, for example clothes that are not produced under sweatshop conditions.

If an express or implied term can be derived from the contract itself, nonconformity of the goods already follows from Article 35(1) CISG. It must be remembered here that, in this day and age, the observance of, at least, basic ethical standards can be regarded as an international trade usage and, thus, as an implied term in every international sales contract. Goods processed under conditions violating the contractually fixed ethical standards are not of the quality asked for by the contract. Quality must be understood as not just the goods' physical condition, but also as all the factual and legal circumstances concerning the relationship of the goods to their surroundings. It is irrelevant whether those circumstances affect the usability of the goods due to their nature or durability. The agreed origin of the goods, which necessarily comprises issues of ethical standards, also forms part of the quality characteristics.[73]

Insofar as the contract does not contain any, or only insufficient details in order to determine the requirements to be satisfied in producing the goods, recourse is to be had to the subsidiary determination of conformity set forth in Article 35(2) CISG.

First of all, the goods must be fit for any particular purpose according to Article 35(2)(b) CISG. In this context one may think of a buyer purchasing goods in order to sell them in specific markets, such as one specializing in organic food, biodynamic agriculture or fair trade. However, this particular purpose must be made known to the seller at the time of the conclusion of the contract, be it expressly or implicitly. This requirement may be fulfilled in cases where the buyer's firm, i.e. the company's name, contains information in this regard or where its reputation in context with ethical values is widely known in the trade sector concerned. The further prerequisite laid down in Article 35(2)(b) CISG, namely that the buyer relied on the seller's skill and judgment and it was reasonable for it to do so, should not cause any problems in these cases.

If a particular purpose in the above-mentioned sense cannot be construed, it might be questionable whether fitness for the ordinary purpose, according to Article 35(2)(a) CISG, presupposes that the goods have been manufactured or processed in accordance with specific ethical standards. Ordinary purpose primarily means that the goods must be fit for commercial purposes. In the resale business, this means that it must be possible to resell them.[74] In general, this purpose of the goods will not be influenced by the mere way in which the goods are manufactured or processed.[75] Thus, in cases not covered by Article 35(1) CISG or Article 35(2)(b) CISG, there will be little chance for the buyer to allege non-conformity of the goods and to hold the seller responsible if ethical standards have not been met.

If the goods are non-conforming, the buyer must notify the seller in accordance with Articles 38 and 39 CISG. However, where the non-conformity results solely from the way in which the goods are manufactured or processed, any eventual examination of the goods themselves will not reveal this fact. Thus, notification can only be required from the buyer after it has actually learned about the violation of ethical standards. Such knowledge may, in an individual case, be inferred from missing certificates relating to the origin of the goods.[76] If the non-conformity is not discovered until more than two years have passed since the handing-over of the goods, however, Article 39(2) CISG prevents the buyer from relying on the non-conformity.

Possible remedies

In the case of non-conforming goods, the buyer may resort to the usual remedies, namely avoidance of the contract, damages and price reduction; all such remedies raise special questions in connection with the violation of ethical standards.

Even if one finds that violation of ethical standards does not result in non-conformity of the goods in accordance with Article 35 CISG, if compliance with certain standards is a duty resulting from the contract, any non-compliance amounts to a breach of contract, giving rise to all remedies that are not specifically limited to cases of non-conformity.

Avoidance of the contract, Art. 49(1)(a) and Art. 25 CISG

Avoidance of the contract is possible only in cases where the non-conformity amounts to a fundamental breach of contract. This presupposes a substantial deprivation of what the buyer is entitled to expect under the contract. Such deprivation can be ascertained, in the first place, from the terms of the contract.[77] If the parties stipulate that certain ethical standards have to be adhered to, the parties have, thereby, sufficiently made clear that compliance is of special interest to the buyer and, therefore, such deprivation can be assumed in the event of a breach. In cases where *basic* ethical standards have been violated, such a fundamental breach also exists, having regard to the fact that damages in these cases are often not sufficient to sanction this breach of contract.[78] Furthermore, if the buyer is not allowed to avoid the contract, its reputation may still be endangered, because the buyer could be seen to be associated with the seller and its unethical behavior. In all other cases, where the alleged violation does not concern *basic* ethical values, whether or not the breach is fundamental has to be determined on a case-by-case basis.

Damages, Art. 45(1)(b) and 74 CISG

The easiest way for the buyer to obtain financial redress in case of violation of ethical standards is where the parties have agreed upon a liquidated damages clause or a contractual penalty, whereby the latter generally functions as both a compensatory remedy as well as a deterrent.[79] Such a clause releases the buyer from its – maybe difficult – obligation of proving whether or not it suffered damage at all and, if so, in what amount. However, parties may not think of such a clause in connection with compliance with ethical standards, or the buyer may not be in a position to force such a clause on the seller. Therefore, it is important to examine what can be considered to be damage within the meaning of Article 74 CISG.

In the first place, if the goods have not been sold before the violation of ethical standards is discovered, lost profits will be likely to occur. This may be because the goods are no longer resalable, or because the buyer decides not to resell them under the given circumstances. The latter behavior cannot be sanctioned as a violation of the buyer's general duty to mitigate damages according to Article 77 CISG, at least not where the buyer cannot be expected to sell the goods elsewhere, possibly at a lower price. This, i.e. whether the buyer can be expected to sell the goods, in turn, has to be decided by taking all the circumstances into account, such as the respective weight of the breach.[80] In addition, further damages accruing from substitute transactions can be recoverable under Articles 75 and 76 CISG in these cases.

If the goods have already been resold prior to discovering the breach, damage in the form of loss of reputation may come into play.[81] As Article 74 CISG recognizes the principle of full compensation, there is no question that loss of goodwill can be recovered under this article.[82] Such a loss should always be foreseen or ought to be foreseen according to Article 74 CISG. It might, however, be difficult to financially quantify a loss of goodwill in an individual case. In assessing the amount, due regard is to be given to the level of public ethical commitment by the individual buyer, such as, for example, participation in one of the above-mentioned private initiatives.

Problems arise, however, where all goods have been resold and the violation of ethical standards by the buyer's supplier has never become public knowledge. Although, even in such a case, one might argue that there is a loss of goodwill that could perhaps materialize in some future sale of the business itself, for example during due diligence proceedings, the loss becomes more and more elusive. Therefore, in these cases, another method of calculating damages is called for if one does not want to allow the seller to get off scot-free. One possibility could be to assess the decrease in value of the goods on an abstract level. The purchase price always reflects the costs of producing the goods and a profit for the seller. If the seller, by violating ethical standards, substantially reduces the costs in production and thus respectively maximizes its own profit, the equilibrium of the contract has become unbalanced. One may well argue that the real value of the goods is decreased by the amount of the – unethically – reduced production costs. The buyer may claim this margin as minimum damages. Although this might appear to be a windfall profit for the buyer, it is the only way to secure that – in the long term – ethical standards can be and actually are enforced by buyers having an incentive to do so. Moreover, in many legal systems today – at least in scholarly writings – the law of damages is regarded as a means for *prevention* and not only for compensation.[83]

It might be necessary to note here that, in cases where the buyer is only willing to pay a price that is so low that ethical production standards are impossible to be applied – and consequently cannot be expected –, it would be against good faith[84] to rely on such an implied term of the contract and to claim damages.

Price reduction, Art. 45(1)(a) and Art. 50 CISG

Finally, the possibility of a price reduction according to Article 50 CISG exists. As has been set out, any reduction of the production costs resulting from a violation of ethical standards can be regarded as causing a decrease in the value of the goods. Thus, the buy-

er may reduce the purchase price in proportion to the lower value
that the goods actually delivered had at the time of the delivery.

4.2 Seller's remedies – avoidance of the contract and damages, Art. 45(1) CISG

The factual situations for sellers who want to assure that their contract partners comply with certain ethical standards are different.
As has been shown above, the main sphere of application for the
seller is the sale of so-called dual-use goods that can be misused
in violation of basic ethical values, such as to produce chemical,
biological or nuclear weapons. If compliance with ethical standards has become part of the contract in the way described above,[85]
any non-compliance would amount to a breach of contract. If such
a misuse becomes apparent, the question again arises as to what
remedies the seller has.

In relation to both avoidance of the contract and damages, the same considerations as those concerning the buyer apply.

Again, it has to be established that the breach by the buyer
is fundamental in order to give rise to the remedy of avoidance. A
claim for damages will predominantly depend on the question of
whether lost profits and loss of goodwill are present. Here, however, any abstract calculation of damages based upon the equilibrium of the contractual obligations is likely to fail. The only way to
construe damages mirroring the buyer's solution outlined above
would be to speculate that goods for the intended unethical use
would have a higher value on the international market. The loss of
the seller would then be that, in relying upon the buyer's contractual promise to comply with ethical standards, the purchase price
did not reflect the real value of the goods.

4.3 Hardship, Art. 79 CISG and Art. 6.2.1 et seq. Unidroit Principles 2004

Ethical questions may also arise where it is not one of the contracting parties that violates ethical standards and thereby breaches the contract, but where the political situation in the buyer's or

the seller's country changes in a way that basic ethical standards are disregarded. Although it must be mentioned again that it is the primary task of the community of states to take the appropriate political measures, prompt action by private companies may be called for prior to such – often time-consuming and long-winded – endeavors. Otherwise, companies carrying on business with partners from states violating basic human rights may later be blamed for being complicit with human rights abuses, be it actively or passively.[86] In this regard, the discussions with regard to doing business in South Africa under the Apartheid-Regime come to mind.[87]

Reasonable action that could be taken by sellers and buyers concerning their contractual relationship with their business partners would be, primarily, to suspend the performance of the contract. In order to escape liability for damages, suspending performance is only possible if the requirements for an exemption under Article 79 CISG are met. According to this Article, firstly, there must be an impediment beyond the party's control. Impediments are usually defined as external circumstances or exogenous causes that impair the promisor's ability to perform.[88] Taken at face value, such an impediment could not be assumed in the cases discussed here. However, there can be no doubt that it would be commercially unreasonable to continue performance of the contract where this would risk causing detriment to one's business reputation. The management may even be under a duty of corporate law, e.g. towards their shareholders, to suspend the performance of such contracts. Whether *ethical hardship,* as present in the described cases, is an impediment within the meaning of Article 79(1) CISG has never been discussed, neither in case law nor in scholarly writing.

To answer this question, recourse is to be had to the legislative intention underlying Article 79 CISG. Although, admittedly, the provision's history, systematic placement and wording imply that an exemption comes into consideration only under very narrow conditions,[89] it reflects the intention of reasonable parties who are willing to take responsibility for risks that are outside their sphere of control only to the extent that they are able to insure against these risks or can take them into account when drafting the contract.[90] The fact that, after the conclusion of the contract, grave violations of basic ethical values – such as human rights – in the country of the obligee occur, certainly falls outside the sphere of risk of the promisor. If, for ethical reasons, it cannot reasonably be expected of the obligor to perform the contract, this certainly amounts to an impediment.

Finally, it has to be stressed, that – assuming that the level of violation of ethical values is sustained – whether the community of states has already reacted by imposing trade bans, or whether such measures are only in their initial phases, cannot make any difference.

The other prerequisites set out in Article 79(1) CISG, namely that the obligor could not reasonably be expected to have taken the impediment into account at the time of the conclusion of the contract or to have avoided or overcome it or its consequences, do not pose any major problems in connection with the cases discussed here.

If, in a given case, the contract could be reasonably performed by, for example, changing the place of performance or origin[91] of the goods without posing undue burden upon the parties, an adaptation of the contract may be called for, if not under CISG then possibly under Article 6.2.3 Unidroit Principles 2004.[92]

5. Conclusion

As has been shown, ethical behavior is becoming increasingly important for businesses and for conducting business. Such importance must necessarily translate into appropriate action, for example, as prescribed in codes of conducts or in contracts.

A crucial question is how those ethical values can be realized and upheld in daily commercial business transactions. In contracts governed by the CISG, ethical norms can be incorporated by several different means. Either they are expressly incorporated into the contract, or they are – in specific cases – incorporated as usages to which the parties have agreed or as practices which they have established between themselves pursuant to Article 9(1) CISG. Fundamental ethical standards – such as the prohibition of forced or child labor – are incorporated into the contract in any case. Such standards can be considered as being applicable to the contract by implication according to Article 9(2) CISG as a usage of which the parties knew or ought to have known and which in international trade is widely known to, and regularly observed by, parties to contracts of the type involved in the particular trade concerned.

The violation of – express or implied – contractual ethical **147** duties by the seller usually leads to non-conformity of the goods under Article 35 CISG. Consequently, the party in breach can face remedies, such as a claim for damages, price reduction or – in the event of a fundamental breach under Article 25 CISG – avoidance of the contract.

If a party wants to claim damages, however, problems can arise. If the buyer has already resold the goods and has not yet suffered any loss of goodwill, a basis upon which to claim damages would not appear to be established. However, it is submitted that, in such cases, the buyer can claim damages in the amount by which the actual value of the goods is reduced. This amount equals the amount by which the seller reduced its production costs by producing the goods in an unethical way – for example, by using forced labor. The same is true if a seller – who is interested in compliance with ethical standards – wants to claim damages from the buyer who does not use the goods in an ethical way. In this regard, it is submitted that the loss of the seller equals the eventual difference between the contractual value of the goods – i.e. the purchase price – and the real value of the goods, taking into account the unethical use that is intended and the possible consequences arising therefrom. Such claims for damages serve two functions. First, the equilibrium of the contract is reestablished. The seller's unethically generated profit is transferred to the buyer who – hypothetically – either would not have concluded the sales contract or would have bought the goods at a much lower price. With respect to unethical behavior by the buyer, any negative external effects on society at large would be internalized and imposed upon the buyer. Second, the objective of observance of ethical standards in international trade would be achieved as, on the one hand, one party loses its interest in unethically maximizing its profit and, on the other hand, the other has a financial incentive to enforce ethical standards.

In cases where the external circumstances change in a way that third parties – such as governments or rebels – severely violate ethical standards, this amounts to an impediment under Article 79(1) CISG. Here, sanctions by the community of states are likely to occur, and – for ethical reasons – it cannot reasonably be expected of the obligor to perform the contract. The obligor, in such cases, is entitled to suspend the performance of the contract without having to fear liability for damages.

Whether the respective prerequisites are actually met in a specific case is, of course, left to be decided by judges or arbitrators. However, the more that care is exercised in drafting the contract and in allocating the risks under it, the more that legal certainty and predictability of the outcome and legal position can be achieved and ensured.

10

HUMAN RIGHTS – BEST PRACTICE IN MAINSTREAM INVESTMENT DECISIONS?

Philippe Spicher

1. Introduction

Human rights, that once were a concern almost only of Non Governmental Organisations (NGO) such as Amnesty International, are now fully part of the business agenda.

In the first part of this paper, as an illustration of how and why human rights can be considered as part of the business agenda, we will mention some of the major worldwide initiatives that link business and human rights. We will then present an overview of current business practices with regard to some selected key human rights issues.

The practice of taking into account human rights concerns when making investment decisions is not new. This was initially the initiative of mostly faith-based organizations. It then spread to a wider audience through the development of socially responsible investment, which experienced a dramatic growth over the past 5 years. What we see now is the emergence of the broadening of (some of) socially responsible investment (SRI) practices to the mainstream arena.

In the second part of this paper, we will start by reviewing this evolution and identify its drivers. We will then expose the various techniques and tools available to investors to integrate human rights issues into their investment decision processes and give an overview of the extent to which investors are doing so.

2. Overview of current CSR business practices

The past five to ten years have seen numerous worldwide initiatives aiming at defining the corporate social responsibility (CSR) agenda and framing the responsibility of business towards society. Among these initiatives some focus particularly on human rights issues.

Major worldwide initiatives with a focus on Human Rights issues:[1]

+ Ethical trading initiative (ETI)
+ Extractive Industries Transparency Initiative (EITI)

+ Kimberly Process
+ Equator Principles
+ UN Global Compact
+ UN Draft Norms on the Responsibilities of Transnational Cor-
  porations (UN Draft Norms)

The Ethical Trading Initiative, the Extractive Industries Transparency Initiative and the Kimberly Process are all sector-specific
and are focusing on a limited number of key human rights issues.
The Equator Principles are also sector-specific but they address a
broader scope of human rights.

 The Global Compact and the UN Draft Norms, both ema-
nating from the United Nations, address more or less the full spectrum of human rights and are valid for all industries and types of
economic activity.

 Another key feature of the UN Draft Norms is that they are
more practical in the sense that they provide some sort of guidance
with regard to how human rights relate to business activities.

 It is important to emphasize that some companies are less
concerned than others by human rights issues, depending on their
size – both in terms of turnover and number of employees – the
sector in which they operate, the location of their operations, the
markets (in geographic terms) they are serving and the places
where they are sourcing from.

 This is well recognized by the UN Draft Norms:

 "Within their respective spheres of activity and influence,
transnational corporations and other business enterprises have
the obligation to promote, secure the fulfillment of, respect, ensure respect of, and protect human rights recognized in international as well as national law."

 The debate over whether and to what extent corporations
can be held responsible for human rights violations, complicity with human rights violations or for failing to protect human
rights is certainly not closed. However, looking at these initiatives
and codes – and at the various ones not mentioned here – there is

no doubt that human rights have definitely become a relevant and important issue for corporations. More importantly, the business and human rights problematic has now reached what can be called the institutionalization stage.

It is useful to get an overview of current business practices with regard to some selected key human rights issues. The analysis presented below is based on SiRi research[2] which delivers environmental, social, governance (ESG) reports and assessments of major international companies. The SiRi research universe consists of 1673 companies representing approximately 75% of the market capitalization of each of the following countries: Australia, Austria, Belgium, Canada, Denmark, Finland, France, Germany, Greece, Hong Kong, Ireland, Italy, Japan, Netherlands, New Zealand, Norway, Portugal, Singapore, Spain, Sweden, Switzerland, United Kingdom, United States.

2.1 Global Compact

Some 13% of the companies in our sample of 1673 companies are participants to the Global Compact. There are important differences both between countries and sectors. By country, French companies clearly lead with 67% having signed the Global Compact, followed by Norway (57%), Spain (55%), Netherlands (48%) and Germany (44%). There are no Global Compact companies in Ireland, New Zealand and Singapore and a very low rate in the United States (2%). By sector, the Household and Personal Products sector leads with 31%, followed by Automobiles and Components (24%), and Banks (22%). There are no Global Compact companies in the Real Estate sector and quite a low rate in Health Care Equipment and Services (3%), Retailing (5%), and Consumer Services (6%).

2.2 Freedom of association and right to collective bargaining

Only 108 companies, representing 6% of our research universe have adopted a formal, clear and detailed policy on freedom of association and right to collective bargaining. Another 26% also address this issue but in rather vague terms or not in a formal policy document.

Some examples of explicit policy statements:

"By signing the Declaration of Employees' Fundamental Rights on October 12, 2004, [the Company] undertakes to respect group employees worldwide and states it enables the strictest respect for freedom of association, regarding the freedom to join a trade union and hold office in a trade union, in compliance with the principles set out by International Labour Organisation (ILO) convention No. 97 of 1948 on the freedom of association and the protection of the right to organize. Recognition of the freedom of association means that each employee has the right to join a trade union or decline membership. [The Company] is also determined to comply with the provisions of ILO convention No. 98 on the right to organize and collective bargaining.

The Company adopted Social Responsibility Principles which are part of the company's Integrity Code. The Social Responsibility Principles are based on the UN Global Compact and ILO Conventions and are valid for all employees worldwide.

Within these principles, 'The Company acknowledges the human right to form trade unions. (...) Freedom of association will be granted even in those countries in which freedom of association is not protected by law.'"

And of some less explicit statements:

"The Company supports an organizational culture that affords its workers the right to associate and take collective action without fear of intimidation, reprisal, or harassment, and to get their questions resolved in a fair and timely manner."

"[...] each country's rules regarding protection of human rights at work, no discrimination, freedom of association and collective bargaining, ban on employing children and forced labor and protection of ethnic minorities, are fulfilled in all the Group's [...] companies."

As for the Global Compact, there are notable differences between countries and sectors.

The freedom of association and right to collective bargaining is formally recognized by 38% of the companies in Finland, 36% in the Netherlands and 31% in Sweden. No company in our sample has such a formal policy in Hong Kong, New Zealand, Ireland or Portugal and only few of them have one in Australia (5%), Singapore (3%), Italy (3%), Japan (1%), Canada (1%) and the United States (1%). With only 14% of companies having no policy at all, France is the country where reference to freedom of association and right to collective bargaining is the most widespread.

With 18%, it is in the Automobiles & Components sector where these rights are the most frequently formally recognized, followed by the Food, Beverage & Tobacco (15%) and the Telecommunication services (11%). Consumer Services and Real Estate are the two sectors in which no single company has adopted a formal policy. At a rate of 94%, Real Estate is again the sector with the highest proportion of companies making no mention at all of these rights.

2.3 Supply chain and human rights

The SiRi research and assessment framework addresses the supply chain and human rights issues at two levels. The first looks at the existence of a general policy on contractors and social issues for all companies, irrespective of the sector they are in. The second also looks at the existence of such policy (but uses stricter requirements with regard to the content of the policy), the extent to which this policy is translated to be made available to contractors' employees and whether the core labor issues from a clause in standard procurement contracts.

Formal policy statement on contractors and social issues

Out of the 1673 companies researched, 426 have adopted a formal policy statement on contractors and social issues and another 190 make a very general statement. This leaves 1057 companies not addressing this issue at all. Not surprisingly, there are some important differentiations between sectors. At a rate of 53%, companies within the Food & Staples Retailing sector address this issue most frequently, followed by Food, Beverage and Tobacco (46%), Consumer Durables and Apparel (41%), and Retailing (40%). By region, Europe shows the highest rate of companies addressing the issue (42%). North America stands at 24% and the Asia-Pacific region records only a low 10%.

Formal policy on core labour issues

Among the companies active in the sectors with high exposure to supply chain and human rights issues – representing 319 companies belonging to sectors such as Retailing, Food, Beverage & Tobacco, or Technology Hardware & Equipment – 18% have adopted a formal and detailed policy addressing all the core labor issues, 27% have a less formal and detailed policy and 55% do not have any kind of serious policy on these issues.

The extract below illustrates the differences between formal and detailed policy (first two examples) and ones that contain weaker commitments (the last two):

"[The Company] adopted Standards of Engagement for its suppliers, based on the conventions of the ILO, the UN conventions relating to human rights and employment [...].
These standards address the following issues:

+ Prohibition of any form of forced labour
+ Prohibition of child labour
+ Non-discrimination
+ Legal minimum wage or industry-specific wage (whichever is higher) and compensation for overtime
+ 60 hours per week at maximum and at least 24 consecutive hours rest within every seven-day period as well as paid annual leave
+ Freedom of association & collective bargaining (at minimum systems to ensure effective communication with employees)
+ No disciplinary practices in any form
+ Safe and hygienic working environment (also relevant for residential facilities if provided to employees)"

"The Code of Conduct addresses contractors and social issues. It is a non-negotiable requirement from [Company's] side that all its suppliers and their subcontractors, without exception, should follow the code.

The Code of Conduct is partly based on the UN Convention on the Rights of the Child and ILO conventions on working conditions and employment rights. The Code of Conduct states the following on child labor: 'We base our policy on child labour on the UN Convention on The Rights of the Child, article 32.1. In countries where the law permits apprenticeship programmes for children between 12 and 15 years of age, we will accept that children of this age work a few hours per day. The total numbers of hours daily spent on school and light work should never exceed 7 (seven) hours (ILO convention No. 33).' Furthermore the Code addresses health and safety, minimum living wages, maximum working hours, freedom of association/right to collective bargaining, acceptable living conditions, non-discrimination, corporate punishment/disciplinary practices and forced labor."

"[The company's] Guide to Ethical Business Practices states that it expects its suppliers to comply with 'all applicable local, national, and international laws and regulations, including those governing environment, health and safety, human rights, and employment conditions.'"

"[The Company] declares that it is 'striving to improve the ethical management of its supply chain, including in the area of human right and labour.'"

Translation and dissemination of the policy statements

A formal policy stating unambiguous commitments with regard to core labor issues in the supply chain can be almost without positive effect if the employees of the suppliers and contractors are not aware of it.

The translation of the policy into relevant languages (i.e. the languages spoken by the contractors' employees) is seen as a basic requirement to make sure the policy can be implemented.

Only 12% of the companies provide clear evidence that their policy is translated in relevant language and made accessible to contractors' employees. The two examples below can be considered as best practice in this area:

"As concerns corporate responsibility, [The Company] implements '[Company]'s Principles of Socially Responsible Trading' in its supplier relations. The company states the following: 'Today, our principles are similar to the Code of Conduct of Business Social Compliance Initiative (BSCI). This Code has been translated into 10 different languages – mainly those used in the Far East – and close to 100% of our suppliers in the social risk area (and their employees) can get the Code both in English and in their own native language.'"

"The company states that the Vendor/Supplier Code of Conduct should be translated into the native languages of the workforce and prominently displayed at each facility where [Company] merchandise is being manufactured."

By region, Europe and North America have respectively 15 and 14% of companies translating their policy and Asia-Pacific a lower 7%. Most of the companies in Japan declare to have their policy in both Japanese and English only.

Labor issues form a clause in standard procurement contracts

Overall, 16% of the companies have procurement contracts that include a clause on respect of labor rights and compliance with the company's policy statements on labor rights. For example:

"Since 2003, a specific clause has been added to the General Purchasing Conditions of [the Company]. Article 21 includes an explicit reference to the obligation of compliance with the Fundamental Social Principles. The article also indicates that audits and verification may be undertaken at any time and that corrective actions may be decided in order to remedy non-compliance."

This overall percentage hides important differences between Asia-Pacific (4%) on one side and Europe and North America (23 and 22% respectively) on the other side.

3. The place of human right issues in investment practices

Even though the term "socially responsible investment" covers many different approaches, it is useful to adopt a general definition: socially responsible investment (SRI) can be defined as the process by which factors other than standard financial ones are affecting the investment decisions.

With the first fund created in 1928 and documented practices of making investment decisions based on moral grounds much before that, socially responsible investment is not new. However, it is generally admitted that the modern area of socially responsible investment started in 1971 when the Episcopal Church presented at the General Motors's annual meeting a shareholder resolution calling the company to withdraw from South Africa.

Since then funds managed under the SRI label have increased dramatically, particularly over the past three years. These funds, however, still represent a minor proportion of the total assets under management in the world. But there are signs that momentum is gathering for the integration of ESG factors into mainstream investment processes.[3] Among those signs, it is worth mentioning the following initiatives:

The Who Cares Win initiative was launched in 2004 by mainstream investment houses representing US$ 6000 billions in assets following an invitation by Kofi Annan to "develop guidelines and recommendations on how to better integrate environmental, social and corporate governance issues in asset management, securities brokerage services and associated research functions."[4]

The Enhanced Analytics Initiative was launched in 2004 by fund managers representing US$ 1000 billions in assets to encourage ESG research by brokers.

The Principles for Responsible Investment were launched in April 2006 by the United Nations and signed by asset owners and investment managers representing more than US$ 2000 billions. One year later, more than 180 institutional investors managing assets worth US$ 8000 billions have signed up to these principles.

In parallel to the institutionalization of business and human rights problemas, we are witnessing an increased interest by major financial institutions and institutional investors with regard to ESG issues.

Human rights issues are part of the broader ESG framework commonly used by specialized research and rating organizations to assess corporate behavior and performance on extra-financial factors, and by investors to take into account these factors into their investment processes.

The different approaches used in integrating environmental, social and governance ESG factors into investment processes fall into the following three broad categories:

+ Exclusion
+ Best-in-class
+ Engagement

There is a continuum between these approaches and two of them or even all three are quite commonly applied together. It is however true that many investors are focusing only on one.

It is worth noting that exclusion and best-in-class techniques affect the selection of the stocks which are held in the portfolio, whilst the third one does not. Ultimately it is the risk-return requirements and the constraints of the end investor which determine which approach – or combination of approaches – should be implemented to build a SRI portfolio.

In the following pages we will review each of these approaches by focusing on the underlining research needed to implement them, the kind of results this research delivers, and to what extent and how investors are actually using these results.

3.1 Exclusion

Exclusion involves the creation of an investable universe. In other words it means defining some companies as eligible for an investment and some others as not. The companies which are not eligible – the excluded companies – are those that do no meet certain criteria, called the exclusion criteria or screen. These criteria can be of three types:

+ activity-based
+ policy-based
+ practice-based

Activity-based criteria focus on the products and services a company is producing and bringing to the market. Some common activity-based criteria include weapons and military contracting, tobacco, alcohol, nuclear power, gambling, pornography, genetically modified organisms.

The case of cluster munitions[5] has recently made its way into the investment world. Cluster munitions raise specific humanitarian concerns related to the fact that many civilians become casualties of non-exploded munitions during and sometimes long after conflicts have ended.

Policy-based criteria seek to identify companies that do not have adopted formal policies on one or several ESG related issues. In that context, the adoption of a formal policy by a company is considered as a necessary condition for investment. Although any kind of issue can fit into these criteria, in practice the most commonly used issues specifically relate to human rights.

Practice-based criteria are intended to capture the actual corporate behavior and not only the corporate commitments. As for policy-based criteria, the practice-based ones are generally aimed at capturing human rights violations by companies. This specific type of exclusion is also sometimes called norm-based screening.

According to Eurosif, € 266 billions are invested in Europe based on simple exclusion screens[6], with arms trade (€ 138 billions) and human rights (€ 61 billions) the most commonly used screens. In the United States, the Social Investment Forum[7] reports that in 2005, a total of US$ 1,679 billions is invested using social screens, among these approximately 17% include a human rights screen. It has to be noted that while the data reported by Eurosif make a clear distinction between exclusion screen and best-in-class strategy (see also the next section), reflecting current practice in Europe, it is not the case for the data reported by the US Social Investment Forum. This makes a direct comparison difficult, as part of the US\$ 1,679 billions reported as using social screens may also include some best-in-class strategies.

3.2 Best-in-class

A best-in-class approach involves the selection or the overweighting of stocks of companies that perform particularly well compared to their peers. A best-in-class approach thus involves the realization of an assessment of corporate ESG performance and behavior. This kind of assessment is conducted by dedicated teams within asset management firms or banks, and, more generally, by specialized research organizations and rating agencies. More recently, brokerage houses, encouraged by the Enhanced Analytics Initiative (see above) and growing demand, have started to deliver interesting pieces of research in this area.

It is important to note here that there is no standardized and generally accepted framework to conduct ESG assessments. However, most of the models currently in use address, not so surprisingly, the same kind of issues and are based on the same type of criteria and indicators. Beyond the model, what really matters with regard to the ability to undertake in-depth research and deliver meaningful results are the expertise, qualification and know-how of the research analysts. This is particularly true as this type of research and assessment is usually based on a mix of quantitative and qualitative criteria which involve a necessary interpretation and analysis. In that context, the development of a certifiable quality standard for ESG research by the AI CSRR[8] has to be welcomed. The aim of ESG research and assessment is not to make a moral judgment upon a company or to say if it is good or bad, but rather to indicate whether and to what extent a company is responsive to society concerns, whether it is recognizing the negative externalities it creates and how it is striving to limit them, and whether it is contributing – strategically and operationally – to a better society.

A best-in-class approach, based on this type of ESG assessment, is therefore very well-suited to take into account into investment decisions less clearly defined human rights; that is human rights whose implementation depends upon numerous actors and factors, and therefore for which there is a shared responsibility.

In that context, the question is not if a company is respecting a given human right, but rather if the way it operates – over its entire value chain – and the strategic choices it makes are contributing to improve the social, political and economical context in a way that human rights can be respected.

The extent to which the use of best-in-class technique to build a portfolio will have an effect on corporate behavior with regard to human rights depends on the following parameters:

+ the assets under management using this approach compared to the total assets under management;
+ the publicity made by those who are implementing this approach, such as public statements by major financial institutions or pension funds declaring they will favor investment in companies showing a relatively good ESG performance.

Also worth noting is the effect coming from the research process itself. The more companies are questioned with regard to their commitment and behavior on human rights issues by research organizations, the more they are aware of the importance of these issues. According to Eurosif, a total of € 29 billions is invested in Europe using best-in-class strategies. This figure may be slightly underestimated as a part of the € 641 billons assets managed using an "integration" approach[9] is most probably using best-in-class technique as defined above.

3.3 Engagement

Engagement is used by investors to apply direct pressure to corporations to improve their social and environmental performance. It encompasses various means to dialogue with management and influence corporate behavior, including letter writing, meetings with top management and board of directors, proxy voting and ultimately filling in shareholder resolutions. In 2005, investment through engagement strategies accounted for US$ 703 billions in United States[10] and for € 730 billions in Europe[11].

Shareholder advocacy is a particular form of engagement that is used by stakeholders other than investors, mainly NGOs (such as Amnesty International and Reporters Without Borders) and unions. Shareholder advocacy is more popular in countries where shareholders' rights require little capital to bring resolutions to an annual general meeting such as in the United States.

To give an overview of the importance of engagement strategies in the US market, we can highlight that in 2005 as reported by the US Social Investment Forum, 348 resolutions were proposed dealing mainly with political contributions (42 resolutions), climate change (35), and equal employment opportunities (32). There were 25 resolutions addressing global labor standards and another 11 addressing human rights. Among these 348 resolutions, 98 were withdrawn, which is an indication of the responsiveness of companies to pre-vote dialogues and negotiations. On average, the shareholders resolutions that have been voted on received 10% of the votes.

4. Conclusion

Human rights issues are at the center of socially responsible investment practices and probably one of the most predominant issues to filter from social investment to the mainstream arena, along with climate change and corporate governance. This trend of taking into account human rights in the investment decision process inevitably makes companies more aware of that issue.

Strengthening and further development of initiatives that aim at better defining corporate responsibilities with regards to human rights will provide additional incentives and guidance for integration of human rights considerations into daily management by companies.

The coming years will be decisive. If the current trends gain momentum, there is little doubt that what is now best practice will become current practice. A huge step towards global respect of human rights would be accomplished. But if investors' pressure over companies fades, those will lose their interest in human rights and return to old practices. Not because the old practice delivers higher returns, but just because it is more convenient to do nothing than to do what is right.

11

CORPORATE RESPONSIBILITY IN THE GLOBAL MARKET

WHY HUMAN RIGHTS ISSUES ARE GROWING MORE RELEVANT FOR SWISS SMALL AND MEDIUM-SIZED COMPANIES

Fritz Brugger & Thomas Streiff

1. Human rights as a challenge and an opportunity for small and medium-sized companies

Small and medium-sized companies are increasingly finding themselves confronted with human rights issues – from three different fronts:

+ **Pressure from clients:** Many small and medium-sized companies supply their products to major trading and consumer goods companies that are clearly visible on the market. These in turn have entered into commitments towards their clients and are now to an increasing extent demanding that their suppliers are able to both guarantee and provide evidence of respect for human rights standards.
+ **Challenges in emerging markets and developing countries:** Globalisation is enabling more and more small and medium-sized companies to operate independently abroad, but at the same time they are also having to face unknown realities: foreign cultural standards, lack of legal security, volatile political situations, unreliable administrative bodies, lack of respect for the environment, violations of human rights. How should small and medium-sized companies behave in such circumstances?
+ **Expectations on the part of stakeholders:** Society expects companies to behave in a responsible manner and to also respect the standards of their home country in the countries in which they purchase and manufacture and to which they export their products, even though these may have less stringent regulatory conditions. As banker Foster Deibert astutely reminds us, "No project is too small or too distant to show up on the radar of attentive interest groups."[1] Labour norms and human rights, corruption and utilisation of resources are especially sensitive issues.

Small and medium-sized companies that prefer to be perceived as part of the solution rather than part of the problem would therefore be well advised to examine their own sense of corporate responsibility and take suitable measures before they, too, find themselves facing such challenges. Precautionary measures are a sound investment in the future: companies that act in an exemplary manner and thus enhance their reputation instead of harming it can create competitive advantages for themselves on the market and secure their continued existence both in the short term and the long term.

In the course of the discussions held at the 2006 annual conference of the Political Affairs Division IV (PD IV) of the Swiss Federal Department of Foreign Affairs (FDFA) it became apparent that, as a rule, internationally active small and medium-sized companies do not have sufficient resources at their disposal for comprehensively clarifying central human rights issues, and in many cases they are not familiar with the practices and circumstances of the country or countries concerned. They therefore have to rely on a pragmatic analysis of their exposure to human rights issues and on the use of risk management and market positioning tools.

In order to respond to these needs, PD IV initiated a platform for small and medium-sized companies together with The Sustainability Forum Zurich, and prepared a management guide. The paper initially takes a look at the question of where and how small and medium-sized companies are exposed to human rights issues, then goes on to provide information concerning specific instruments, methods and options for action relating to a focused approach to dealing with human rights issues in the course of daily business activities.

The citations often concern multinationals, even though this paper is addressed to small and medium-sized companies, but the reason for this can be quickly explained: multinationals have been confronted with human rights issues for many years. Initially these were regarded as internal processes, but recently human rights have increasingly developed into a more public issue. By contrast, human rights issues are relatively new to small and medium-sized companies, and are not discussed in public as much as they are in the case of multinationals. Nonetheless, they are just as pressing, despite this delay. The authors hope that this working guide will help the management of small and medium-sized companies to familiarize themselves with the subject.

2. Human rights and small/medium-sized companies
2.1 The impacts of human rights issues on small and medium-sized companies (SMEs)

Negative impacts on company management: Health risks at the workplace, discrimination, prohibition of the activities of associations, unions and trade organisations, child labour and other human rights violations can interfere with good corporate governance, lead to major demands as well as to difficulties in obtaining credit facilities.

Negative market response to corporate behaviour: A company can only be successful if it enjoys the confidence of its relevant stakeholders (employees, clients, suppliers, investors etc.). If the perception of these groups is positive, the company is able to benefit from significant competitive advantages:

+ A sound internal reputation manifests itself through the degree of **identification** with the company by its employees; it promotes commitment to quality as well to innovation and performance. In particular with SMEs, each employee has a major influence on the company's reputation.
+ A company that is perceived to be **attractive** and to possess a strong sense of responsibility is regarded as a desirable employer and business partner, as well as a wor-

"In the past, clients only cared about quality and price. But now people also want to know about the social conditions under which a product has been manufactured."

VADAR O'HARA, NIKE CORPORATE RESPONSIBILITY

CR describes responsible corporate behaviour. The prerequisites for the credible implementation of corporate responsibility include:
+ Clarification of corporate values. The written definition of this clarification, e.g. in the form of an ethical code of behaviour (social responsibility) is a positive indicator here.
+ Definition of management processes for the systematic consideration of social issues (social responsiveness).

thy company to invest in.

+ If a company has a sound **external reputation,** it is able to break through onto the market more easily and benefit from more stable prices for its products and services. Clients and employees demonstrate greater loyalty, and the company's ability to procure capital is greatly enhanced.

Stakeholders also respond to the behaviour of a company's suppliers. Increasing transparency and the greater availability of information have given rise to increased social awareness. Major corporations in particular have undertaken commitments towards their clients to respect human rights, and have passed on these commitments to their suppliers – which are often small and medium-sized companies – with the added requirement that the latter not only demonstrate that they themselves respect human rights, but that they make sure their own suppliers do so too.

2.2 The most relevant human rights for small and medium-sized companies

All human rights are important, of course, and all are described in binding conventions under international law. Although they are signed by national governments, these conventions also address actions on the part of private individuals and companies, and this leads to five aspects that are of relevance to corporate activities[2]:

a) **Equal opportunities and non-discrimination:** Companies may not through their activities demean or otherwise disadvantage groups of people, especially women, children, the elderly, the disabled, foreign workers, etc., or ethnic groups (minorities, indigenous peoples etc.).

b) **Safety of persons:** Companies are obliged to guarantee the safety of people who are involved in work and production processes. This also applies to people who are in-

+ The creation of transparency and verifiability of corporate behaviour (social accountability).

+ Proof of verifiable, where possible, measurable performance (social performance).

The overlying and most important requirement with respect to corporate responsibility is that the company's owners and management play an exemplary role by putting ethical values into practice.

directly involved, e.g. if they protest peacefully against a company and security personnel intervene, or if the company is protected by external security providers.

c) **Labour standards**: Labour standards include the prohibition of child labour, forced labour (e.g. as punishment for a different ideology, to work off debt or in the form of enforced overtime), the provision of acceptable workplace conditions, fair wages, the right to assembly, to join a union and to collective negotiations.

d) **Protection of the environment**: Most Swiss small and medium-sized companies are aware of the relevance of, and their responsibility for, the protection and efficient utilisation of natural resources. Here a connection with human rights exists in that an intact environment is a vital factor for human existence and development, and it therefore has to be protected accordingly.

e) **Corruption**: Bribery and corruption, and the failure on the part of local governments to respect applicable institutional obligations, are contrary to the principles of self-determination and sovereignty called for within the scope of human rights.

2.3 Can small and medium-sized companies be held partially to blame in human rights issues even though they comply with the relevant legal provisions?

This question is gaining of importance in view of the growing focus on the legal aspects and consequences[3] of corporate responsibility, and it encompasses several dimensions:

+ Direct **complicity** applies if a company directly supports human rights violations, for example in the form of enforced relocation of persons in association with its business activity. But it also applies if a company makes a substantial contribution, e.g. if it provides information

"The guiding principle of Switzerland's foreign policy is 'Do no harm.' This principle could also be applied by companies."

FEDERAL COUNCILLOR MICHELINE CALMY-REY

+ More than 12 million people throughout the world perform forced labour.

+ According to UNICEF, more than 190 million children between the ages of 5 and 14 are being forced to work, the majority under exploitative conditions. Between 5 and 10 % work for companies that export goods, e.g. in textile factories, quarries, cocoa and coffee plantations.

+ The ILO estimates that at least 10 % of employees in the world's tourism industry are children.

about private individuals to the state or third parties and thus has to anticipate that the recipient(s) thereof will commit human rights violations on the basis of the supplied information.

+ If a company directly **benefits** from human rights violations by other parties, it is also guilty of complicity. A frequently cited example of this is the violent suppression of protests against a company; another example concerns the case in which a company enters into a joint venture even though it could have known in advance that the partner concerned will violate human rights within the scope of the collaboration. The consequences of complicity may range from damage to the company's reputation through to legal disputes.

+ Finally, a company may be **tacitly implicated** if it becomes aware of systematic human rights violations but fails to report them to the relevant authorities. This may apply, for example, if a law discriminates against groups of persons due to their origin or sex.

2.4 Is a company responsible for human rights violations by suppliers and in society?

Consumers are well aware that a company is not an isolated entity that has no influence on its surroundings. Stakeholders therefore expect companies to use their influence to ensure respect for human rights.

+ Doing nothing while citing legally defined company limits is not sufficient, as Nike discovered when it tried to deny its responsibility for the working conditions of its suppliers.

+ Glossy brochures quickly give rise to questions regarding the truth of their content, as Nike again discovered when a court classified its "Social Responsibility" report as false publicity.

"It is not easy, but dealing with dilemmas is a core competency that companies have to develop. They have to make a decision, then be aware of what they have decided in favour of."

LISE KINGO,
NOVO NORDISK

+ Experience has shown that, while it is major brands that first appear in the spotlight, investigations rapidly extend to other players in the value chain. For example, as importer of Toys "R" Us products, the Swiss company was accused of insufficient transparency. According to a rating of toy manufacturers by a coalition of NGOs, Toys "R" Us does not pay attention to socially acceptable production standards. Far-sighted small and medium-sized companies seized on this as an opportunity in that they are drawing the attention of their business partners to the aspect of responsible behaviour and are thus able to influence their human rights policy, which in turn enhances their credibility and reputation.

+ Responsibility applies not only to the manufacturing of products, but also – and to an increasing extent – to their use, as lawsuits brought against tobacco companies, weapons manufacturers, casinos, fast-food chains and providers of high-tech products, etc. clearly illustrate.

"If companies – no matter how large or small – no longer view themselves as victims when it comes to human rights, they will discover that actively dealing with human rights issues opens up new opportunities for them."

GARY STEEL, ABB

Even if clear boundaries do not exist, drawing attention to the sphere of influence of a company makes it possible to view things pragmatically: the more pronounced and direct the political, economic, contractual and geographical proximity to people, the greater the moral or "specific" responsibility of the company, and this responsibility diminishes as the degree of proximity and thus the sphere of influence diminish. Every company, including the smallest, has a sphere of influence.

3. Methods and instruments available to small and medium-sized companies for dealing with human rights issues
3.1 Priorities for companies in dealing with human rights issues
Three levels of priority can be identified for companies with

respect to dealing with human rights issues.[4]

+ The lowest (and fundamental) level concerns **"must norms:"** respecting the existing laws and regulations, even in situations where the local government is either incapable or unwilling to meet its own obligations.

+ The next level concerns **"ought-to norms"**, i.e. precautions that a company should take in order to meet the legitimate expectations of stakeholders and assume an appropriate level of co-responsibility for the observance of human rights. What this involves in concrete terms has to be clarified for each individual company.

+ While the above levels more or less explicitly serve to minimise risk, the third level – **"can norms"** – concerns a long-term commitment by means of which a company can positively differentiate itself by demonstrating genuine leadership and far-reaching commitment in the area of human rights. This may, for example, take the form of a joint project with stakeholders, financial support or a philanthropic commitment.

The potential consequences here also need to be taken into account. For example, new expectations and demands may arise, and by imposing ambitious commitments, a company can also render itself vulnerable. Sufficient attention therefore needs to be paid to suitable communication.

3.2 How does a company find out whether it is in conflict with human rights standards?

Knowing that a company has to respect human rights is not sufficient. In order to act responsibly and to verify the effectiveness of corresponding measures, companies also need to use instruments and methods that can be applied.

First and foremost, the company has to focus on core questions, e.g. which human rights issues are of relevance to the company, and what are the specific risks associated with human rights violations? By examining these aspects, the company management is able to obtain a decision-making basis on which it can define the right priorities. Here, useful instruments include:

+ **Analysis of the immediate environment:** Identifying all relevant partners and interest groups provides an initial overview of potentially involved circles. By weighting these on the basis of degree of influence, a company can identify potential fields of action. In any case, the employees are an important factor, followed by suppliers, unions, business locations and society.
+ **Internal human rights audit:** The Danish Institute for Human Rights has developed an instrument in close collaboration with private sector companies and industry organisations that enables companies to audit their activities from the point of view of compliance with central human rights aspects.[5]

A checklist comprising 28 questions covers the areas of employee policy, supply chain management and the impacts on the relevant social groups. In addition, indicators are provided that can be used for answering the various questions and which can easily be verified.

> "Leaving a country because human rights problems arise is not necessarily the best solution. With the commitment on the part of all stakeholders, it is possible for small and medium-sized companies in particular to meet the bottom-line requirements, namely economic growth, social responsibility, environmental protection and respect for human rights."
>
> SCOTT MORRISON, METALOR

3.3 How should a company go about optimising its dealings with human rights issues and observing their development?

In order for a company to successfully deal with human rights issues it has to systematically integrate them into its management process instead of treating them as an isolated matter. In this way the company can make sure that it does not lose sight of its objectives and values.

The most important steps are as follows:
+ Consciously respecting and complying with the principles

of human rights is a **strategic decision.** This includes the formulation of objectives as well as the definition of specific measures and realistic planning of resources.

+ **Integration into processes and corporate structure** (e.g. into the company's risk analysis, human resource policy, code of behaviour): practical implementation can be supported with the aid of written guidelines and through the clear allocation of responsibilities.

+ **Communication** relating to human rights is primarily an internal matter:

  • Providing information to employees and business partners concerning the company's human rights policy, criteria and measures. Putting the defined criteria and standards into practice is the most effective form of communication.

  • Providing institutionalised options so that employees and business partners can report violations without fearing negative consequences (e.g. hotline, whistle-blowing scheme).

+ Customised **training** of key personnel – including suppliers and business partners – guarantees the effective implementation of the company's human rights policy.

+ **Periodical audits** of human rights practice on the basis of clearly defined criteria that have been adjusted to the company's sphere of influence, together with the reporting of the findings, form the basis for further improvements.

"Make the observance of human rights part of your normal 'good management practice' criteria – but treat this as a process, not as a project, since society's expectations and demands will change."

KLAUS LEISINGER, NOVARTIS FOUNDATION FOR SUSTAINABLE DEVELOPMENT

3.4 Do opportunities exist for companies to benefit from previous findings relating to human rights issues?

The systematic processing of human rights issues in companies is still very much in its infancy, in particular in the cases of small and medium-sized companies.

This means that existing management tools are conceived in somewhat general terms, and instruments and aids designed to meet the needs of specific sectors and small and medium-sized companies are practically non-existent.

There are also very few opportunities for small and medium-sized companies to exchange experiences with similar companies. On the other hand, numerous small and medium-sized companies have gathered practical experience concerning human rights issues from their business activities.

In order to close this gap, the Political Affairs Division PD IV of the Swiss Federal Department of Foreign Affairs and The Sustainability Forum Zurich have joined forces to create a platform that focuses on the principles of the UN Global Compact and sets out to support small and medium-sized companies in their efforts to deal with human rights issues. This platform provides interested companies with an opportunity to exchange experiences and to provide or develop management aids designed to meet specific requirements. The *UN Global Compact learning platform for Swiss small and medium-sized companies* and its events are structured so that they offer participants the maximum benefits.[6] The concept is as follows:

+ Each event focuses on case studies that are presented by company representatives. These are followed by hearings with two to three other experts with the aim of identifying the strengths and weaknesses of the presented solutions, and the sessions are rounded off with plenary or group discussions during which proposals are developed to improve and define management criteria.
+ The results of these events are turned into learning aids and placed at the disposal of the participants in anonymous form.
+ Events are primarily attended by company representatives, and experts are called on as required. They are held in an atmosphere of confidentiality, are need-oriented and focus specifically on management support.

"It is appropriate to consider all options for action, but companies often do this in too isolated a manner for themselves alone."

ALAN DETHERIDGE, SHELL

12

ACTIONS SPEAK LOUDER THAN WORDS

Danièle Gosteli Hauser

The inclusion of Human Rights on the agenda of business forums seems to be taken for granted nowadays, but in fact this is the result of a hard process of gaining recognition, carried out only over the past ten years.

If you Google the words "corporate social responsibility" you'll get about 55 million references (for human rights, there are about 570 million). What are the reasons for this trend? What place do human rights have in corporate social responsibility? Do they really matter to business, or are they purely a cosmetic attempt to enable companies to "sell" their products more successfully and enhance their corporate reputation? Why did an organization like Amnesty International (AI), known for its expertise and analysis of governmental failures with respect to human rights, decide to direct its attention to the private sector? What do we expect of companies and what challenges will face us in future?

1. Corporate social responsibility and human rights

When I started to work for Amnesty International fifteen years ago, corporate social responsibility and human rights were not a topic of discussion, not even within our own organization. Corporate social responsibility was limited to corporate philanthropy, and companies were "doing good" by financially supporting development projects in Southern/Eastern countries.

John Elkington, the environmentalist and business consultant, developed the concept of the Triple Bottom Line in 1998 as a guideline for companies. He believed companies had to manage their impacts in all three areas of sustainable development: economic, social, and environmental. Today more and more companies publish corporate social responsibility reports in addition to environmental ones, and some of them have dared to include a reference to human rights issues.

The reasons for the trend in corporate social responsibility can certainly be found in the emergence of economic globalization since the end of the Cold War. Since then there has been an explosion in international trade and financial relationships, with companies merging to become huge transnational corporations, so powerful economically that they could influence the regulatory capacities of any national system. Suddenly, transnational companies had the power of doing good, but also evil.

At the same time, as the result of the increasing pervasiveness of the Internet and a rather well-organized and well-informed civil society, companies have been exposed to greater external scrutiny. In recent years, a number of corporations have been embarrassed by human rights controversies that they were unable to address adequately.

2. Why did Amnesty International devote its resources to the private sector?

The new human rights challenges arising from globalization have impelled Amnesty International to take on new areas of work, namely socio-economic rights and economic actors. Amnesty International has broadened its mission, recognizing that there are many more prisoners of poverty than prisoners of conscience, and that millions endure the torture of hunger and slow death from preventable disease. Some have questioned our choice, arguing that Amnesty International would become distracted from its core mission. This is absolutely not the case. There is a close interrelationship between civil, political, economic, social and cultural rights. The rights to adequate food and to the highest attainable standards of health and education are as much human rights as are freedom of expression or the right to a fair trial.

For people in Zimbabwe who have been forcibly evicted, the right to housing is no less real than the right to be free from police brutality. To the women raped in conflicts in, for example, ex-Yugoslavia or Rwanda, their claim to medical care was no less a priority than their demands for justice. And as we showed in our report on North Korea, food can be used as a powerful weapon to starve dissidents. For more than a decade, the people of North Korea have suffered from famine and acute food shortages. Hundreds of thousands have died and many millions more have suffered from chronic malnutrition. North Koreans who have sought desperately to find food, by moving around the country to search for it or by crossing the border into China, have been subjected to other human rights violations, such as arrest, detention, and by some accounts even torture and execution, by the North Korean authorities.

In 1998, on the 50th anniversary of the Universal Declaration of Human Rights (UDHR), Amnesty International reiterated the importance of the interdependence and indivisibility of human rights. We have stressed that the UDHR not only addresses governments, but calls upon "every individual and every organ of society" to promote respect for these rights and freedoms and to secure their observance. We have published a set of Human Rights Principles for companies, to encourage them to uphold international human rights standards in their activities.

For the first time in 1998, and after very intense and hard lobbying – I can testify to this because I was personally involved in that project – we managed to get an invitation for our Secretary-General Pierre Sané to participate in the World Economic Forum in Davos. I say "hard lobbying," because human rights were still not considered an integral part of the corporate agenda of economic actors. We insisted on being invited because we believed that opportunities to speak directly to those who hold real power in the business world could be useful both in raising the profile of human rights and in pressing individual cases. Since then, Amnesty International has argued that companies should protect human rights, and set up codes of conduct to be verified independently and reported on publicly.

3. Do human rights really matter to business?

As a representative of Amnesty International, I can tell you without doubt that the answer is: very much so!

The end of the Cold War was hailed by many as the start of a new world order that would bring freedom and prosperity to all.

The global economy offered unprecedented opportunities to business, and has led to enormous economic expansion. But the expected euphoria has been dampened by a counter-effect: the gap between rich and poor has widened to a huge canyon. While some have seen their welfare improved, for millions of people globalization has brought destitution and despair. Currently, at least 1.3 billion people struggle to survive on less than a dollar a day. Deregulation, privatization and the dismantling of social welfare provisions have led to widening inequalities in many countries. The almost inevitable consequence of this growth in poverty has been a parallel escalation in violations of human rights.

Yet the international community has failed to meet its obligations to respect and fulfill the human rights of the victims. Governments were keen to encourage investment but have often failed to ensure that big business respect its human rights responsibilities. Companies have exposed populations to danger through pollution (as in Nigeria or during the Bhopal tragedy) and to exploitation through denial of the right to a fair wage and decent working conditions. Acting alone or with the help of international financial institutions, some governments became obsessed with building giant projects such as the construction of huge dams, which resulted in social unrest, forced displacement of populations, widespread homelessness and violations of the rights of indigenous peoples.

Companies have also been faced with serious threats. Operating in conflict zones, under regimes with a weak rule of law where human rights were systematically violated and where corruption was rife, proved to be destabilizing for the investment climate. Some companies have discovered to their disadvantage that their relationship with security forces put them at risk of contributing to human rights abuses and damaged their reputations. BP in Colombia is one example. The local company used by BP to protect its oil installations (OCENSA/DSC) was reportedly passing intelligence information about the local population to the Colombian military. Together with its paramilitary allies, it was accused of targeting those considered subversive, resulting in extrajudicial executions and "disappearances."

Other companies have experienced how easy it is to get involved in political conflicts. For instance, Amnesty International criticized Caterpillar for selling bulldozers to the Israeli army, as these bulldozers have been modified and used to destroy Palestinian homes.[1] The activist Rachel Corrie was killed by such a bulldozer in March 2003, when she tried to stop the destruction of homes in Gaza. In our eyes, Caterpillar cannot simply reject its responsibility by arguing that it has "neither the legal right nor the means to police" individual use of its equipment.

Another threat is the increasing risk of litigation for those who are found to be complicit in human rights abuses. For example, Cape Plc has been sued in the UK over allegations that it exposed its workers to asbestos in South Africa. UNOCAL and Coca Cola have faced lawsuits for complicity in human rights violations in Myanmar and Colombia, respectively. Other examples relate to pharmaceutical and chemical companies: a lawsuit was filed against Pfizer in the US in 2001 by Nigerian families who claimed that the company did not obtain their informed consent for a clinical trial, in violation of international treaties. ICI and Monsanto discovered that the use of chemical agents by security forces in contexts where human rights are violated may be linked to them, as was the case in Colombia with the use of herbicides by security forces.

4. What are Amnesty International's expectations of the business world?

States have the primary responsibility to respect, protect and promote human rights. The focus on the state as the primary duty-bearer for human rights is due to the nature of the development of human rights standards, which emerged after World War II when the state had the most important influence on people's lives. But it is increasingly recognized that companies are also duty-bearers. The growing acceptance of international human rights laws and standards made it inevitable that companies would have to face their responsibilities towards human rights and recognize that they have the responsibility to promote and secure the human rights set forth in the UDHR, and not to encourage or be complicit in human rights abuses committed by governments and others.

4.1 What do we seek from companies?

We expect them to:

+ Give effect to the UDHR (through a public commitment)
+ Develop codes of conduct and policies that refer explicitly to human rights ›
+ Integrate human rights considerations into all decision-making processes
+ Protect human rights within all areas of their operations (suppliers, contractors, subsidiaries, workers and their family members, local communities, and other parties affected by the company's activities)
+ Make sure that the codes of conduct and policies are implemented across all functions of the company, and that the managers and staff, as well as suppliers and sub-contractors, are specifically trained on these codes and policies
+ Establish on-going dialogue with local stakeholders to improve the protection of the local communities' human rights
+ Conduct a human rights impact assessment in areas of potential operation
+ Have the code of conduct audited regularly by an external third party
+ Put in place corrective measures in cases of abuse
+ Disclose publicly and transparently the implementation of the policy/code of conduct
+ Undertake advocacy work with governments and act collectively with other companies to raise human rights concerns with government authorities
+ Avoid complicity with human rights violations

5. How does Amnesty International work with the corporate sector?

Before explaining how we work with the corporate sector, let me briefly explain how Amnesty International is organized and how we work.

5.1 Amnesty International's overall mission

Amnesty International is a 46-year-old worldwide movement of people, who campaign for internationally recognized human rights.

Our vision is of a world in which every person enjoys all of the human rights enshrined in the Universal Declaration of Human Rights and other international human rights standards.

In pursuit of our vision, our mission is to undertake research and action focused on preventing and ending grave abuses of the rights to physical and mental integrity, freedom of conscience and expression, and freedom from discrimination, within the context of our work to promote all human rights.

Amnesty International is independent of any government, political ideology, economic interest, or religion. It does not support or oppose any government or political system, nor does it support or oppose the views of the victims whose rights it seeks to protect. It is concerned solely with the impartial protection of human rights.

Our organization has a varied network of members and supporters around the world. At the latest count, there were more than 2.2 million members, supporters, and subscribers in over 150 countries and territories in every region of the world. Although they come from many different backgrounds and have widely different political and religious beliefs, they are united by a determination to work for a world where everyone enjoys human rights.

5.2 Amnesty International's work on economic relations and human rights

When we began to target the corporate sector a decade ago, we devoted our time mainly to lobbying, promoting human rights within companies, presenting our business principles, and convincing our interlocutors that human rights were indeed "their business" and had to be integrated into a company's agenda. Initially, our views were received with skepticism and reluctance.

To illustrate our purpose, in 2002 the UK Section of Amnesty International, together with the International Business Leaders Forum, issued the "Geography of Corporate Risk," a series of seven detailed world maps depicting where human rights abuses and violations existed and where leading North American and European multinational companies were at risk of being associated with them. The set of maps covered different sectors: extractive; food and beverages; pharmaceutical and chemical; infrastructure and utilities; heavy manufacturing and defence; and IT hardware and telecommunications.

This document was very useful because it illustrated concretely the extent to which a particular company was exposed to risk, depending on where it operated and on the types of activity it was engaging in. It made clear that the corporate sector could no longer ignore human rights violations such as torture, disappearances, extrajudicial killings, denial of freedom of assembly and association, forced and bonded labour, forcible relocation, denial of freedom of expression, arbitrary arrest and detention, etc. This mapping showed clearly that any transnational corporation operating in repressive countries could be caught and risk litigation (with significant costs and damage to its reputation) if it failed to develop a transparent and properly enforced human rights policy.

5.3 Amnesty International's research on the corporate sector[2]

Amnesty International has also developed its research on the corporate sector. Of course, we are still far from reaching the level of research we have attained in our "traditional" government approach. For that, we would need twice the personnel resources that we currently have.

Here are two examples of reports on the corporate sector that show how host government agreements can undermine the governments' obligations to protect the human rights of local communities, and that expose human rights violations linked to the projects.

Report on the Baku-Tbilisi-Ceyhan (BTC) pipeline project

The report focuses on the ways in which the legal agreement between the Turkish government and the BP-led consortium of oil companies in effect creates a human rights free corridor for the pipeline. The project is established under a framework of special agreements between the three states concerned (Azerbaijan, Georgia and Turkey), and between each state and the consortium. The latter agreements are known as Host Government Agreements (HGA). The HGA between the Turkish government and the consortium makes clear that the consortium is to be protected from, among other things, the consequences of any changes in national or international legislation that might hamper the construction and subsequent operation of the pipeline. In its report Amnesty International argues that such a project should go ahead only if it incorporates basic rights as a central operational feature of the project. It should not treat human rights as items to be negotiated. Our organization denounced the fact that mechanisms for protecting human rights were being systematically undermined.

Report on the Chad-Cameroon pipeline project

In this case, Amnesty International shows that companies should uphold their human rights responsibilities within their sphere of influence. These responsibilities are particularly relevant when the companies operate in countries where grave violations of human rights take place.

A consortium of oil companies is extracting oil from the Doba oilfields in southern Chad and transporting it 1,070 km by pipeline to Cameroon's Atlantic coast, in one of the largest private sector investment projects in Africa. The consortium is led by the

US company ExxonMobil, and includes Chevron (another US corporation) and Petronas, the Malaysian state oil company. The project has been promoted by investors, agreed to by governments and supported by lenders such as the World Bank, export credit agencies and private banks. While some of the parties have voluntarily adopted social and environmental standards, the agreements could hold back the governments of Chad and Cameroon, which have poor track records on human rights, from taking steps to improve the human rights protection of those affected by the pipeline project. The framework of agreements could also make it more difficult to hold the consortium to account for abuses of human rights that result from its activities.

Amnesty International's report highlights the potential dangers to human rights posed by the investment agreements underpinning the pipeline project. In Chad and Cameroon, human rights are largely disregarded. Both countries have ineffective judicial systems. The courts and the police are not properly equipped to uphold the human rights of people who might be adversely affected by the construction of the pipeline. The risk of exacerbating social unrest, abuses, and corruption must not be underestimated. Amnesty International calls on the governments, international financial institutions, and companies involved in the Chad-Cameroon pipeline project to revise the investment agreements. They should include an explicit guarantee that the agreements will not be used to undermine either the human rights obligations of the states or the human rights responsibilities of the companies.

5.4 Research combined with campaigning activities

As mentioned above, Amnesty International has the potential to mobilize activists worldwide to publicly denounce the implication in human rights violations by public as well as private actors. Often we do this jointly with other Non-Governmental Organizations (NGO) working on the same issues. Here are some examples.
The Bhopal disaster 20 years on

In December 1984, over 7000 people died in the course of a few days when toxic gases leaked from the chemical plant of Union Carbide in Bhopal, India. Since then, another 15,000 have died from exposure to the toxins, and thousands of others have suffered from chronic, debilitating illnesses. The plant site has not been cleaned up, so toxic wastes continue to pollute the environment and groundwater.

Survivors have been denied adequate compensation, appropriate and timely medical assistance, and rehabilitation. The leak devastated Bhopal's poorest communities. Its impact reverberated across the globe, raising questions about government and corporate responsibility for large-scale industrial accidents.

In 2004, Amnesty International issued a report on Bhopal, looking back through a human rights lens over the 20 years since the tragedy occurred. Our organization exposed the failure by UCC/Dow Chemical (which took over UCC in 2001) and the Indian government to prevent the gas leak, to address its consequences, and to prevent the continuing pollution of the environment and water through the dispersal of toxic and hazardous substances. The report also demonstrated the need to establish a universal human rights framework that could be applied to companies directly.

In conjunction with the publication of the report, Amnesty International country sections organized worldwide public activities, including sit-ins in front of Dow Chemical's offices and supporting shareholders' resolutions at Dow's annual general meetings in the United States of America. In Switzerland we participated in a common demonstration with Greenpeace and trade unions in front of the office of Dow Europe.

Caterpillar bulldozers to destroy houses in Israel and the OT

Caterpillar bulldozers (redesigned and armed) have been used by the Israeli army and security forces to destroy Palestinian homes, land and other properties for many years. Thousands of families have had their homes and possessions destroyed under the blades of the Israeli army's US-made Caterpillar bulldozers.

As the pace of the destruction increased in recent years, a number of pressure groups have made Caterpillar aware of concerns about the use of its equipment to commit such violations. Amnesty International conducted public campaigns against Caterpillar, expressing its concern about the use of Caterpillar products in human rights violations committed by the Israeli army and pointing out that the Universal Declaration of Human Rights proclaims that "every organ of society" shall promote human rights and strive "to secure their universal and effective recognition and observance." The company denied all responsibility and said that it could not control the use to which its products were put by buyers, adding that the sale was not direct to the Israel Defense Forces, but that there were intermediaries involved. We believe that Caterpillar has the duty to ensure that its bulldozers are not used to commit human rights violations, including the unlawful destruction of homes, land and other properties.

Guantanamo: secret flights, torture and "disappearances"

In 2006 Amnesty International released a report exposing the CIA's use of private aircraft operators and front companies to preserve the secrecy of so-called "rendition" flights.[3]

Our organization showed that the CIA has exploited aviation practices in order to avoid declaring the flights to aviation authorities. The report listed dozens of destinations around the world where planes associated with "rendition" flights have landed and taken off, and listed private airlines with licenses to land at US military bases worldwide. It also detailed the destinations and ownership of specific aircraft allegedly used to illegally transfer people interviewed by Amnesty International. One particular aircraft is known to have made over 100 stops in Guantanamo Bay. Another took Abu Omar to Egypt from Germany after he was kidnapped in Italy. The aircraft's owners have admitted leasing the plane to the CIA, but have said it is not used exclusively by the agency. There are 488 relevant recorded landings or take-offs between February 2001 and July 2005.

The report uncovers part of the mystery surrounding the practice of renditions. Because of the secrecy surrounding rendition operations, it is impossible to know how many people have been arrested or abducted, transferred across borders, held in secret detention or tortured in the "war on terror." Information from governments themselves indicates that the number is likely to be in the hundreds.

Amnesty International called on *governments* to:

+ Insist that any plane or helicopter used to carry out the missions of the intelligence services be declared a "state" flight, even if it is a civilian aircraft
+ Prohibit the use of airspace and airports for renditions
+ Actively investigate suspected rendition cases
+ Disclose the full extent of these practices and the fate of those whose whereabouts are still unknown

Amnesty International called on the *aviation sector* to take specific and immediate action to ensure that aviation companies do not lease their aircraft in circumstances in which they may be used in renditions. The onus is on companies to ensure that they are aware of the end use of any aircraft they lease or operate, and that they do not facilitate human rights violations.

IT Technologies: a force for human rights – and for human rights abuse

In the early days of the Internet, many people felt that this new technology had a kind of "revolutionary" power to help the expression of human rights, such as freedom of expression, democracy, and cross-cultural collaboration, free from political restrictions. Suddenly, people had wide-ranging and rapid access to information around the world, and could organize common activities very quickly. I remember having been overloaded by emails when civil groups sent out an appeal to demonstrate against the WTO in Seattle in 1999. The same happened during G8 meetings and at the World Economic and World Social Forums.

Communication has always been at the heart of Amnesty International's work, and therefore the Internet is also important to us. The advancement in popularity of online communication in the past ten years has completely changed the way we work. Through our website, we can communicate directly to the public, we can distribute our material instantly to media organizations around the world, and we can communicate with NGOs all over the world who can give us timely warnings about human rights violations taking place in their countries. We now have access to information and testimonies from people we might never have been able to reach.

The development of internet applications allowed human rights defenders to tell the world about the human rights abuses in their country, even in countries with poor human rights records. Alas, this "freedom" appeares to be a "short-lived dream." Governments did not take long to begin repressing the people identified as authors of politically sensitive messages. Internet users were imprisoned or had their freedom of movement restricted in countries such as Tunisia, Israel, Vietnam, Iran, Saudi Arabia, Cuba and China.

Because of the anonymity of the Internet and the difficulty of tracing targets, these governments needed help to find those they wanted to stop speaking out. They found an ally in companies who had previously put themselves forward as champions of free speech and freedom of information. In November 2002, Amnesty International reported that foreign companies, including Websense, Sun Microsystems, Cisco Systems, Nortel Networks and Microsoft, had provided technology to the Chinese authorities to help them censor the Internet. Far from denying this, the companies argued that they had no control over how their equipment was used. A Cisco Systems spokesperson said that "if the government of China wants to monitor the Internet, that's their business. We are basically politically neutral." We do not share this view. In our eyes, companies have a duty to ensure they do not help governments in violating human rights.

Other Internet companies have compromised their principles in order to gain lucrative slices of the market. For instance, Microsoft launched a portal in China that blocked the use of words such as "freedom" in "blog" text, Google launched a self-censoring Chinese search engine, and Yahoo! revealed email account details of the journalist Shi Tao to the Chinese authorities. Shi Tao was then prosecuted and sentenced to 10 years in prison.

Amnesty International launched a campaign called "freedom of expression and information." Thousands of people signed the pledge at http://irrepressible.info/ on our Web site. In the USA, a bill that would impose strict new obligations on American technology companies doing business with "Internet-restricting countries" like China is making its way through the US political system. Media and campaign organizations around the world have criticized the actions of these companies. The court of public opinion likely will have an effect on the policy of Internet companies, because their business depends on widespread public use of their services and their share price is vulnerable to negative publicity. Companies that provide services or products that help governments to abuse human rights risk facing the claim that they are complicit in these violations, which could prove bad for their business.

In January 2007, Amnesty International joined a "multi-stakeholder initiative" on Internet freedom of expression with academics, socially responsible investment firms, NGOs, other experts and companies including Microsoft, Google, and Yahoo!, to develop a set of voluntary principles to promote and respect human rights on the Internet. Though welcoming the initiative, we warned that it would not stop our movement from campaigning against Internet companies that participate with governments in human rights abuses. We also stated that any talks with respect to this initiative would continue in parallel with our support for proposed legislative measures in the USA (the Global Online Freedom

Act[4]) and elsewhere to combat Internet repression worldwide.

Campaigning for a global Arms Trade Treaty

Amnesty International, together with Oxfam and the International Action Network on Small Arms (IANSA), is campaigning for a global Arms Trade Treaty to bring the trade in weapons under control.

There are around 640 million small arms and light weapons in the world today. Eight million more are produced every year. For many years Oxfam, Amnesty International and IANSA have witnessed the human cost of arms abuses and campaigned for tougher arms controls. Thousands of people are killed, injured, raped and forced to flee from their homes as a result of the unregulated global arms trade.

Globalization has changed the arms trade. Arms companies, operating from an increasing number of locations, now source components from across the world, with no single company or country responsible for the production of all the different components. Companies are setting up offshore production facilities, foreign subsidiaries and other collaborative ventures. Their products are often assembled in countries with lax controls on where they end up. Too easily, weapons get into the wrong hands – to embargoed destinations, to parties breaching international law in armed conflict, and to those who use them to flagrantly violate human rights. Without strict control, such weapons will continue to fuel violent conflict, state repression, crime, and domestic abuse.

Existing arms regulations are dangerously out of date. Faced with an arms industry that operates globally, governments cannot rely solely on traditional national or regional export control systems. Effective control of a global arms trade requires new international standards and regulations based on international law.

The "Control Arms campaign" is calling for an international, legally-binding arms trade treaty to ease the suffering caused by irresponsible weapons transfers. Since its beginning in October 2003, Control Arms has gathered the support of over one million people worldwide. In December 2006, 153 governments voted at the United Nations to start work on developing an international Arms Trade Treaty. Unless governments act to stop the spread of arms, more lives will be lost, more human rights violations will take place, and more people will be denied the chance to escape poverty.

Conflict diamonds are still a reality

"Conflict diamonds" (or "blood diamonds") are diamonds that fuel conflict, civil wars and human rights violations and abuses. They have been responsible for funding recent conflicts in Africa that re- sulted in the death and displacement of millions of people. During these conflicts, profits from the illegal trade in diamonds, worth billions of dollars, were used by warlords and rebels to buy arms. An estimated 3.7 million people died in Angola, the Democratic Republic of the Congo (DRC), Liberia and Sierra Leone, in conflicts fuelled by diamonds.

In 2003, an international certification scheme called the Kimberley Process was launched, making it illegal to trade in conflict diamonds. A Kimberley Process certificate, guaranteeing diamonds as conflict-free, accompanies all official shipments of rough diamonds to and from participating countries. To support this, the international diamond industry agreed to a voluntary system of warranties to ensure diamonds continued to be tracked right up to the point of sale. All invoices for the sale of diamonds and jewelry containing diamonds should now include a written guarantee that states they are conflict-free.

Despite making significant progress, both governments and the diamond industry are still falling short in combatting the trade in conflict diamonds. In many participating countries, government controls in the diamond trade from mining to polishing are still inadequate and poorly enforced due to the lack of binding common minimum internal control standards, effective monitoring, capacity and political will.

Moreover, while the wars in Angola and Sierra Leone are now over and fighting in the DRC has decreased, the problem of conflict diamonds has not gone away, despite the existence of the

Kimberley Process. The United Nations reported in 2006 that poor controls are allowing up to US$ 23 million of conflict diamonds from Côte d'Ivoire to enter the legitimate trade through Ghana, where they are being certified as conflict-free, and through Mali. The Kimberley Process was set up to stop the trade in conflict diamonds, but it still is not strong enough to achieve its aim.

Angola, the Democratic Republic of the Congo (DRC), Liberia and Sierra Leone are still recovering from widespread devastation resulting from wars funded by diamonds. The number of conflict diamonds has been significantly reduced because peace agreements have been signed in countries in Western and Southern Africa. But more diamond-fuelled wars could occur in the future unless the Kimberley Process strengthens government controls and the diamond industry cleans up its act.

Amnesty International and Global Witness produced a diamond buyer's guide in 2006. We wanted to encourage all customers shopping for a diamond to put pressure on retailers and make sure they could give assurances that the diamonds sold were conflict-free.

The launch of the film "Blood Diamond," directed by Edward Zwick, at the beginning of 2007, was a timely reminder that governments and the diamond industry must ensure that no conflict diamonds find their way into the consumer market. It helped us to inform and sensitize the public broadly about this little known problem.

6. What are the challenges to be faced in the future?

Here are just a few of the numerous challenges.

6.1 The reluctance of companies to carry out advocacy work

One of the challenges for the corporate sector relates to the limits of business responsibilities when we ask them to "use their influence." Most companies are reluctant to lobby governments on human rights issues, even if those governments have a very poor human rights record. When in 1994 we urged Shell to use its influence on the Nigerian government to prevent the killing of Ken Saro Wiwa, the leader of the Ogoni people, the corporation reacted by arguing that as a business actor it could not interfere with the political processes and decisions of its respective host countries. Ken Saro Wiwa and eight of his companions were executed by the state for campaigning against the devastation of the Niger Delta by oil companies, especially Shell and Chevron.

Many corporations use the argument that seeking to influence governments is a political act that goes beyond their mandate. But this does not prevent them from lobbying vigorously on corporate tax reduction and tariff protection! We do not ask companies to step into the shoes of governments; we ask them to carry out advocacy work to enable governments to establish, at their national level, the conditions for guaranteeing the fundamental rights of their peoples. It is in the interest of corporate leaders to promote a safer, more stable world and to use their influence to promote human rights in the countries in which they work.

6.2 Breaking the silence of the corporate sector in a context of human rights violations

In many countries, companies work in a context of human rights violations committed by governments. When faced with human rights violations, they are reluctant to publicly express their concern towards the governments, arguing that for the safety of their investment they have to remain "neutral." This is illusory.

Moreover, silence might be interpreted by the world as complicity, as acquiescing in oppression for the sake of profit. In the context of human rights violations, neutrality – and silence – will support a government's assumption that the corporate sector accepts anything it does. The silence of Shell in Nigeria in 1995 cost Ken Saro Wiwa and eight of his companions their lives.

6.3 The risk of using human rights purely for public

relations purposes

Another challenge we face is the risk that human rights are considered to be useful simply for public relations and marketing purposes, like a new consumer good to be sold to enhance a corporation's reputation. I mean a risk, because most of the time human
rights issues are under the responsibility of corporate communication teams, who have even set up new functions, for example
"Head of Reputation." Corporate communication teams usually
deal with the media, and NGOs are the new target of those who
have developed the so-called stakeholder dialogue. For NGOs, it is
often difficult to know if our preoccupations really go beyond corporate communication and reach the management of a company.

6.4 The limits of self-regulation

The threat of damaged reputations, of legal action, and of investor
and consumer boycotts, has clearly been a spur for voluntary codes
and initiatives, such as the GRI, the Kimberley Process (on conflict
diamonds), the Global Compact or the Voluntary Principles on Security and Human Rights for the extractive industries.

Our experience has shown that while interest in social development might be widespread, serious commitment to human
rights has been patchy.

Voluntary initiatives have limits. They are insufficient because they work only for the well-intentioned. Moreover, the mul-
tiplicity of codes and standards is counterproductive: companies
take "self-service," picking up some of the rights and leaving others,
like, for instance, the rights to collective bargaining and freedom
of association. Voluntary initiatives generally offer very limited
leverage for victims of abuse. They do not allow a systematic review of the human rights performance of companies, which would
enhance their capacity to put in place corrective procedures.

Commitments made to human rights have to be meaning
-ful, and there must be some system of enforcing accountability.
That is why our organization has decided to champion legal accountability mechanisms, based on international human rights

13

HUMAN RIGHTS AND CORPORATE GOVERNANCE

Katharina Pistor

1. Introduction

Major efforts have bee made in recent times to bring human rights, environmental concerns, and labor rights back into corporate law and corporate governance. This trend was already well under way when two of the leading corporate law scholars in the United States pronounced "the end of history in corporate law," namely the convergence on the idea that corporate law – hence corporate governance – is (or will be) focused exclusively on maximizing shareholder value, whereas all other issues should be addressed in legislation or other measures targeted accordingly (Hansmann and Kraakman 2001). In other words, while some were already celebrating the externalization of all non-shareholder-related issues from corporate governance, others were working hard on re-introducing these issues into corporate decision making all the way to the board level, i.e. to ensure that these concerns were once more internalized. The chosen means for this renewed internalization, however, were not legislation or regulation, but voluntary codes of conduct with only reporting requirements attached to them. This essay seeks to assess these two trends: the externalization through law and the internalization through voluntary codes. The core thesis of the paper is that the formal legal governance framework for multinational corporations – including corporate law, choice of law rules, and the legal investment regime – that has emerged in the international market place is not conducive to the internalization project and might in fact create *disincentives* for corporations to effectively address concerns typically associated with "corporate social responsibility." Soft law interventions, such as the Global Compact or similar voluntary commitment devices that seek to commit corporations to adhere to basic human rights, labor or environmental protection standards, have to be assessed against this background of extensive legal entitlements that protect investor rights.

A note on what this essay is *not* about seems in order. This essay does not analyze the extent to which international norms of human rights are directly or indirectly applicable to corporations. Nor does it address corporations' criminal responsibility under do-governments or international organizations (the OECD) to complement formal law. How effective self-regulation or soft law is in protecting *investor* rights, and how it interfaces with legal or market mechanisms, however, remain largely unexplored issues.

Most contributors to this literature, however, agree on one thing: They believe that stakeholder interests should not be regulated by corporate law (Hansmann and Kraakman 2001) – or even any law (Easterbrook 1997). The major argument is that this would interfere with investor rights and leave directors and officers in a control vacuum created by competing stakeholder interests (Coffee 1988; Pistor 1999). In this context, it is typically pointed out that corporations not subject to mandatory rules requiring stakeholder participation in firm governance (as the German co-determination model, for example, does) do *not* adopt such mechanisms voluntarily as a matter of empirical evidence (Jensen and Meckling 1979). While this statement may have been true in the late 1970s, it does not appear to be entirely correct anymore today. Over the last 10 to 15 years we have seen the proliferation of governance arrangements that benefit stakeholders other than shareholders, and sometimes even commit a company to monitoring and enforcement devices by non-shareholder constituencies. These arrangements take various forms, including codes of conduct governing stakeholder interests, monitoring arrangements, as well as disclosure and reporting agreements – to mention just a few. The majority of these arrangements are – from the perspective of the firm – voluntary in the sense that there was no mandatory law requiring them to enter into them or design them in a particular way. This does not imply that firms necessarily commit to such standards without external pressure, but includes the possibility that they respond largely to the threat of shaming, consumer boycotts, or even litigation. The most prominent examples for such quasi-voluntary arrangements is the UN Global Compact, which has influenced codes adopted by individual firms. The Global Compact commits corporations to basic principles of human rights, labor protection, and environmental standards. To date, 2981 companies have registered on the Global Compact's web page as having adopted these standards.

These voluntary arrangements are hailed by some as evidence for greater recognition of stakeholder interests without relinquishing the overall notion of profit maximization and shareholder supremacy (Ruggie 2004), or as a learning experience with different players bound together in networks (Kell and Levin 2003). Others suggest that they are at best signaling devices and at worse a disguise for the continuing shareholder primacy (Sagafi-Nejad 2005). At this point in time it seems too early to assess the effect the Global Compact has had on firm behavior and stakeholder interests it seeks to address – although the recent delisting of companies for failure to comply with the GC's communication policy and, perhaps even more, the silence with which the delisting has been greeted – is a little disconcerting.[1] Instead, this paper seeks to place the nature of these arrangements – voluntary codes without tangible enforcement mechanisms into the broader context of firm governance in the context of the emerging global economic order.

3. Setting the stage: corporate law, regulatory competition and the role of stakeholders

The role corporations – firms that enjoy independent personality, limited liability and the benefits associated with these features, in particular limited risk exposure and asset partitioning between owners and the firm (Hansmann and Kraakman 2000) – shall play in society has been debated since the emergence of the large private corporate enterprises. Until the mid 19th century, only few jurisdictions allowed private firms to incorporate and thus to benefit from the status as legal entity that could act, sue and be sued in its own name and from limited liability for its shareholders without specific state approval. Jurisdictions that liberalized entry earlier, such as the state of New York in 1811, did so only for companies in particular sectors (manufacturing), of a maximum size (not more than US$ 100,000 in capital), and with inbuilt sunset provision (20 years).[2] By the beginning of the 21st century, few jurisdictions have retained administrative entry barriers, such as state approval requirements, for firms wishing to incorporate. Most substantive entry requirements, such as minimum capital requirements, minimum number of shareholders, have been equally eroded (Pistor et al. 2002). More importantly, corporations are now largely free to choose the place where they wish to incorporate without having to fear lack of recognition in the jurisdictions where they maintain operations. Advocates of "regulatory competition" have carried the day not only in the United States – where the fear of a race to the bottom was voiced in the 1970s (Winter 1977; Cary 1974), but has been silenced by advocates of regulatory competition (Romano 1993). The same can now be said for the European Union. Certainly after the most recent decisions by the European Court of Justice – Überseering[3] and Inspire Art[4] – there is little doubt that the seat theory, which forced companies to incorporate in the jurisdiction where they maintained their headquarters and/or major operations, is being relegated to history.[5]

The trend towards free choice of the law that shall govern corporate affairs endorses a certain model of the nature of the corporate enterprise.[6] This model seeks to optimize decision making at the firm level and to externalize issues not directly related to the profit maximization maxim of business. It also assumes that those in charge of the incorporation decision – typically management in coalition with shareholders – are best able to assess the pros and cons of alternative corporate law regimes and that their choice should prevail over other interests. In fact, the attractiveness of the state of Delaware in the US, the paradigmatic case for regulatory competition, was in large parts determined by the absence of other well organized constituencies in that state, such as labor unions (Arsht 1976).

Regulatory competition over *corporate law* thus tends to eliminate corporate law rules aimed at protecting the interests of non-shareholder constituencies. The protection of these interests now becomes exclusively the realm of separate state legislation.

This is precisely what advocates of the end of history for corporate law were hoping for (Hansmann and Kraakman 2001). While corporations can focus on the profit maximization maxim, the state protects non-shareholder constituencies through *other* law. This argument assumes that the political process is independent from corporate interests. In fact, – and this point is crucial for the argument advanced here – corporations do play a critical role in shaping public opinion and influencing lawmaking processes. Streamlining corporate interests by promoting their exclusive focus on profit maximization is likely to reduce the influence of other constituencies not only in corporate law, but also in the political market place where laws are made.

Firms frequently do make concessions not prescribed by law to non-shareholder constituencies. They may do so either because of a general commitment to a community or societal interests, or out of pure self-interest, because they need societal or labor support to advance their agenda. Post et al. (2002) have documented how companies, such as Cummins and Motorola have benefited in the long term from stakeholder engagement. It has allowed these companies to respond effectively to crises that resulted in part from management flaws, and in part from changes in the market for their products (Post, Preston, and Sachs 2002). Heal has shown that environmental policies pursued by firms have not only improved their image but led to substantial cost cutting (Heal 2004). But overall, these firms are the exception, not the rule. The Social Investment Forum, for example, reports that in 2005 only about 9.5% of the US$ 24.4 trillion assets under professional management in the Unites States used socially responsible investment strategies.[7] Moreover, few corporations institutionalize such policies by introducing provisions into their charters or bylaws or creating councils or other bodies within the corporation that would give these constituencies a greater voice in corporate affairs. This kind of institutionalization might face legal scrutiny (certainly in the US) as in the famous case Dodge v. Ford.[8] Still, this decision, which stated that the essence of the corporate enterprise is profit maximization and that a decision by the controlling owner (Henry Ford) not ever to pay dividends again was in violation of this fundamental principle, should not be over-interpreted. Corporations have been allowed, even encouraged, to make contributions to charitable funds, institutions of higher education, and even party finance, without any substantial oversight by shareholders.[9] Moreover, in recent years courts have increasingly noted that in today's world, corporations are subjects, to a host of laws and regulations, including environmental law, labor law, or laws aimed at controlling corruption, etc. In order to avoid penalty under such laws, companies may not only be allowed, but in fact be obliged to create governance structures that monitor deviant practices and address them.[10] A similar argument could be made for governance mechanisms that ensure compliance with voluntary codes of conduct – at least if there is a looming threat of liability. Institutionalizing commitments to stakeholders does, of course, create costs. Most importantly, it places constraints on the ability of firms to flexibly shift alliance with different stakeholder in response to changes on the market place. Indeed, Post et al. (2002) show how over the course of a firm's life the governance challenges changed, and with it the allegiance to stakeholders they were dependent on and/or willing to negotiate with.[11]

The picture that emerges is one where corporations are committed by law to advance shareholder interests and where the pursuit of other objectives requires specific justification. The extent of legal liability in turn depends on the willingness of politicians to give voice to non-shareholder constituencies and create mechanisms for enforcing them – which, as argued before, is not exogenous to corporate interests, as they influence the political process. Corporations are not prevented by law from acting in compliance with basic CSR norms, but given the strong bias in favor of shareholders, the burden of proof will be on them to justify the scope of such actions if they affect the position of shareholders.

4. The emerging global investor rights regime

Whereas corporations crave flexibility in order to be able to respond to new challenges as they arise, they are reluctant to afford the same flexibility to governments in countries where they operate. The emerging global investment regime subjects governments increasingly to a straitjacket committing them to protecting the property rights of foreign investors, irrespective of changing domestic preferences and policy concerns lest they face huge liabilities imposed by transnational tribunals.[12] And while corporations have often advocated the retreat of the state in order to enhance economic efficiency, they have not been shy to get states involved in creating a new *legal* regime that protects their interests by promoting the adoption of bilateral investment treaties between their home government and governments around the globe, which create legal rights for foreign direct investors against host governments. In fact, the propensity for developing countries to adopt a Bilateral Investment Treaty appears to be higher in countries that already have a substantial amount of foreign investment than those seeking to attract FDI from scratch (Swenson 2006).

Bilateral investment treaties are not new, but their usage has become much more common after the failure of the Multilateral Agreement on Investment (the MAI) in 1999 (Tobin and Rose-Ackerman 2006; Elkins, Guzman, and Simmons 2004). Today, more than 2000 BITs are in effect, with countries committing in bilateral agreements vis-à-vis other countries to largely similar principles,[13] namely to open their borders to investment by firms located in the other country and to afford them similar protection as domestic firms; not to expropriate either directly or indirectly; and to ensure that disputes between the foreign investor and the host country are settled in established procedures.[14] The dispute settlement arrangements are critical for understanding the impact BITs are having on host countries' policy choices, administrative and regulatory laws (Dolzer 2005). Typically, BITs provide a choice between dispute resolution in the country that is party to the dispute (i.e. the host country of the foreign investment) or referring a dispute to an international arbitration tribunal, including (but not limited to) the Center for the Settlement of Investment Disputes (ICSID) at the World Bank. Under the standard BITs, foreign investors can refer disputes directly to tribunals outside the host country if their rights have been infringed upon. The rationale for this regime is clear. The dispute is between a private party and a foreign government. Judicial independence in the host country might be questionable. Even if guaranteed in principle, there might be a bias against foreign players. Arbitration in international tribunals may therefore level the playing field and give foreign investors sufficient assurance that they will have a fair hearing should they be adversely affected by government action.

The flip side of this arrangement, however, is that arbiters are not attuned to any of the social concerns of the country, and are in fact asked to settle the dispute in isolation of such concerns. The liabilities they may impose on a country can have a huge impact on that country's government finances and is therefore likely to affect its policies and legislation (Peterson 2004). Imagine that the extensive case law on "regulatory takings" in the US, the "enteignungsgleicher Eingriff" in Germany, or their functional equivalents in other countries had been decided not by domestic courts, but by international tribunals. Would they have engaged in the kind of balancing of diverse interests in deciding whether or not a particular measure would be deemed an expropriation and would therefore be subject to liability? What impact would their decisions have had on the effectiveness and legitimacy of law in resolving conflicts between the interests of investors and broader social issues?

One might argue that developing countries could actually benefit from the outsourcing of dispute resolution (Bjorklund 2005). First, given that local institutions are weak and often corrupt, the credibility of legal arrangements could be enhanced. Second, competition between domestic courts and foreign tribunals may improve the overall quality of local courts. And third, developing countries benefit greatly from foreign direct investment, which in turn has been boosted by legal commitments host countries have made under BITs.

On the first point, foreign investors undoubtedly benefit from outsourcing dispute resolution. However, we have no evidence that outsourcing dispute resolution enhances legal governance back home. It is not clear that domestic courts will perceive the outsourcing as competition to their activities and therefore respond to the threat by improving their own performance. This argument rests on the assumption that judges and courts operate like entrepreneurs and compete for case load (or at least interesting cases) – an assumption that might have some credibility with regards to US courts, but would not adequately describe the operation of courts in most other countries. Finally, there is substantial evidence that foreign investment is associated with economic growth[15] and that economic growth in turn is positively correlated with improved "rule of law" indicators.[16] However, the relation with BITs is tenuous at best. While some studies assert that the adoption of BITs has increased foreign direct investment (Elkins, Guzman, and Simmons 2004), a review of these studies by Swenson (2006) suggests that the causal relation is rather doubtful. According to Swenson, many BITs were entered into by countries that had already received substantial foreign investments, suggesting that foreign investors may have acted as important lobbyists to stimulate the adoption of BITs.

Even if BITs do promote FDI flows, it is worth asking what impact FDI might have on governance – including the protection of basic human rights, labor rights and the environment in the host countries. Unfortunately, the only systemic evidence we have on this specific question is limited to former socialist countries (Hellmann, Jones, and Kaufmann 2002). In this study, Hellman et al. do find that FDI flows are lower in countries with high levels of corruption and other indicators for governance ailments. When they do flow, they tend to exacerbate governance problems as companies engage in corruption to promote their comparative advantage. Put differently, corporations tend to converge in their practices on the norms of the environment in which they operate rather than engaging in the improvement of such norms and practices. This finding is consistent with a recent study by Lock et al. (2006) investigating the effectiveness of NIKE's monitoring system of subcontractors and supply companies in Asia. The study finds that even after several years of systematic monitoring and ranking based on CSR performance indicators, few operations had improved their performance on these indicators. Interestingly, CSR performance turned out to be highly correlated with rule of law indicators and other measures of institutional quality in the countries where NIKE's sub-contractors operated. Neither result should come as a surprise. Given the incentives under which corporations operate they will seek ways to maximize profits wherever they are located and adapt to their environment.

5. Legal entitlements: human rights vs. investor rights

The previous section analyzed the creation of a global investor rights regime based on a patch-work of BITs. These rights are anchored in law and tied into an already existent network of arbitration tribunals. By the end of 2005, over 200 international investment arbitration cases were pending at ICSID and other arbitration sites (such as the Stockholm Chamber of Commerce). 48 cases alone had been filed in 2005.[17] The overall numbers as well as the steep increase of suits (from less than 10 in 1999 to over 2000 five years later) suggests that this system is actively used. Compliance rates by governments appears to be quite high, as countries often feel compelled to pay up lest they lose the much desired foreign investment flows.[18]

It is worth comparing this regime with the international regime for the enforcement of human rights violations. Some countries have allowed their own courts to become a forum for resolving human rights atrocities committed by governments and/or private actors elsewhere. An example is the US Alien Tort Statute and Belgium's assertion of universal jurisdiction of its criminal courts over human rights atrocities. However, these examples remain exceptions rather than the rule and come with many strings attached. ATS litigation has produced some highly visible cases, but the threshold for invoking ATS is rather high and requires major human rights atrocities, such as torture, genocide, and the like.[19] In addition, suits against foreign heads of governments are often dismissed because of immunity of foreign heads of state or the state department asserting its political jurisdiction over the matter, thus denying justiciability. And Belgium has been pressured (by the US among others) to backtrack and limit private party initiation of criminal suits under the universal jurisdiction doctrine.

At the international level, the number of transnational tribunals with jurisdiction over human rights has increased, resulting in some "outsourcing," most notably among them, of course the ICTY, the ICTR as well as the International Criminal Court. However, victims cannot formally initiate proceedings in those courts. Their ability to do so is limited to only few tribunals. The European Court of Human Rights now permits individuals to bring suits before the court without government permission, but still requires that these individuals first exhaust the domestic judicial process (Koehane, Moravcsik, and Slaughter 2000). The same applies in principle to the Inter-American Commission on Human Rights (IACHR, although the interpretation of what it means to exhaust domestic judicial remedies is somewhat more relaxed) (Koehane et al., ibid).

The enforcement of human rights violations against *private* actors is limited to domestic courts – and consistent with conflict of law rules – primarily in the locality where the violation occurred, even though advocacy groups are seeking to sue corporations in the country where the parent corporation is incorporated. An exception is the Alien Tort Claim Act in the US, which gives US courts jurisdiction over suits brought by aliens for violation of the law of nations or a treaty of the United States.[20] The ATCA has been used to sue a number of private corporations in recent years, including among others the US oil company UNOCAL for complicity in the Burmese government's human rights abuses, in particular the use of forced labor for building a pipeline from Burma to Thailand; in a suit against the Canadian company Talisman for its complicity with genocide in Sudan; and against the Anglo-Dutch Shell Corporation for human rights abuses in Ogoniland, Nigeria.[21] The critical issue in most of these cases is that corporations were accused not necessarily of directly committing human rights abuses, but of aiding and abetting in such abuses by taking advantage of human rights violations committed by government officials of the host country. The extent of such tort liability under US law still remains to be clarified as both the UNOCAL and Talisman cases were settled out of court.

The contrast between the legal regime established for corporations to protect their property rights in foreign countries and individuals who suffered human rights abuses in connection with (some) corporation's investments in their home country is striking. Whereas individuals are at best relegated to US statute dating back to 1789, corporations have ready access to transnational arbitration tribunals in order to protect their property rights.

6. Soft law and corporate governance

In order to bring the interests and rights of non-shareholder constituencies back into corporate decision making, the Global Compact offers a soft law approach to corporations wishing to signal their willingness to comply with basic human rights, labor, and environmental standards.[22] Companies voluntarily register and commit to comply with a communication policy that requires them to report annually on progress in achieving the self-set goals. This soft law approach seems rather timid given the extent to which shareholder and investor rights have been legally fortified. But before dismissing it, it is worth considering the debate about the relevance of hard vs. soft law, codes and norms in the corporate governance literature.

The conventional literature on corporate governance has witnessed an interesting turn-around over the past ten years. Legal scholars in the law and economics tradition, particularly in the US, have long emphasized the superiority of "enabling" over "mandatory" rules as governance devices. While enabling rules are "hard" law, in the sense that they are enacted by state legislatures, they offer a good benchmark case for assessing the efficacy of soft law, such as the Global Compact.

In an influential paper, Bernard Black argued that corpo- rate law is "trivial" (Black 1990). He argued that rules that conflicted with the economic rationale of the market place would be arbitraged around and that those that were consistent with it were in fact trivial, as firms would adopt them voluntarily anyhow. Consistent with Jensen and Meckling's notion that the corporation is nothing but a nexus of contracts (Jensen and Meckling 1976), private autonomy of contracting should apply within firms as it does outside firms (Easterbrook and Fischel 1991). Within this framework, legal rules are only one mechanism to address the agency problem between managers who control but do not own the firm and shareholders as their principals. Other mechanisms include market mechanisms (product market competition, labor market competition, capital market competition and the market for corporate control). In addition, a growing literature has pointed to the importance of social norms in governing corporations (Eisenberg 1999).

While lawyers in the law and economics tradition have been preoccupied with demonstrating the relative unimportance, if not triviality of law, economists have discovered the importance of legal rules aimed at protecting investor interests. Various empirical studies suggest that better protection of shareholder and creditor rights is positively correlated with better developed financial markets. The results are particularly pronounced for shareholder rights/stock markets (La Porta, Lopez-de-Silanes, and Shleifer 2004; La Porta et al. 2000; La Porta et al. 1997), but extend to credit markets and creditor rights (La Porta et al. 1998; Levine 1998).[23]

The studies typically don't distinguish between mandatory and enabling rules. Instead they assume that the rules on the books used as independent variables affect outcomes, i.e. that they are by and large followed even if they are not mandatory. At least implicitly they thereby endorse the notion that hard legal rules matter for economic outcome. Moreover, there is broad agreement that the protection of investors in publicly traded firms should take the form of mandatory law with enforcement not only left to private parties, but backed by enforcement agencies, such as securities regulators (Black 2000).

If shareholder rights require legal endorsement even though their interests are more likely to be aligned with corporate interests and they tend to benefit from other non-legal governance mechanisms, including capital markets and the market for corporate control – the case for protecting human rights with mechanisms that have some "legal teeth" appears to be even stronger. One might hold against this, first that investors might be in need of stronger protection, because their input to the firm is so crucial (Hansmann 1996); and second that it might politically not be feasible to effectively protect human rights through hard law, rendering soft law better than no law.

Regarding the first point, it is important to note that analyses of the importance of legal protection for various stakeholders or "patrons" (Hansmann, ibid) of the firm are typically framed as an optimization exercise that focuses exclusively on the firm. In order to effectively address human rights, environmental and similar concerns, a broader lens of social, rather than firm level, optimality is in order. From that perspective it seems difficult to argue that the value increase for shareholders is more precious than the protection of basic human rights or the environment. In fact, precisely because human rights and similar violation are often "externalities" of the firm's conduct of its "normal" business (take for example Unocal's alleged toleration or encouragement of human rights abuses by the government of Burma), mechanisms might be needed to induce firms to internalize the costs of their action.

In light of the strong legal rights investors typically enjoy, and the stronger legal protection of firm's property rights over human rights in the international arena, a soft law approach is likely to be insufficient.

Turning to the political feasibility of legal rights protection, it should be noted that multilateral agreements or concerted efforts to standardize bilateral agreements on a particular matter, whether investor or human rights, is only one of several ways in which human rights could be better protected globally. An alternative would be for countries to enter into regulatory competition by giving their domestic courts universal jurisdiction in civil and/or criminal matters over human rights violations by corporations. The Alien Tort Statute would then be only one of several avenues and countries could compete for improving the human rights protection they grant to individuals from around the globe. As the discussion of the evolution of corporate law has suggested, regulatory competition has often been instrumentalized to advance the interest of one particular group of stakeholders – those of shareholders. There is no reason to believe that the same mechanism could not be used to advance the interests of other stakeholders. No doubt, the danger of strike suits looms in the background – but that problem is not unique to human rights cases and thus not a reason to dismiss it outright.

7. Concluding comments

The paper has identified the imbalance in rights protection between shareholders/investors on one hand, and individuals or groups who suffered from human rights abuse on the other. It argued that relying on soft codes is unlikely to achieve the objectives stated by the framers of the Global Compact. While it is not inconceivable for soft law approaches to work as a governance mechanism, their efficacy needs to be assessed in the context of other opportunities as well as constraints a corporation faces in the domestic and global market places. We therefore need to take into consideration the strong entrenchment of investor rights in domestic corporate law on the one hand, and the strong legal protection of firm's property rights through bilateral investment treaties on the other. Combined, these strong legal rights create disincentives for firms to embrace other norms, such as human rights or environmental protection. In fact, with BITs, corporations now have a mechanism at their disposal that allows them to challenge domestic policies aimed at promoting such norms if these policies can be interpreted to violate investors' interests and expectations. Against this background, human rights will have to be better fortified with legal remedies – domestically and/or internationally. If that were to happen, the Global Compact could play a critical role – not only as a signaling device, but as a way for corporations to defend themselves against accusations of abuse in a court of law – not only in the court of public opinion, which is short lived and highly volatile.

14

THE 2007 GLOBAL COMPACT LEADERS SUMMIT:

MAJOR OUTCOMES AND PRELIMINARY CONCLUSIONS

Georg Kell

The 2007 Global Compact Leaders Summit, held in Geneva on 5–6 July 2007, was a milestone in the evolution of the Global Compact initiative and the related UN-business agenda. With over 1100 participating leaders and representatives from business, government, civil society, labour, academia and the United Nations, the Leaders Summit was the largest high-level event ever held on the topic of corporate responsibility. Through the launch of various reports, action platforms and learning resources, as well the convening of dialogues across all core issue areas, the Leaders Summit succeeded in bringing together the Global Compact's multi-stakeholder base to candidly assess the initiative's progress, renew commitment to the principles and project the Compact's future course.

Chaired by Secretary-General Ban Ki-moon, the Leaders Summit produced numerous outcomes that have significant bearing on the future of the Global Compact. Among the most fundamental conclusions from the Summit was a consensus among all stakeholders that organizing corporate practices around universal principles can be a winning proposition for both business and society.

1. Major outcomes
1.1 Global Compact governance fully implemented and thriving

The Leaders Summit fulfilled its role as the Global Compact's chief governance mechanism – one that is designed to provide maximum ownership of the initiative by its stakeholders. In doing so, the Leaders Summit brought to a successful conclusion a two-year effort to fully implement the Global Compact's unique multi-centric governance framework adopted in August 2005: Triennial Global Compact Leaders Summit, Global Compact Board, Local Networks, Annual Local Networks Forum, Global Compact Office, and UN Inter-Agency Team. All elements of the Global Compact's unique governance framework are now fully implemented and thriving.

1.2 Leaders Summit participants renew and deepen commitment to advance Global Compact principles

Summit participants deepened their collective commitment to embedding universal values in economies and markets. The 21-point "Geneva Declaration" carries forward the philosophy that through responsible business practices a more sustainable and inclusive global economy can be realized. The declaration identifies priority actions for participants, such as mobilizing subsidiaries to engage in Global Compact Local Networks and encouraging supply chains to commit to the ten principles. Additionally, it contains actions for governments, including cultivating enabling environments for business and supporting responsible business practices.

In addition, the Summit exposed chief executives to learning and dialogue opportunities in many of the Global Compact's priority areas through round-table discussions on human rights, labour, environmental responsibility, anti-corruption, responsible investment and UN-business partnerships. For example, in the area of human rights, business was challenged to introduce human-rights-specific policies in advance of the 60th anniversary of the Universal Declaration on Human Rights in 2008. The round-table discussions provided important content which will shape the future direction of the Global Compact's work programs in these areas.

1.3 Diversity of Leaders Summit participants – across geography, industry and stakeholder groups – results in rich exchange of experiences and perspectives

With participants from approximately 90 countries, the Leaders Summit reinforced the truly global nature of the Global Compact and the unifying commitment of companies from vastly different social and economic environments to corporate responsibility. For example, the delegation of 100 top Chinese executives hosted a breakfast meeting on corporate action to combat climate change.

Nearly 200 representatives from civil society, labour and academia added important voices and views in plenary and break-out sessions, furthering their critical role as constructive and necessary partners of the Global Compact who seek to hold businesses accountable for their commitments.

1.4 Government ministers adopt "Chairperson's Summary of Ministerial Round-table on the Role of Governments in Promoting Responsible Corporate Citizenship"

Ministers and other high-level government officials participating in the Leaders Summit held a round-table on the role of governments in promoting responsible corporate citizenship. Chaired by H.E. Sheikha Haya Rashed Al Khalifa, President of the 61st Session of the United Nations General Assembly, the Ministerial Round-table was attended by governments from North and South. Consensus was reached on the Chairperson's Summary of the round-table which lays out ways in which governments can support responsible business practices, including by creating enabling environments, raising awareness, developing tools and providing funding for voluntary initiatives.

1.5 Leaders Summit serves as launching pad for numerous action initiatives, stock-taking reports and learning resources

A bounty of new initiatives, studies and resources launched at the Leaders Summit will help the Global Compact continue to provide issue leadership and guidance on matters related to the implementation of universal values into business practices, as well as cross-sector partnerships.

Reports

In preparation for the Summit, two stock-taking reports were prepared to stimulate discussion and debate among participants. The Global Compact released its first annual review which contains the results of an in-depth survey of business participants regarding their efforts to implement the ten principles, engage in partnerships and work with local networks. Also, McKinsey & Company presented findings from its first comprehensive global CEO survey on the topic of business and society, looking specifically at the key socio-economic and political mega-trends shaping the leadership agenda.

Action platforms

Through the "Caring for Climate" platform, chief executives of 150 companies from around the world pledged to speed up action on climate change and called on governments to agree as soon as possible on Kyoto follow-up measures to secure workable and inclusive climate market mechanisms.

The Principles for Responsible Management Education is the first large-scale initiative developed for academic institutions to advance corporate responsibility through the incorporation of universal values into curricula and research. The PRME was co-convened by leading business management organizations and developed by an international task force of sixty deans and official representatives of leading business schools.

The CEO Water Mandate is designed to help companies better manage water use in their operations and throughout their supply chains.

Resources and tools

Numerous publications and online tools were released to aid Global Compact participants in implementing the ten principles, engaging in partnerships and communicating progress on corporate responsibility actions, including:

+ Inspirational Guide to Implementing the Global Compact
+ Operational Guide for Medium-sized Business
+ A Guide to Human Rights Impact Assessment and Management
+ Human Rights and Business E-Learning Tool
+ A Human Rights Framework

- Caring for Climate: Tomorrow's Leadership Today
- Business Guide to Partnering with NGOs and the United Nations
- Enhancing Partnership Value: A Tool for Assessing Sustainability and Impact
- Joining Forces for Change: Demonstrating Innovation and Impact through UN-Business Partnerships
- Measuring Business Success from Sustainability Certification

1.6 Mainstreaming of responsible investment practices provides compelling incentive for business to address environmental, social and governance issues

New research by Goldman Sachs launched at the Leaders Summit greatly bolsters the emerging argument that addressing environmental, social and governance (ESG) issues is an important element for ensuring a company's long-term value. After applying an ESG research and investment framework in six sectors (energy, mining, steel, food, beverages, and media), Goldman Sachs found that companies considered leaders in implementing ESG policies have outperformed the general stock market by 25% since August 2005. In addition, 72% of these companies have outperformed their peers over the same period.

Another key indicator of the mainstreaming of responsible investment is the astounding growth of the Principles for Responsible Investment (PRI) in just over one year since launching, with more than 200 institutional investors representing over US$ 9 trillion in assets signed on to the initiative. A report released at the first annual PRI meeting, held in Geneva in conjunction with the Leaders Summit, shows that the PRI signatories, many of whom rank among the global giants of investing, are now actively integrating ESG issues into their investment policies and engagement strategies – with 88% of investment managers and 82 % of asset owners conducting at least some shareholder engagement on ESG issues.

Together, the growth of PRI and Goldman Sachs' ESG investment findings greatly underscore and contribute to the business case for corporate responsibility – serving as a powerful catalyst for increased efforts by business to implement universal principles into their operations.

1.7 UN-business agenda receives recognition and gains momentum

Chaired by Secretary-General Ban Ki-moon, the Leaders Summit **226** gave fresh impetus to the UN-business agenda. It bolstered the case for system-wide UN-business engagement by showing the ability of corporate responsibility and cross-sector cooperation to contribute enormously to UN goals. Importantly, the Summit also reflected the ability of the UN to engage with business to meet common challenges in today's globalized world and demonstrated why and how the UN is making business an active partner. Additionally, the importance of practical UN-business partnerships – in areas such as development, education, financial markets and water – was reinforced.

In an effort to improve the capacity of the UN to engage with business, several resources and tools were launched during the Leaders Summit, including a new UN-business website, a partnership assessment tool and a guide for partnering with NGOs and the UN. In addition, a meeting of high-level representatives of UN agencies, funds and programmes, was held during the Summit to discuss ways to enhance UN-business collaboration. Such a meeting is an excellent indicator of increased collaboration and cooperation with business across the UN system in the future.

2. Preliminary conclusions

The major outcomes of the Leaders Summit – renewed multi-stakeholder commitment, deepening of business engagement, growing financial market incentives, increased governmental support and strengthening of the broader UN-business agenda – all point to the conclusion that working with business in a principled and pragmatic approach is one effective means for the United Nations to achieve its goals of global security, development and realization of human rights. Further developing the linkages between the Global Compact and the UN could provide for increased effectiveness of the broader UN-business agenda. In addition, continued leadership of the Global Compact by the Secretary-General remains essential for ensuring that this agenda not only makes lasting changes in economies and societies everywhere, but also throughout the United Nations system.

The Leaders Summit outcomes also highlight the need to strengthen the Global Compact's integrity measures – for example through quality management and brand protection – in order to ensure the continued growth and increased effectiveness of the initiative. It is equally important for the Global Compact to continue to identify and facilitate, when possible, market-based incentives for companies to implement the ten principles into their operations. An increased scale of responsible corporate practices is the only way that the Global Compact can help achieve a new phase of globalization which provides opportunities and wealth in all corners of the earth.

The main outcomes of the Leaders Summit also underscore the importance of continued caretaking of the Global Compact's unique, multi-centric governance framework. It will be a challenge to ensure that all its elements – the Leaders Summit, Local Networks, the Annual Local Networks Forum, the Global Compact Board, the Global Compact Office and the Inter-Agency Team – reinforce one another and operate in a synergistic manner. Maintaining the right balance between governmental support, UN mandate and outward business orientation will be critical.

Certainly, additional implications for the Global Compact's future will emerge given the variety of outputs from the Leaders Summit, including the Geneva Declaration, the Chairperson's Summary of the Ministerial Round-table, new action initiatives on environment and education, surveys of business implementation, issue-focused working groups, and renewed multi-stakeholder commitment. Tangible adjustments and updates to the Global Compact's strategy and day-to-day operations will undoubtedly result in due course. However, the core objective of the Global Compact is unwavering: to ensure that businesses everywhere contribute to a more sustainable and inclusive global economy through embedding universal principles into operations and corporate culture.

15

UNITED
NATIONS

A

General Assembly

Distr.
GENERAL

A/HRC/4/035
9 February 2007

Original: ENGLISH

HUMAN RIGHTS COUNCIL
Fourth session
Item 2 of the provisional agenda

IMPLEMENTATION OF GENERAL ASSEMBLY RESOLUTION 60/251 OF 15 MARCH 2006 ENTITLED "HUMAN RIGHTS COUNCIL"

"Business and Human Rights:
Mapping International Standards of Responsibility and Accountability
for Corporate Acts"

Report of the Special Representative of the Secretary-General (SRSG)
on the issue of human rights and transnational corporations and other
business enterprises

Summary

This report responds to various elements of subparagraphs (a) through (c) as well as (e) of the mandate (Commission on Human Rights resolution 2005/69): "standards of corporate responsibility and accountability…with regard to human rights"; "the role of States in effectively regulating and adjudicating" business activities; the subject of corporate "complicity"; and identifying some prevailing if not "best" practices by states and companies. The four addenda to this report provide greater detail. A companion report (A/HRC/4/74) explains the key issues involved in conducting human rights impact assessments, as per subparagraph (d).

Business and human rights: mapping international standards of responsibility and accountability for corporate acts*
John Ruggie

1.   There is no magic in the marketplace. Markets function effi-
ciently and sustainably only when certain institutional parameters
are in place. The preconditions for success generally are assumed
to include the protection of property rights, the enforceability of
contracts, competition, and the smooth flow of information. But
a key requisite is often overlooked: curtailing individual and social harms imposed by markets. History demonstrates that without adequate institutional underpinnings markets will fail to deliver their full benefits and may even become socially unsustainable.[1]

2.   In recent decades, especially the 1990s, global markets expanded significantly as a result of trade agreements, bilateral investment treaties, and domestic liberalization and privatization.
The rights of transnational corporations became more secure-
ly anchored in national laws and increasingly defended through
compulsory arbitration before international tribunals. Globalization has contributed to impressive poverty reduction in major
emerging market countries and overall welfare in the industrial-
ized world. But it also imposes costs on people and communities –
including corporate-related human rights abuses, for reasons detailed in the SRSG's interim report.[2]

3.   These are challenges posed not only by transnational corporations and private enterprises. Evidence suggests that firms operating in only one country and state-owned companies often are
worse offenders than their highly visible private sector transnational counterparts. Clearly, a more fundamental institutional misalignment is present: between the scope and impact of economic
forces and actors, on the one hand, and the capacity of societies to
manage their adverse consequences, on the other. This misalignment creates the permissive environment within which blamewor-
thy acts by corporations may occur without adequate sanctioning

or reparation. For the sake of the victims of abuse, and to sustain globalization as a positive force, this must be fixed.

4.   Realigning the relationships among social institutions is a long-term process. While governments representing the public interest must play key roles, they need to be joined by other social actors and to utilize other social institutions to achieve this goal, including market mechanisms themselves. The Commission on Human Rights recognized the scope and complexity of the challenge when it established this multifaceted mandate.   **232**

5.   The mandate asks the SRSG to "identify and clarify," to "research" and "elaborate upon," and to "compile" materials – in short, to provide a comprehensive mapping of current international standards and practices regarding business and human rights. Resolution 2005/69 also invites him to submit his "views and recommendations" for consideration by the Council. This report is devoted to the first task: mapping evolving standards, practices, gaps and trends.

6.   The report is organized into five clusters of standards and practices governing orporate "responsibility" (the legal, social, or moral obligations imposed on companies) and "accountability" (the mechanisms holding them to these obligations). For ease of presentation, the five are laid out along a continuum, starting with the most deeply rooted international legal obligations, and ending with voluntary business standards. A brief discussion of trends and gaps concludes the report. The clusters are:

I.   State duty to protect;
II. Corporate responsibility and accountability for international crimes;
III. Corporate responsibility for other human rights violations under international law;
IV. Soft law mechanisms;
V.   Self-regulation.

7.   This report draws on some two-dozen research papers produced by or for the SRSG.[3] He also benefited from three regional multi-stakeholder consultations in Johannesburg, Bangkok, and Bogotá; civil society consultations on five continents; visits to the operations of firms in four industry sectors in developing countries; four legal expert workshops; two multi-stakeholder consultations, on the extractive and financial services industries; and discussions with representatives of all relevant multilateral institutions and some government officials.[4]

8.   Addenda 1 through 4 provide greater detail on some of the issues posed in resolution 2005/69. A companion report (A/HRC/4/74) addresses the important subject of human rights impact assessments, as requested in subparagraph (d) of the mandate.

9. Because the SRSG has had fewer than 18 months to pursue this mandate, the job is not yet completed. For instance, research to date on "corporate spheres of influence" (subparagraph (c)) suggests only that it lacks legal meaning; further work is required to see if it can become a useful policy tool. More important, because factual claims about corporate obligations in the prior debate were so entangled with normative preferences and institutional interests, the SRSG has focused on producing a solid and objective evidentiary foundation. However, this has afforded him little opportunity to develop the "views and recommendations" he was invited to submit and which should rightly form part of this mandate's conclusion. Therefore, the SRSG would welcome the opportunity of an additional year to build on the extensive work already done and submit clear options and proposals for the Council's consideration.

1. State duty to protect

10.   Many claims about business and human rights are deeply contested. But international law firmly establishes that states have a duty to protect against nonstate human rights abuses within their jurisdiction, and that this duty extends to protection against abuses by business entities.[5] The duty to protect exists under the

core United Nations human rights treaties as elaborated by the treaty bodies, and is also generally agreed to exist under customary international law.[6] Moreover, the treaty bodies unanimously affirm that this duty requires steps by states to regulate and adjudicate abuses by all social actors including businesses.[7]

11. The earlier UN human rights treaties, such as the International Convention on the Elimination of All Forms of Racial Discrimination (ICERD), the International Covenant on Economic, Social and Cultural Rights (ICESCR), and the International Covenant on **234** Civil and Political Rights (ICCPR), do not specifically address state duties regarding business. They impose generalized obligations to ensure the enjoyment of rights and prevent nonstate abuse. Thus, ICERD requires each state party to prohibit racial discrimination by "any persons, group or organization" (Art. 2.1(d)). And some of the treaties recognize rights that are particularly relevant in business contexts, including rights related to employment, health, and indigenous communities.

12.   Beginning with the Convention on the Elimination of All Forms of Discrimination Against Women (CEDAW), adopted in 1979, and including the Convention on the Rights of the Child (CRC) and the recently adopted Convention on the Rights of Persons with Disabilities, business is addressed more directly. CEDAW, for example, requires states to take all appropriate measures to eliminate discrimination against women by any "enterprise" (Art. 2(e)), and in the context of "bank loans, mortgages and other forms of financial credit" (Art. 13(c)). The treaties generally give states discretion regarding the modalities for regulating and adjudicating nonstate abuses, but emphasize legislation and judicial remedies.

13.   The treaty bodies elaborate upon the duty to protect. General Comment 31 by the Human Rights Committee is one recent example. It confirms that under the ICCPR "the positive obligations on states parties to ensure Covenant rights will only be fully discharged if individuals are protected by the state, not just against violations of Covenant rights by its agents, but also against acts

committed by private persons or entities ..."[8] It further explains that states could breach Covenant obligations where they permit or fail "to take appropriate measures or to exercise due diligence to prevent, punish, investigate or redress the harm caused by such acts by private persons or entities."

14.   The Committees express concern about state failure to protect against business abuse most frequently in relation to the right to non-discrimination, indigenous peoples' rights, and labor and health-related rights. But the duty to protect applies to all substan- tive rights. The Committees tend not to specify the precise content of required state action, but generally recommend regulation through legislation and adjudication through judicial remedies, including compensation where appropriate.

15.   Current guidance from the Committees suggests that the treaties do not require states to exercise extraterritorial jurisdiction over business abuse. But nor are they prohibited from doing so.[9] International law permits a state to exercise such jurisdiction provided there is a recognized basis: where the actor or victim is a national, where the acts have substantial adverse effects on the state, or where specific international crimes are involved.[10] Extraterritorial jurisdiction must also meet an overall reasonableness test, which includes non-intervention in other states' internal affairs.[11] Debate continues over precisely when the protection of human rights justifies extraterritorial jurisdiction.

16.   The regional human rights systems also affirm the state duty to protect against nonstate abuse, and establish similar correlative state requirements to regulate and adjudicate corporate acts.[12] Indeed, the increasing focus on protection against corporate abuse by the UN treaty bodies and regional mechanisms indicates growing concern that states either do not fully understand or are not always able or willing to fulfil this duty.

17.   The SRSG's questionnaire survey of states, asking them to identify policies and practices by which they regulate, adjudicate, and otherwise influence corporate actions in relation to human rights, reinforces those concerns.[13] No robust conclusions can

be drawn because of the low response rate. But of those states responding very few report having policies, programs or tools designed specifically to deal with corporate human rights challenges. A larger number say they rely on the framework of corporate responsibility initiatives, including such soft law instruments as the OECD Guidelines or voluntary initiatives like the Global Compact. Very few explicitly consider human rights criteria in their export credit and investment promotion policies or in bilateral trade and investment treaties, points at which government policies and global business operations most closely intersect.[14]

18.   In sum, the state duty to protect against nonstate abuses is part of the international human rights regime's very foundation. The duty requires states to play a key role in regulating and adjudicating abuse by business enterprises or risk breaching their international obligations.

2. Corporate responsibility and accountability for international crimes

19.   But states are not the only duty bearers under international law.[15] Individuals have long been subject to direct responsibility for the international crimes of piracy and slavery, although in the absence of international accountability mechanisms they could be held liable only by national legal systems. The International Military Tribunals established after World War II confirmed that individuals bear responsibility for crimes against peace, war crimes, and crimes against humanity, and also imposed accountability on those within their jurisdiction – including corporate officers. With the entry into force of the Statute of the International Criminal Court (ICC) in 2002, a permanent forum now exists in which individuals can be held directly accountable for genocide, crimes against humanity, and war crimes if states parties fail to act.[16]

20.   Long-standing doctrinal arguments over whether corporations could be "subjects" of international law, which impeded conceptual thinking about and the attribution of direct legal responsibility to corporations, are yielding to new realities. Corporations

increasingly are recognized as "participants" at the international level, with the capacity to bear some rights and duties under international law.[17] As noted, they have certain rights under bilateral investment treaties; they are also subject to duties under several civil liability conventions dealing with environmental pollution. Although this has no direct bearing on corporate responsibility for international crimes, it makes it more difficult to maintain that corporations should be entirely exempt from responsibility in other areas of international law.

21.   The ICC preparatory committee and the Rome conference itself debated a proposal that would have given the Court jurisdiction over legal persons (other than states), but differences in national approaches prevented its adoption. Nevertheless, just as the absence of an international accountability mechanism did not preclude individual responsibility for international crimes in the past, it does not preclude the emergence of corporate responsibility today.

22.   Indeed, corporate responsibility is being shaped through the interplay of two developments: one is the expansion and refinement of individual responsibility by the international ad hoc criminal tribunals and the ICC Statute; the other is the extension of responsibility for international crimes to corporations under domestic law. The complex interaction between the two is creating an expanding web of potential corporate liability for international crimes – imposed through national courts.

23.   Individual responsibility under international law may arise by directly committing or instigating a crime, or for crimes committed by subordinates that a superior had reason to know would be committed but failed to prevent. The international tribunals have also imposed liability for "aiding and abetting" a crime, or for engaging in a "common purpose" or "joint criminal enterprise."[18] No one-to-one mapping can be assumed between standards for natural and legal persons. But national courts interpreting corporate liability for international crimes have drawn on principles of individual responsibility – as the US Court of Appeals for the Ninth Circuit did in its Unocal ruling.[19]

24. At the same time, the number of jurisdictions in which charges for international crimes can be brought against corporations is increasing, as countries ratify the ICC statute and incorporate its definitions into domestic law. Where national legal systems already provide for criminal punishment of companies the international standards for individuals may be extended, thereby, to corporate entities.[20] Even some ICC nonparties have incorporated one or more of the statute's crimes into their domestic laws, with potential legal implications for corporations.[21]

25. Domestic incorporation may also have an extraterritorial dimension. Several countries provide for extraterritorial jurisdiction with respect to international crimes committed by or against their nationals; and a few rely on "universal jurisdiction" to extend their laws regardless of nationality links.[22] Again, if they also permit criminal punishment of firms, those extraterritorial provisions could be extended to corporations.

26. Apart from national incorporation of international standards, a number of legal systems are evolving independently towards greater recognition of corporate criminal liability for violations of domestic law. Most common law countries have such provisions, at least for economic and some violent crimes. Many European civil law countries have moved beyond purely administrative regulation to adopt some form of criminal responsibility for corporations.

27. In this fluid setting, simple laws of probability alone suggest that corporations will be subject to increased liability for international crimes in the future. They may face either criminal or civil liability depending on whether international standards are incorporated into a state's criminal code or as a civil cause of action (as under the US Alien Torts Claims Act, or ATCA). Furthermore, companies cannot be certain where claims will be brought against them or what precise standards they may be held to because no two national jurisdictions have identical evidentiary and other procedural rules. Finally, civil proceedings may be brought for related wrongs under domestic law, such as assault or false imprisonment.[23] In short, the risk environment for companies is expanding slowly but steadily – as are remedial options for victims.

28.   Adding to the uncertainty for corporations, significant national variation remains in modes of attributing corporate liability. Given the difficulty of establishing a corporate "mind and will" in criminal cases, a number of jurisdictions have adopted a "corporate culture" approach. In Australia, where a firm's culture expressly or tacitly permitted the commission of an offence by an employee, the firm may be held liable.[24] In the US, federal sentencing guidelines take corporate culture into account in assessing monetary penalties.[25]

29.   There are also national differences in attributing liability within transnational corporate structures. The doctrine of separate corporate personality treats each member of a corporate group as a legally distinct entity. No uniform formula exists for "piercing the corporate veil" that separates a subsidiary from its parent company in order to hold the parent responsible for the subsidiary's acts. One alternative that has attracted attention is for the home country to impose civil liability on the parent company for its acts and omissions regarding activities by its subsidiaries abroad.[26] The rules governing extraterritorial jurisdiction suggest that such provisions are permissible.

30.   Few legitimate firms may ever directly commit acts that amount to international crimes. But there is greater risk of their facing allegations of "complicity" in such crimes. For example, of the more than forty ATCA cases brought against companies in the US – now the largest body of domestic jurisprudence regarding corporate responsibility for international crimes – most have concerned alleged complicity, where the actual perpetrators were public or private security forces, other government agents, or armed factions in civil conflicts.[27]

31.   Corporate complicity is an umbrella term for a range of ways in which companies may be liable for their participation in criminal or civil wrongs. With nuanced differences, most national legal systems appear to recognize complicity as a concept. The internation-

al tribunals have developed a fairly clear standard for individual criminal aiding and abetting liability: knowingly providing practical assistance, encouragement or moral support that has a substantial effect on the commission of the crime.[28] Where national courts adopt this standard it is likely that its application to corporations would closely track its application to individuals, although the element of "moral support" may pose specific challenges.[29]

32.   "Moral support" can establish individual liability under international law, and the tribunals have extended it to include silent presence coupled with authority. But a company trying in good faith to avoid involvement in human rights abuses might have difficulty knowing what counts as moral support for legal purposes. Mere presence in a country and paying taxes are unlikely to create liability. But deriving indirect economic benefit from the wrongful conduct of others may do so, depending on such facts as the closeness of the company's association with those actors. Greater clarity currently does not exist. However, it is established that even where a corporation does not intend for the crime to occur, and regrets its commission, it will not be absolved of liability if it knew, or should have known, that it was providing assistance, and that the assistance would contribute to the commission of a crime.

3. Corporate responsibility for other human rights violations under international law

33.   The emerging corporate responsibility for international crimes is grounded in growing national acceptance of international standards for individual responsibility. Although it continues to evolve, there is observable evidence of its existence. In contrast, what if any legal responsibilities corporations may have for other human rights violations under international law is subject to far greater existential debate.[30]

34.   At national levels, there is enormous diversity in the scope and content of corporate legal responsibilities regarding human rights.[31] A systematic mapping would require a comprehensive country-by-country study not only of the direct applicability of in-

ternational law, but also of a range of relevant national measures: constitutional protections of human rights, legislative provisions, administrative mechanisms, and case law. However, preliminary research has not identified the emergence of uniform and consistent state practice establishing corporate responsibilities under customary international law.[32]

35. The traditional view of international human rights instruments is that they impose only "indirect" responsibilities on corporations – responsibilities provided under domestic law in accordance with states' international obligations. In contrast, some observers hold that these instruments already impose direct legal responsibilities on corporations but merely lack direct accountability mechanisms. For example, the UN Sub-Commission on the Promotion and Protection of Human Rights, explaining that its proposed Norms "reflect" and "restate" existing international law, attributed the entire spectrum of state duties under the treaties – to respect, protect, promote, and fulfil rights – to corporations within their "spheres of influence."

36. This section looks for evidence of direct corporate legal responsibilities under the international sources featured in this debate: the International Bill of Human Rights – the UDHR and the two Covenants – and the other core UN human rights treaties and the ILO core conventions. It also notes major trends within the regional human rights systems. Nothing prevents states from imposing international responsibilities directly on companies; the question is whether they have already done so.

37. The UDHR occupies a unique place in the international normative order. Its preamble proclaims that "every individual and every organ of society ... shall strive by teaching and education to promote respect for these rights and freedoms and by progressive measures, national and international, to secure their universal and effective recognition and observance."[33] In Professor Louis Henkin's famous words: "Every individual includes juridical persons. Every individual and every organ of society excludes no one, no company, no market, no cyberspace. The Universal Declaration ap-

plies to them all."[34] Henkin surely is correct that the Declaration's aspirations and moral claims were addressed, and apply, to all humanity – and as we shall see in section V, companies themselves invoke it in formulating their own human rights policies. But that does not equate to legally binding effect.

38.   Many UDHR provisions have entered customary international law. While there is some debate, it is generally agreed that they currently apply only to states (and sometimes individuals) and do not include its preamble. Most of its provisions have also been incorporated in the Covenants and other UN human rights treaties. Do these instruments establish direct legal responsibilities for corporations? Several of them include preambular, and therefore non-binding, recognition that individuals have duties to others. But the operational paragraphs do not address the issue explicitly.[35]

39.   The treaties do say that states have a duty to "ensure respect" for and "ensure the enjoyment" of rights. Some have argued that this implies a direct legal obligation for all social actors, including corporations, to respect those rights in the first place. How can this claim be tested? One means is by examining the treaty bodies' commentaries, as they are charged with providing authoritative interpretations. Although their mandate is to define state responsibilities, several have exhibited growing interest in the role of business itself with regard to human rights.

40.   Where the treaty bodies discuss corporate responsibilities, it is unclear whether they regard them as legal in nature. CESCR's most recent General Comment on the right to work, for example, recognizes that various private actors, including national and multinational enterprises, "have responsibilities regarding the realization of the right to work" – that they "have a particular role to play in job creation, hiring policies and non-discriminatory access to work."[36] But then, in the same Comment, the Committee appears to reiterate the traditional view that such enterprises are "not bound" by the Covenant. Similarly, the HRC's most recent General Comment concludes that the treaty obligations "do not ... have

direct horizontal effect as a matter of international law" – that is, they take effect as between nonstate actors only under domestic law.[37]

41.   In short, the treaties do not address direct corporate legal responsibilities explicitly, while the treaty bodies' commentaries on the subject are ambiguous. However, the increased attention the Committees are devoting to the need to prevent corporate abuse acknowledges that businesses are capable of both breaching human rights and contributing to their protection.[38]

42.   On purely logical grounds, a stronger argument could be made for direct corporate responsibilities under the ILO core conventions: their subject matter addresses all types of employers, including corporations; corporations generally acknowledge greater responsibility for their employees than for other stakeholders; and the ILO's supervisory mechanism and complaints procedure specify roles for employer organizations and trade unions. But logic alone does not make law, and corporations' legal responsibilities under the ILO conventions remain indirect.

43.   At the regional level there is greater diversity. The African Charter is unusual because it imposes direct duties on individuals, but opinions vary on their effect and whether they apply to groups, including corporations. Expert commentary suggests that the Inter-American Court may have moved away from the traditional view when it recognized that non-discrimination "gives rise to effects with regard to third parties," including in private employment relationships, "under which the employer must respect the human rights of his workers."[39] The Inter-American Commission has limited itself to condemning nonstate actor abuses. The European Court of Human Rights has generally adopted the traditional view, imposing far-reaching obligations to protect on states but leaving to them the choice of means.[40]

44.   In conclusion, it does not seem that the international human rights instruments discussed here currently impose direct legal responsibilities on corporations. Even so, corporations are under growing scrutiny by the international human rights mech-

anisms. And while states have been unwilling to adopt binding international human rights standards for corporations, together with business and civil society they have drawn on some of these instruments in establishing soft law standards and initiatives. It seems likely, therefore, that these instruments will play a key role in any future development of defining corporate responsibility for human rights.

4. Soft law mechanisms 244

45.   Soft law is "soft" in the sense that it does not by itself create legally binding obligations. It derives its normative force through recognition of social expectations by states and other key actors.[41] States may turn to soft law for several reasons: to chart possible future directions for, and fill gaps in, the international legal order when they are not yet able or willing to take firmer measures; where they conclude that legally binding mechanisms are not the best tool to address a particular issue; or in some instances to avoid having more binding measures gain political momentum.

46.   This section maps three current types of soft law arrangements that address corporate responsibility and accountability for human rights: the traditional standardsetting role performed by intergovernmental organizations; the enhanced accountability mechanisms recently added by some intergovernmental initiatives; and an emerging multi-stakeholder form that involves corporations directly, along with states and civil society organizations, in redressing sources of corporate-related human rights abuses.[42]

47.   A prominent example of soft law's normative role is the ILO Tripartite Declaration of Principles Concerning Multinational Enterprises and Social Policy, endorsed not only by states but also global employers' and workers' organizations. It proclaims that all parties, including multinational enterprises, "should respect the Universal Declaration of Human Rights and the corresponding international Covenants."[43]

48.   The OECD Guidelines for Multinational Enterprises perform a similar role. They acknowledge that the capacity and will-

ingness of states to implement their international human rights obligations vary. Accordingly, they recommend that firms "respect the human rights of those affected by their activities consistent with the host government's obligations and commitments"[44] – the commentary expressly indicating that these include the host state's international commitments.[45]

49.   Both instruments are widely referenced by governments and businesses and may, in due course, crystallize into harder forms. Thus, soft law's normative role remains essential to elaborating and further developing standards of corporate responsibility.[46]

50.   Several intergovernmental initiatives recently have focused not only on promulgating standards for companies, but also on ways to enhance accountability for compliance. For example, due to civil society demands, anyone can now bring a complaint against a multinational firm operating within the OECD Guidelines' sphere to the attention of a National Contact Point (NCP) – a non-judicial review procedure. Some NCPs have also become more transparent about the details of complaints and conclusions, permitting greater social tracking of corporate conduct, although the NCPs' overall performance remains highly uneven. And the OECD Investment Committee has expanded its oversight of the NCPs, providing another opportunity to review their treatment of complaints.

51.   For its part, the International Finance Corporation (IFC) now has performance standards that companies are required to meet in return for IFC investment funds. They include several human rights elements.[47] Depending on the project, the IFC may require impact assessments that include human rights elements, and community consultation. Client compliance is subject to review by an ombudsman, who may hear complaints from anyone adversely affected by an IFC-funded project's social or environmental consequences.[48] The IFC standards also have accountability spillover effects, as they are tracked by banks adhering to the Equator Principles, which are responsible for some two-thirds of global

commercial project lending.[49]

52.   Beyond the intergovernmental system, a new multi-stakeholder form of soft law initiatives is emerging. Most prominent among them are the Voluntary Principles on Security and Human Rights (VPs), promoting corporate human rights risk assessments and training of security providers in the extractive sector; the Kimberley Process Certification Scheme (Kimberley) to stem the flow of conflict diamonds; and the Extractive Industries Transparency Initiative (EITI), establishing a degree of revenue transparency in the taxes, royalties and fees companies pay to host governments.

53.   Driven by social pressure, these initiatives seek to close regulatory gaps that contribute to human rights abuses. But they do so in specific operational contexts, not in any overarching manner. Moreover, recognizing that some business and human rights challenges require multi-stakeholder responses, they allocate shared responsibilities and establish mutual accountability mechanisms within complex collaborative networks that can include any combination of host and home states, corporations, civil society actors, industry associations, international institutions and investors groups.

54.   These hybrids seek to enhance the responsibility and accountability of states and corporations alike by means of operational standards and procedures for firms, often together with regulatory action by governments, both supported by transparency mechanisms. Kimberley, for instance, involves a global certification scheme implemented through domestic law, whereby states ensure that the diamonds they trade are from Kimberley-compliant countries by requiring detailed packaging protocols and certification, coupled with chain-of-custody warranties by companies.

55.   In these collaborative ventures, there is no external legislative body that sets standards and no separate adjudicative body to assess compliance. Both functions are internalized within the operational entity itself. But without such mechanisms, how can they be judged?

56.   These initiatives may be seen as still largely experimental

expressions of an emerging practice of voluntary global administrative rulemaking and implementation, which exist in a number of areas where the intergovernmental system has not kept pace with rapid changes in social expectations. Because they are relatively new and few in number, no definitive standards yet exist by which to assess them. But among the key criteria suggested by those who study them professionally are the perceived credibility of their governance structures, and their effectiveness.[50]

57.   The credibility of their governance structures, in turn, is said to hinge on three factors: participation, transparency, and ongoing status reviews. Thus, regarding participation, civil society and industry members collaborated with states to develop the standards for, and now participate in, the governance of the VPs, EITI, and Kimberley. Concerning transparency, EITI and Kimberley have established detailed public reporting requirements for participants as well as multi-stakeholder monitoring. And in terms of participant compliance, Kimberley carries out peer reviews of member states, often spurred by civil society reports of government-related performance shortfalls; EITI recently established a validation process by which non-compliant members may have their status publicly reduced; and Kimberley actually removed one government, effectively shutting it out of the international diamond trade – a measure permitted under World Trade Organization rules.

58.   None of the initiatives examined here embodies all of these standards fully. But each exhibits some, and participants appear to realize, albeit sometimes reluctantly, that the initiatives' credibility rests on them.[51]

59.   The effectiveness of these initiatives can be measured in two ways. One is their operational impact on the ground. It is generally acknowledged that Kimberley has reduced the flow of conflict diamonds to one percent of the total market, from three or four; the Nigeria Extractive Industries Transparency Initiative reports that it gained taxpayers the equivalent of US$ 1 billion in 2004 and 2005;[52] and the VPs have been implemented most extensively at the country level in Colombia – which is not yet even a formal par-

ticipant in the process, but where several thousand armed forces members have gone through company-supported human rights training.[53] Thus, even though their participants admit that substantial improvements are required, these initiatives have a significant operational impact.

60.   A second measure of effectiveness is whether they serve as examples for others. Indeed, the relative ease with which they can be established, in contrast with treatybased instruments, together with their perceived potential have directly inspired parallel efforts in related fields, including rules regarding private security forces and also for businesses beyond the extractive sector.[54]

61.   One final feature of recent innovations in soft law arrangements – both the intergovernmental and multi-stakeholder variety – should be noted. As they strengthen their accountability mechanisms, they also begin to blur the lines between the strictly voluntary and mandatory spheres for participants. Once in, exiting can be costly. No company has to accept IFC financing or Equator banks' loans, but if they do, certain performance criteria become required for continued funding. Countries are free to join the EITI or not, but if they do then extractive companies are required to issue public reports of their payments to governments. Suspension or expulsion from Kimberley has a direct economic impact on countries and companies. VPs language – and in some cases the actual text – has been incorporated into legal agreements between governments and companies. And once the VPs adopt participation criteria, noncompliance similarly could lead to expulsion.

62.   In sum, the standard-setting role of soft law remains as important as ever to crystallize emerging norms in the international community. The increased focus on accountability in some intergovernmental arrangements, coupled with the innovations in soft law mechanisms that involve corporations directly in regulatory rulemaking and implementation, suggests increased state and corporate acknowledgment of evolving social expectations and a recognition of the need to exercise shared responsibility.

5. Self-regulation

63.   In addition to legal standards, hard or soft, the SRSG's mandate includes evolving social expectations regarding responsible corporate citizenship, including human rights. One key indicator consists of the policies and practices that business itself adopts voluntarily, triggered by its assessment of human-rights-related risks and opportunities, often under pressure from civil society and local communities. This section maps such standards of self-regulation.[55]

64.   However, mapping the entire universe of "business enterprises" is impossible. More than 77,000 transnational corporations currently span the globe, with roughly 70,000 subsidiaries and millions of suppliers.[56] Those numbers are dwarfed by local firms, and an even bigger informal sector in developing countries.

65.   Therefore, the SRSG conducted studies of a subset of business entities to determine how they perceive corporate responsibility and accountability regarding human rights. One was a questionnaire survey of the Fortune Global 500 firms (FG500), which are under social scrutiny as the world's largest companies. The second "business recognition study") consisted of three parts: actual policies, rather than questionnaire responses, of a broader cross-section of firms from all regions (including developing countries) screened as likely to have policies that include human rights; eight collective initiatives that include human rights standards, like the Fair Labor Association (FLA) or the International Council on Metals and Mining (ICMM); and the rights criteria employed by five socially responsible investment funds (SRI).[57]

66.   Such a mapping barely could have been done five years ago because few corporate human rights policies existed. Uptake has been especially rapid among large global firms, a group still predominantly domiciled in Europe, North America, and Japan. Newer entrants from other regions lag behind, though it is unclear whether this lag reflects a fundamental difference or merely timing. Numerous firms in the business recognition study only recently joined initiatives like the Global Compact and are only beginning to develop human rights policies. And the FG500 survey demonstrates that there is substantial policy diffusion in this domain: fewer than half of the respondents indicate having experienced "a significant human rights issue" themselves, yet almost all report having policies or management practices in place relating to human rights.

67.   All FG500 respondents, irrespective of region or sector, include nondiscrimination as a core corporate responsibility, at minimum meaning recruitment and promotion based on merit. Workplace health and safety standards are cited almost as frequently. More than three-fourths recognize freedom of association and the right to collective bargaining, the prohibition against child and forced labor, and the right to privacy. European firms are more likely than their US counterparts to recognize the rights to life, liberty, and security of person; health; and an adequate standard of living.

68.   The survey asked the FG500 firms to rank order the stakeholders their human rights policies or practices encompass – in effect, to indicate the companies' conception of their "sphere of influence." Employees were ranked highest (99 percent); suppliers and others in their value chain next (92.5 percent); then the communities in which companies operate (71 percent); followed by countries of operation (63 percent). The only significant variations are that the extractive sector ranks communities ahead of suppliers, while US and Japanese firms place communities and countries of operations far lower than European companies.

69.   Companies reference international instruments in formulating their policies. Among the FG500, ILO declarations and conventions top the list, followed by the UDHR. UN human rights treaties are mentioned infrequently. The Global Compact is cited by just over half, the OECD Guidelines just under. More than 80 percent also say they work with external stakeholders on their human rights policies. NGOs top that list, followed by industry asso-

ciations. Intergovernmental organizations are a distant third – except for US firms, which rank them fifth, behind labor unions and governments.

70. The broader cross-section of companies parallels the FG500 in recognizing labor standards. But their recognition of other rights is consistently lower: the highest, at 16 percent, is the right to security of the person, encompassing both the right to life and the freedom from cruel and unusual punishment.[58] For areas covered by social, economic, and cultural rights these companies tend to emphasize their philanthropic contributions.

71. Firms in both samples participate in one of the eight collective initiatives.[59] The recognition of rights by these initiatives closely reflects industry sectors: for example, those in manufacturing focus more on labor rights, whereas the extractive initiatives emphasize community relations and indigenous rights. Moreover, they draw on international standards: the FLA and Social Accountability 8000 meet or exceed most core ILO rights, while Equator banks track the IFC's performance standards. The SRI indices mirror the overall high recognition of labor rights, and several exhibit a particular concern for rights related to indigenous peoples, as well as the right to a family life.

72. How do these companies and other business entities respond to social expectations regarding accountability? Most FG500 firms say they have internal reporting systems to monitor their human rights performance. Three-fourths indicate that they also report externally, but of those fewer than half utilize a third-party medium like the Global Reporting Initiative (GRI). Some form of supply chain monitoring is relatively common. But only one-third say they routinely include human rights criteria within their social/environmental impact assessments. The business recognition study generally matches this pattern.

73. Similarly, each of the collective initiatives requires some form of reporting; the ICMM utilizes the GRI. Most have remediation requirements for noncompliant participants, and four pre-

scribe grievance mechanisms for employees or community members. Five extend human rights requirements to supply chain practices, with accountability mechanisms ranging from periodic audits to certifying individual factories or global brands.

74.   In short, leading business players recognize human rights and adopt means to ensure basic accountability. Yet even among the leaders, certain weaknesses of voluntarism are evident. Companies do not necessarily recognize those rights on which they may have the greatest impact. And while the rights they do recognize typically draw on international instruments, the language is rarely identical. Some interpretations are so elastic that the standards lose meaning, making it difficult for the company itself, let alone the public, to assess performance against commitments.

75.   There are also variations in the rights companies emphasize that seem unrelated to expected sectoral differences, which appear instead to reflect the political culture of companies' home countries. For example, European-based firms are most likely to adopt a comprehensive rights agenda, including social and economic rights, with US firms tending to recognize a narrower spectrum of rights and rights holders.

76.   Where self-regulation remains most challenged, however, is in its accountability provisions. The number, diversity, and uptake of instruments have grown significantly. But they also pose serious issues about the meaning of accountability and how it is established. Only three can be touched on here: human rights impact assessments, materiality, and assurance.

77.   For businesses with large physical or societal footprints, accountability should begin with assessments of what their human rights impact will be. This would permit companies and affected communities to find ways of avoiding negative impacts from the start. Several SRI funds strongly promote human rights impact assessments coupled with community engagement and dialogue. However, relatively few firms conduct these assessments routinely – and only a handful seem ever to have done a fullyfledged human rights impact assessment (HRIA), in contrast to including select-

ed human rights criteria in broader social/environmental assessments.[60] And apparently only one company – BP – has ever made public even a summary of an HRIA. No single measure would yield more immediate results in the human rights performance of firms than conducting such assessments where appropriate.

78.   The concept of materiality refers to the content of company reporting – whether it conveys information that really matters. The number of firms reporting their social, environmental and human rights profiles – called "sustainability reporting" – has risen exponentially.[61] But quality has not matched quantity. Far fewer companies report systematically on how their core business strategies and operations impact on these "sustainability" issues. Instead, anecdotal descriptions of isolated projects and philanthropic activity often prevail. Moreover, only a handful of companies combine social and financial reporting, despite the fact that the former has "sustainability" implications for the latter.[62] The GRI provides standardized protocols to improve the quality and comparability of company reporting, but fewer than 200 firms report "in accordance with" GRI guidelines, another 700 partially, while others claim to use them informally.[63]

79.   Assurance helps people to know whether companies actually do what they say. A growing proportion of sustainability reports (circa 40 percent) include some form of audit statement, typically provided by large accounting firms or smaller consultancies.[64] Two global assurance standards have emerged, one giving companies more control over what is assured (ISAE3000), and the second empowering the assurance provider to consider stakeholder concerns in determining what is material and therefore should be included in public reports (AA1000AS).[65] Both help the public determine whether the information reported is reasonably likely to be accurate, based on such factors as the quality of the management, monitoring, data collection, and other systems in place to generate it, as well as its materiality. A growing but still small fraction of the largest companies use these standards.

80.   Supply chain assurance faces the greatest credibility chal-

lenges. Global brands and retailers, among others, have developed supplier codes to compensate for weak or unenforced standards in some countries – because global social expectations require them to demonstrate adherence to minimum standards. But without independent external assurance of some sort these systems lack credibility, especially for companies with questionable performance records. Standards for supply chain auditing are highly variable. Among the most trusted are the FLA's brand certification and SA8000 factory certification systems, both of which involve multi-stakeholder governance structures. Similar to the hybrid initiatives discussed in the previous section, the credibility of voluntary accountability mechanisms is enhanced by processes involving participation, transparency, and review – which these two systems embody.[66]

81.   For several reasons, the initiatives described in this section have not reached all types of companies. First, because many of the tools were developed for large firms, national and transnational, they are not directly suitable for small and medium sized enterprises. Existing tools need to be adapted or new ones developed. Second, as noted even large developing country firms are just beginning to be drawn into this arena. Third, a more serious omission may be major state-owned enterprises based in some emerging economies: with few exceptions, they have not yet voluntarily associated themselves with such initiatives, nor is it well understood when the rules of state attribution apply to their human rights performance.[67] Finally, as is true of all voluntary – and many statutory – initiatives, determined laggards find ways to avoid scrutiny. This problem is not unique to human rights, nor is it unprecedented in history. But once a tipping point is reached, societies somehow manage to mitigate if not eliminate the problem. The trick is getting to the tipping point – a goal to which this mandate is dedicated.

Conclusion

82.   The permissive conditions for business-related human

rights abuses today are created by a misalignment between economic forces and governance capacity. Only a realignment can fix the problem. In principle, public authorities set the rules within which business operates. But at the national level some governments simply may be unable to take effective action, whether or not the will to do so is present. And in the international arena states themselves compete for access to markets and investments, thus collective action problems may restrict or impede their serving as the international community's "public authority." The most vulnerable people and communities pay the heaviest price for these governance gaps.

83.   There are lessons to be drawn from earlier periods. The Victorian era of globalization collapsed because governments and business failed to manage its adverse impact on core values of social community. Similarly, the attempt to restore a laissez-faire international economy after World War I barely made it off the ground before degenerating into the destructive political "isms" that ascended from the left and right, and for which history will remember the first half of the twentieth century – all championed in the name of social protection against economic forces controlled by "others." There are few indications that such extreme reactions are taking root today, but this is the dystopia states and businesses need to consider – and avoid – as they assess the current situation and where it might lead. Human rights and the sustainability of globalization are inextricably linked.

84.   This report has identified areas of fluidity in the business and human rights constellation, which in some respects may be seen as hopeful signs. By far the most consequential legal development is the gradual extension of liability to companies for international crimes, under domestic jurisdiction but reflecting international standards. But this trend is largely an unanticipated by-product of states' strengthening the legal regime for individuals, and its actual operation will reflect variations in national practice, not an ideal solution for anyone. No comparably consistent hard law developments were found in any other areas of human

rights, which leaves large protection gaps for victims as well as predictability gaps for companies – who may still get tried in "courts of public opinion."

85.   Considerable innovation was found in soft law initiatives, both intergovernmental and, even more so, the multi-stakeholder hybrids. In the latter, individual states most directly concerned with a pressing problem collaborate directly with business and civil society to establish voluntary regulatory systems in specific operational contexts. In addition, self-regulation by business through company codes and collective initiatives, often undertaken in collaboration with civil society, also exhibits innovation and policy diffusion. All of these approaches show some potential, despite obvious weaknesses. The biggest challenge is bringing such efforts to a scale where they become truly systemic interventions. For that to occur, states need to more proactively structure business incentives and disincentives, while accountability practices must be more deeply embedded within market mechanisms themselves.

86.   Judging from the treaty body commentaries, and reinforced by the SRSG's questionnaire survey of states, not all state structures as a whole appear to have internalised the full meaning of the state duty to protect, and its implications with regard to preventing and punishing abuses by nonstate actors, including business. Nor do states seem to be taking full advantage of the many legal and policy tools at their disposal to meet their treaty obligations. Insofar as the duty to the protect lies at the very foundation of the international human rights regime, this uncertainty gives rise to concern.

87.   Lack of clarity regarding the implications of the duty to protect also affects how corporate "sphere of influence" is understood. This concept has no legal pedigree beyond fairly direct agency relationships. But in exploring its potential utility as a practical policy tool the SRSG has discovered that it can not easily be separated operationally from the state duty to protect. Where governments lack capacity or abdicate their duties, the corporate sphere of influence looms large by default, not due to any principled underpin-

ning. Indeed, disputes between governments and businesses over just where the boundaries of their respective responsibilities lie are ending up in courts. The soft law hybrids have made a singular contribution by acknowledging that for some purposes the most sensible solution is to base initiatives on the notion of "shared responsibility" from the start – a conclusion some moral philosophers have also reached with regard to global structural inequities that cannot be solved by individual liability regimes alone.[68] This critical nexus requires greater clarification.

88.   The extensive research and consultations conducted for this mandate demonstrate that no single silver bullet can resolve the business and human rights challenge. A broad array of measures is required, by all relevant actors. Mapping existing and emerging standards and practices was an essential first step. What flows logically from the current report is the need for a strategic assessment of the major legal and policy measures that states and other social actors could take, together with views and recommendations about which options or combinations might work best to create effective remedies on the ground. But because the mandate made only 18 months available to the SRSG, it has not been possible for him to build on his work and submit to the Council the "views and recommendations" Resolution 2005/69 invited. Therefore, he would welcome a one-year extension to complete the assignment. As has been his custom throughout, he would continue to hold transparent consultations with all stakeholders during this process and in advance of submitting his views and recommendations in his next (and final) report to the Council.

Annex

Selection of guidelines, certificates and tools

AA1000

Certifiable social standards of Accountability

http://www.accountability21.net/default.aspx?id=228

Business and Human Rights Resource Centre

Independent site providing information on business and human
rights behaviour of companies

http://www.business-humanrights.org

Conflict-Sensitive Business Practices: Guidance for
extractive industries

Guidance for companies to act conflict-sensitive

http://www.international-alert.org/our_work/themes/csbp.php

Equator Principles

Banking industry framework for addressing environmental
and social risks in project financing

http://www.equator-principles.com

Ethical Trading Initiative

Initiative that collectively seeks to improve working conditions
in supply chains.

http://www.ethicaltrade.org/Z/home/index.shtml

Extractive Industries Transparency Initiative

This initiative supports improved governance in resource-rich
countries through the verification and full publication of company
payments and government revenues from oil, gas, and mining.

http://www.eitransparency.org/

FTSE4Good

The FTSE4Good Index Series has been designed to measure
the performance of companies that meet globally recognised
corporate responsibility standards, and to facilitate investment
in those companies.

http://www.ftse.com/ftse4good/index.jsp

Global Reporting Initiative

Guidelines for reporting in the area of corporate and social
responsibility

http://www.globalreporting.org

Human Rights Compliance Assessment (HRCA)
Comprehensive and reliable tool for helping companies deal
with human rights issues relevant for their particular operations
http://www.humanrightsbusiness.org/040_hrca.htm

Guide to Human Rights Impact Assessment and Management
Guide which provides companies with a practical process to assess
their business risks, enhance their due diligence procedures and
effectively manage their human rights challenges.
http://www.iblf.org/resources/general.jsp?id=123946   **259**

ILO (International Labour Organisation)
Tripartite Declaration of Principles concerning Multinational
Enterprises and Social Policy (MNE Declaration)
http://www.ilo.org/public/english/employment/multi/overview.htm

Kimberley Process
The Kimberley Process is a joint government, international diamond
industry and civil society initiative to stem the flow of conflict
diamonds – rough diamonds that are used by rebel movements to
finance wars against legitimate governments.
http://www.kimberleyprocess.com/

OECD: The OECD Guidelines for Multinational Entreprises
Guidelines for multinational companies
http://www.oecd.org/topic/0,2686,en_2649_34889_1_1_1_1_
37439,00.html

Principles for Responsible Investment
The Principles for Responsible Investment aim to help integrate
consideration of environmental, social and governance (ESG) issues
by institutional investors into investment decision-making and
ownership practices.
http://www.unpri.org/

Social Accountability International
Social standard SA8000: Certifiable management system and
implementation of workers' rights along the value chain
www.sa-intl.org

Special Representative of the UN Secretary-General on the issue of human rights and transnational corporations and other business enterprises
http://www.business-humanrights.org/Gettingstarted/UNSpecial-
Representative

The UN Draft Norms on the Responsibilities of Transnational Corporations and other Business Enterprises with regard to Human Rights

Intended as assistance to companies in framing the human rights responsibilities for business.

http://daccessdds.un.org/doc/UNDOC/GEN/G03/160/08/PDF/
G0316008.pdf?OpenElement

UN Global Compact

Principles of human rights, employment, environmental protection and corruption to which companies can undertake a voluntary commitment.

http://www.unglobalcompact.org

UN/BLIHR A Guide for Integrating Human Rights into Business Management

This guide allows business to implement the Global Compact principles without undermining their other business goals.

http://www.blihr.org/Pdfs/GIHRBM.pdf

Voluntary Principles on Security and Human Rights

Initiative that introduced a set of principles to guide extractives companies in maintaining the safety and security of their operations within an operating framework that ensures respect for human rights and fundamental freedoms.

http://www.voluntaryprinciples.org/

Notes

01 Swiss Foreign Policy and Business — *Micheline Calmy-Rey*

★ This article is based on the speech made by the President of the Swiss Confederation, Micheline Calmy-Rey, at the Annual Conference of the Political Affairs Division IV of the Federal Department of Foreign Affairs, which took place in Bern, in September 2006 and was entitled "Political Risks in a Globalized Marketplace: Company Approaches to Conflict Prevention and Human Rights".   **261**

02 Human Security and Business – A Contradiction in Terms?
— *Marc Probst*

★ The opinions expressed in this editorial do not represent the official position of the Federal Department of Foreign Affairs.

1 Speech of German President Johannes Rau on the impact of globalisation, 13 May 2002, Berlin.

2 A definition of "neoliberalism" can be found, for example, in: Peter Ulrich, Integrative Wirtschaftsethik – Grundlagen einer lebensdienlichen Ökonomie, Bern/Stuttgart/Wien, 3. Auflage, 2001, S. 344–348.

3 World Development Indicators 2007, press release No:2007/159/DEC, http://web.worldbank.org/WBSITE/EXTERNAL/NEWS/0,, contentMDK:21299914~pagePK:64257043~piPK:437376~theSite PK:4607,00.html, 15 April 2007.

4 Food and Agriculture Organization of the United Nations, State of Food Insecurity in the World 2006, http://www.fao.org/docrep/009/a0750e/a0750e00.htm, 2006.

5 Human Security Center, Human Security Report 2005 – War and Peace in the 21st Century, Oxford University Press, 2005.

6 Report of the Secretary-General of the United Nations for Decisions by Heads of State and Government in September 2005, In: Larger Freedom – Towards Development, Security and Human Rights for All, New York 2005.

7 World Summit Outcome, Resolution adopted by the General Assembly, A/Res/60/1, 25.10, 2005, http://daccessdds.un.org/doc/UNDOC/GEN/N05/487/60/PDF/N0548760.pdf?OpenElement

8 E.g. "Norms on the Responsibility of Transnational Corporations and Other Business Entreprises with Regard to Human Rights"; E/CN.4/Sub2/2003/12/Rev 2, preamble (noting that transnational corporations "have the capacity to foster economic well being ... and wealth as well as the capacity to cause harmful impacts on the human rights and lives of individuals ...").

9 Ballentine, Karen and Virginia Haufler, Enabling Economies of Peace – Public Policy for Conflict-Sensitive Business, New York: UN Global Compact, 2005, S. 4, www.unglobalcompact.org/content/NewsDocs/ enabling_econ.pdf

10 Mike Moore, Director of the WTO, 1999–2003, Frankfurter Allgemeine, 28.20.2001, S. 38.

11 Hans Ruh, Ethik und Erfolg verbünden sich, in: Hans Ruh & Klaus M. Leisinger (eds.), "Ethik im Managment. Ethik und Erfolg verbünden sich", Zürich 2004, S. 17.

12 Nachhaltige Kollektivanlagen wachsen 2006 fünf Mal stärker als der gesamte schweizerische Fondsmarkt, Medienmitteilung, http://www.sam-group.com/downloads/about/sam_press_releases/ ina_medienmitteilung_märz07.pdf, März 2007.

13 Barbara Bleich, University of Zurich Centre of Ethics, in: Manager entdecken Ethik-Kurse, Neue Zürcher Zeitung, 12.06.2007, S. 50.

14 http://ec.europa.eu/enterprise/csr/campaign/index_de.htm

15 Report of the Special Representative of the Secretary-General (SRSG) on the issue of human rights and transnational corporations and other business enterprises. 9 February 2007, A/HRC/4/035.

16 Final report of the Panel of Experts on the Illegal Exploitation of Natural Resources and Other Forms of Wealth of the Democratic Republic of the Congo, Annex 3, United Nations, UN Doc: S/2002/1146, 16 October 2002.

17 Example from: The Role of the Private Sector in Supporting Human Security – Opportunities for the Human Security Network, John Bray, 2007, unpublished, a report prepared for the Swiss Department of Foreign Affairs, John Bray, Control Risk.

18 UN Charter, Article 55.

19 see http://www.ohchr.org/english/countries/ratification/3.htm.

20 Report of the Special Representative of the Secretary-General (SRSG) on the issue of human rights and transnational corporations and other business enterprises. 9 February 2007, A/HRC/4/035, S. 7..

21 Report of the Special Representative of the Secretary-General (SRSG) on the issue of human rights and transnational corporations and other business enterprises. 9 February 2007, A/HRC/4/035, S. 23.

22 http://www.icrc.org/Web/Eng/siteengo.nsf/htmlall/private_
sector?OpenDocument

23 Quoted by Novo Nordisk, in: Anthony P. Ewing, Understanding the
Global Compact Human Rights Principles, in: Global Compact,
Embedding Human Rights, New York, 2004, S. 31.

24 Draft Norms on the Responsibilities of Transnational Corporations
and Other Business Enterprises with regard to Human Rights, State
Responsibilites to Regulate and Adjudicate Corporate Activities under
the United Nations Core Human Rights Treaties (John Ruggie),
at: http://daccessdds.un.org/doc/UNDOC/GEN/G03/160/08/PDF/
G0316008.pdf?OpenElement, The Guide to Human Rights Impact
Assessment and Management, IFC, Global Compact, IBLF, 2007 provides
a good overview of "Business sector issues and human rights funda-
mentals for business" as well as a current overview of relevant initiatives.

25 http://www.blihr.org

26 Richard Gerster, Die Schweiz in der Welt – die Welt in der Schweiz,
Switzerland in the World, the World in Switzerland, 2007, at (dt/fr/it):
http://www.deza.admin.ch/de/Home/Dokumentation

27 See for example: Die Nachhaltigkeitsleistungen deutscher Grossunter-
nehmen, The Sustainability Performance of Large German Companies,
2005, at: http://www.scoris.de/download/scoris_dax30_studie_2005.pdf

03 Corporate Responsibility for Human Rights —
Klaus M. Leisinger

1 Draft Interim Report of the Secretary-General's Special Representative on the issue of human rights and transnational corporations and
other business enterprises. February 2006, at: www.ohchr.org/english/
bodies/chr/docs/62chr/E.CN.4.2006.97.pdf, p.4.

2 Report of the Special Representative of the Secretary-General (SRSG)
on the issue of human rights and transnational corporations and other
business enterprises. 9 February 2007, A/HRC/4/035.

3 GlobeScan: 2005 CSR Monitor, at: www.EnvironicsInternational.
com/sp-csr.asp.

4 M. Weber: "Politik als Beruf". In: "Gesammelte Politische Schriften".
J.C.B. Mohr (Paul Siebeck), Tübingen, 4th ed., 1980, p. 545 et seq.

5 InterAction Council, Universal Declaration of Human Responsibilities. September 1997, at: www.interactioncouncil.org/udhr/declaration/
udhr.pdf

6 Henkin L.: "The Universal Declaration at 50 and the Challenges of Global Markets." In: Brooklyn Journal of International Law, Vol. XXV (1999), No. 1 (April), p. 25.

7 See www.amnesty.org.uk

8 For example in New Academy Review, vol. 2, no. 1 (spring 2003): "Business interests … have been antagonistic to human rights" (p. 50) or "MNCs can now pose a significant threat to human rights, and also undermine the ability of individual states to protect people from human rights abuses" (p. 92).

9 See the detailed reports at www.state.gov/g/drl/hr/c1470.htm

10 U.N. Development Programme (UNDP), Human Development Report 2005. International Cooperation at a Crossroads (New York: Oxford University Press, 2005), p. 24.

11 Birchenhall J.A.: Economic Development and the Escape from High Mortality. In: World Development Vol.35 (2007) No.4 pp.543–568;
For the record: Policies to improve income distribution in the context of economic growth will help to "lift more boats". For an introduction to this debate see Chenery. H.: Redistribution with Growth. (Oxford University Press/World Bank) New York 1974.

12 See J. Wieland (ed.), Handbuch Wertemanagement (Hamburg: Murmann Verlag, 2004).

13 For this distinction according to different degrees of obligation for social norms, see R. Dahrendorf, Homo Sociologicus (Cologne: Opladen, 1959), p. 24 et seq., see also Caroll A.B.: Business & Society. Ethics and Stakeholder Management. South-Western Publishing Co., Cincinnati, 2nd edition 1993, p.14.

14 See R.T. De George, Competing with Integrity in International Business (New York: Oxford University Press, 1993).

15 See www.unglobalcompact.org

16 See the symposium reports at: www.novartisfoundation.com/de/symposium/2003/index.htm and www.novartisfoundation.com/de/symposium/2004/index.htm

17 A notion that also shines clearly through the Draft Interim Report of the Secretary-General's Special Representative on the issue of human rights and transnational corporations and other businesses, Boston, February 2006.

18 R. Sullivan (ed.), Business and Human Rights. Dilemmas and Solutions (Sheffield: 2003).

19 For example, Amnesty International UK/Prince of Wales International Business Leaders Forum, Business & Human Rights. A Geography of Corporate Risks (London: 2002); see also the excellent Web sites www.business-humanrights.org/Home and www.blihr.org

20 On the special problem of "failing states" and "failing markets," see K.M. Leisinger, The Right to Health: A Multi-Stakeholder Task, in Novartis Foundation for Sustainable Development, The Right to Health: A Duty for Whom? International Symposium Report 2004 (Basel: 2005) (available at www.novartisfoundation.com). With its voluntary commit-   **265** ment to action, Novartis far exceeds the obligations stipulated by law.

21 See Brokatzky-Geiger J. / Sapru J. / Streib M.: Implementing a Living Wage Globally – The Novartis Approach. In: UN Global Compact: Embedding Human Rights in Business Practices II, New York 2007, (forthcoming).

22 See, e.g., www.novartisfoundation.com and www.nitd.novartis.com

23 See also BLIHR/UN Global Compact, A Guide for Integrating Human Rights into Business Management (New York: 2006) and UN Global Compact / Office of the United Nations High Commissioner for Human Rights (UNHCHR), Embedding Human Rights in Business Practice (New York: November 2004).

24 See www.humanrightsbusiness.org/040_hrca.htm

25 CSR Europe / Business for Social Responsibility, Measuring and Reporting Corporate Performance on Human Rights (San Francisco: 2001).

26 For diverse corporate experiences, see the excellent Web site of Christopher Avery and his colleagues at www.business-humanrights.org, as well as BP's "position on difficult issues involving human rights," at: www.bp.com/liveassets/bp_internet/globalbp/STAGING/global_assets/downloads/H/Human_rights_guidance.pdf

27 See www.novartisstiftung.com

28 P. Drucker, Post Capitalist Society (New York: Harper Business, 1993), pp. 57f.

29 K.M. Leisinger, Business and Human Rights, in M. McIntosh, S. Waddock, and G. Kell (eds.), Learning To Talk: Corporate Citizenship and the Development of the UN Global Compact (London: Greenleaf Publications, July 2004), pp. 72–100.

30 BLIHR /UN Global Compact, op. cit. note 20, p. 8.

31 See The 2005 Business & Human Rights Seminar Report: Exploring Responsibilities and Complicity (London: December 2005), p. 15.

32 P. Watchman, Complicity: Charting a Path Through the Conceptual Minefield. See The 2005 Business & Hu¬man Rights Seminar Report, op. cit. note 29.

33 See The 2005 Business & Human Rights Seminar Report, op. cit. note 29.

34 See OHCHR Briefing Paper, The Global Compact and Human Rights: Understanding Sphere of Influence and Complicity, in UN Global Compact/UNHCHR, op. cit. note 20, p. 19.

35 See in this context Lawyers, Corporations and the International Human Rights Law, The Corporate Lawyer, vol. 25, no. 10 (2004), pp. 298–302.

36 See Compact Quarterly March 2007.

37 The fact that there remains a 'metaphysical' guilt which lies beyond criminal, political, or moral guilt, is discussed by Karl Jaspers in Die Schuldfrage (Heidelberg: 1949). Jaspers sees the existence of solidarity among men as human beings that makes each co-responsible for every wrong and every injustice in the world, especially for crimes committed in his presence or with his knowledge. "If I fail to do whatever I can to prevent them, I too am guilty. If I was present at the murder of others without risking my life to prevent it, I feel guilty in a way not adequately conceivable either legally, politically or morally ... jurisdiction rests with God alone" (p. 63). On a more modest scale, but nonetheless qualifying as Jasper's "guilt," is what human rights advocates define as "silent complicity" – that is, the failure by a company to raise the question of systematic or continuous human rights violations in stakeholder interactions.

38 See Y. Lunau and F. Wettstein, Die Soziale Verantwortung der Wirtschaft. Was Bürger von Unternehmen erwarten (Bern: Haupt Verlag, 2004), p. 140.

39 R. Brennan and P. Baines, Is There a Morally Right Price for Antiretroviral Drugs in the Developing World? Business Ethics: A European Review, vol. 15, no. 1 (2006), pp. 29–43. The authors answer the question affirmatively by advocating for enlightened self-interest.

40 Draft Interim Report of the Secretary-General's Special Representative on the issue of human rights and transnational corporations and other business enterprises. February 2006, available at www.ohchr.org/english/bodies/chr/docs/62chr/E.CN.4.2006.97.pdf, p.4.

41 See www.ohchr.org/english/law/index.htm

42 For a discussion of these risks see K.M. Leisinger and K.M. Schmitt,

Corporate Ethics in a Time of Globalization (Colombo, Sri Lanka: Sarvodaya Vishva Lekha Publication, 2003), pp.154 ff. Given that for companies listed on the stock exchange, reputation accounts for at least 50% of total value, the scale of potential damage inherent in such risks becomes clear; see Business Week, 2 August 2004. For new developments relating to the failure to comply with human rights minima moralia, see I. Schwenzer and B. Leisinger, Ethical Values and International Sales Contracts. In Jan Ramberg et al., Commercial Law Challenges in the 21st Century, Jan Hellner in Memoriam (Stockholm: forthcoming).

43 According to figures published by the Prince of Wales International Business Leaders Forum, calls for boycotts alone cause economic damage of almost 4 billion euros; see IBLF, Human Rights: It is Your Business (London: 2005), p. 4.

44 www.unhchr.ch/development/poverty-01.html

45 See J. Birkinshaw and G. Piramal (eds.), Sumanthra Goshal on Management. A Force for Good (London: Prentice Hall/Financial Times, 2005).

46 Commission on the Private Sector & Development: Unleashing Entrepreneurship. Making Business Work for the Poor (New York: 2004)

47 UNDP, Human Development Report 2000: Human Rights and Development (New York: Oxford University Press, 2000).

48 Report of the Secretary-General of the United Nations for Decisions by Heads of State and Governments, in: Larger Freedom. Towards Security, Development and Human Rights for All (New York: September 2005), see at: www.un.org/largerfreedom

49 UNDP, op. cit. note 46, p. 19.

06 Promoting Human Rights and Business in China —
Mads Holst Jensen

GoTone-Nanchang, 2005: "Declaration of The 2005 GoTone-Nanchang International Forum of Constructing Harmonious Society and Corporate Social Responsibility", 15 October 2005, at: http://www.cpdc.org.cn/major05.asp

ICFTU, 2006: Internationally Recognised Core Labour Standards in the People's Republic of China – Report for the WTO General Council Review of the Trade Policies of the People's Republic of China. Geneva, 4 and 6 April.

Liu Xiusheng, 1995: "时代呼唤商业道德中英市场文化研讨会侧记".

商业文化, no. 1, pp. 26–28

Sun Ruizhe, 2006: "CSC9000T: A Uniquely Chinese Social Compliance
Management System". Business for Social Responsibility: Leading
Perspectives, Summer, pp. 20–23.

UN Press release, 2004: "Annan Calls on Chinese Business Leaders to
Join the Global Compact on Shared Values and Practices", 12 October
2004, retrieved 12 May 2005, at: http://www.unchina.org/news/
Businessleaders.htm

Xinhuanet, 2005: "Harmonious Society Crucial for Progress", Xinhuanet, **268**
26 June 2005, retrieved 29 February 2006, at: http://news.xinhuanet.
com/english/2005-06/26/content_3139097.htm

07 Best Intentions Cannot Go Far Enough — *Salil Tripathi*

★ Based on a speech at the symposium, Human Rights Values and International Business, at the University of Basel in January 2007.

09 Ethical Values and International Sales Contracts — *Ingeborg Schwenzer & Benjamin Leisinger*

1 See Milton Friedman, *The Social Responsibility of Business is to Increase
its Profits,* The New York Times Magazine, 13 September 1970, online at
http://www.colorado.edu/studentgroups/libertarians/issues/
friedman-soc-respbusiness.html (08 March 2006).

2 See Milton Friedman, *Capitalism and Freedom,* Chicago/London 1982,
p. 133. See also Peter Muchlinski, *The Development of Human Rights
Responsibilities for Multinational Enterprises,* in: Rory Sullivan (ed.),
Business and Human Rights, Sheffield 2003, p. 33–51, p. 35, listing the
arguments against the extension of human rights responsibilities to
transnational corporations.

3 See Milton Friedman, *Capitalism and Freedom,* op. cit. (fn 2), p. 135.

4 See Geoffrey Chandler, *The Evolution of the Business and Human Rights
Debate,* in: Rory Sullivan (ed.), op. cit. (fn 2), p. 22–32, p. 24.

5 Survey cited in Douglas Galbi, *Child Labor and the Division of Labor
in the Early English Cotton Mills,* in: J. Pop. Econ. 1997, Vol. 10, pp. 357–375,
p. 357, online at http://www.galbithink.org/child.pdf (08 March 2006).

6 See Beth Stephens, *The Amorality of Profit: Transnational Corporations
and Human Rights,* Stefan A. Riesenfeld Symposium 2001, in: Berkeley
J. Intl. L. 2002, Vol. 20, pp. 45–88, p. 82.

7 See the study by Anita Chan, *Globalization and China's 'Race to the*

Bottom' in Labour Standards, Research School of Pacific and Asian Studies,
online at http://rspas.anu.edu.au/ccc/morrison/morrison02.pdf
(08 March 2006). But see the 'race to the top' noticed by the World Bank
with regard to environmental standards in: The World Bank (ed.),
Is Globalization Causing a 'Race to the Bottom' in Environmental Standards,
in: Assessing Globalization, World Bank Briefing Papers, Part 4, online at
http://www1.worldbank.org/economicpolicy/globalization/documents/
AssessingGlobalizationP4.pdf (08 March 2006).

8 See Claude Fussler, *Responsible Excellence Pays!,* in: JCC 16 (2004),
pp. 33–44, online at http://www.unglobalcompact.org/docs/news-events/
9.5/jcc16fussler.pdf (08 March 2006).

9 The DJSI track the financial performance of the leading
sustainability-driven companies worldwide. For more details see
http://www.sustainability-indexes.com (08 March 2006).

10 See René Kim/Erik Van Dam, *The Added Value of Corporate Social Responsibility,* 2003, online at http://triple-value.com/addedvalueofCSR.pdf
(08 March 2006).

11 See Klaus Leisinger, *Unternehmensethik in Zeiten der Globalisierung:
Idealistische Verirrung, Wettbewerbsnachteil oder Marktchance?,* in:
Schwäbische Gesellschaft (ed.), Schriftenreihe 44–47, Stuttgart 2003,
pp. 49–89, p. 74.

12 See Klaus Leisinger/Karin Schmitt, *Corporate Ethics in a Time of
Globalization,* 2nd ed., Basel/Colombo 2003, p. 78.

13 See this case outlined by David Weissbrodt, *Corporate Human Rights
Responsibilities,* in: zfwu 2005, pp. 279–297, p. 281. For more information
regarding this case, see http://www.bhopal.com (08 March 2006).

14 See report online at http://www.institutionalshareowner.com/news/
article.cgi?sfArticleId=1897 (08 March 2006).

15 See Klaus Leisinger, *Unternehmensethik in Zeiten der Globalisierung,*
op. cit. (fn 12), p. 76.

16 See Peter Pruzan, *Corporate Reputation: Image and Identity,* in:
Corporate Reputation Review, Vol. 4, 2001, No. 1, pp. 50–64, p. 53 et seq.

17 Cf. Carola Gilinski/peter Rott, *Umweltfreundliches und ethisches
Konsumverhalten im harmonisierten Kaufrecht,* in: EuZW 2003,
pp. 649–654, p. 653.

18 See Laura Ho/Catherine Powell/Leti Volpp, *(Dis)Assembling Rights of
Women Workers Along the Global Assembly Line: Human Rights and the
Garment Industry,* in: Harv. C.R.-C.L. L. Rev. 1996, Vol. 31, pp. 383–414,

p. 409, citing Charles Kernaghan, *A Call to Action/We Have More Power than We Realize,* in: The U.S. in Haiti: How to Get Rich on 11 [Cents] an Hour, Nat'l Comm. Educ. Fund 1996, p. 51 et seq., p. 60.

19 See Klaus Leisinger/Karin Schmitt, op. cit. (fn 11), p. 79.

20 See David Kinley/Junko Tadaki, *From Talk to Walk: The Emergence of Human Rights Responsibilities for Corporations at International Law,* in: Va. J. Intl. L. 2004, Vol. 44, pp. 931–1022, p. 953.

21 See Klaus Leisinger, *Unternehmensethik in Zeiten der Globalisierung,* op. cit. (fn 12), p. 77; Claude Fussler, *Responsible Excellence Pays!,* op. cit. (fn 8), p. 35.

270

22 See the report of: Siri Company (ed.), *Green, Social and Ethical Funds in Europe 2005,* October 2005, online at http://www.siricompany.com/pdf/SRI_Funds_Europe_2005.pdf (08 March 2006).

23 The study is available online at http://www.eurosif.org/pub2/lib/2003/10/srirept/eurosif-srireprt-2003-all.pdf (08 March 2006).

24 See online at http://www.socialinvest.org/areas/research/1999-Trends.htm (08 March 2006).

25 See: Social Investment Forum (ed.), *2005 Report on Socially Responsible Trends in the United States – 10 Year Review, 24 January 2006,* p. iv, online at http://www.socialinvest.org/areas/research/trends/sri_trends_report_2005.pdf (08 March 2006).

26 See U.N. Doc. E/CN.4/Sub.2/2003/L.11. The Norms submitted by the Working Group, E/CN.4/Sub.2/2003/12/Rev.2, online at http://documents.un.org/ (08 March 2006).

27 See: United Nations Sub-Commission on the Promotion and Protection of Human Rights (ed.), *Commentary on the Norms on the Responsibilities of Transnational Corporations and Other Business Enterprises with Regard to Human Rights,* UN Doc. E/CN.4/Sub.2/2003/38/Rev.2, online at http://documents.un.org/ (08 March 2006).

28 "The Norms do not change international law; they do not create new law. They bring together what already exists and point the direction towards a common, universal set of benchmarks." See Nicholas Howen, *Business, Human Rights and Accountability,* Speech delivered at the 'Business and Human Rights' Conference organized by the Danish section of the ICJ, Copenhagen, 21 September 2005, online at http://www.icj.org/IMG/pdf/NICK_Speech_DK_2.pdf (08 March 2006).

29 See David Weissbrodt/Muria Kruger, *Current Development: Norms on the Responsibilities of Transnational Corporations and Other Business*

Enterprises with Regard to Human Rights, in: Am. J. Intl. L. 2003, Vol. 97, pp. 901–922, p. 913.

30 The Guidelines that were revised in 2000 are online at http://www.oecd.org/dataoecd/56/36/1922428.pdf (08 March 2006).

31 See Implementation Procedures of the OECD Guidelines for Multinational Enterprises, Procedural Guidance, I. National Contact Points, C. Implementation in Specific Instances.

32 See: OECD Watch (ed.), *The OECD Guidelines for Multinational Enterprises and Supply Chain Responsibility – A Discussion Paper,* December 2004, p. 2, online at http://www.corporate-accountability.org/docs/OW_SupplyChain.pdf (08 March 2006). **271**

33 See Cornelia Heydenreich, *Die Umsetzung der OECD-Leitsätze für multinationale Unternehmen in Deutschland,* in: VENRO (ed.), Unternehmensverantwortung zwischen Dialog und Verbindlichkeit, p. 21 et seq., online at http://www.globalpolicy.org/eu/de/publ/venrocorpacc.pdf (08 March 2006).

34 See: OECD Watch (ed.), op. cit. (fn 32), p. 3.

35 See Mary Robinson, *Beyond Good Intentions: Corporate Citizenship for a New Century,* London, 7 May 2002. Speech available online at http://www.unglobalcompact.org/NewsAndEvents/speeches_and_statements/rsa_world_leaders_lecture.html (08 March 2006).

36 This list can be consulted online at http://www.fairlabor.org (08 March 2006).

37 The Global Reporting Initiative is a multi-stakeholder process aimed at the development and dissemination of globally applicable Sustainability Reporting Guidelines. For more information see http://www.globalreporting.org (08 March 2006).

38 For a brief introduction to these standards, see http://www.iso.org/iso/en/iso9000-14000/understand/inbrief.html (08 March 2006).

39 For an article giving an overview and showing concrete case studies, see Deborah Leipziger/Eileen Kaufman, *SA 8000: Human Rights at the Workplace,* in: Rory Sullivan (ed.), op. cit. (fn 2), p. 197–206.

40 For more information see http://www.sa-intl.org/ (08 March 2006).

41 See: United Nations (ed.), *What is the Global Compact?,* online at http://www.unglobalcompact.org/AboutThe GC/index.html (08 March 2006).

42 This is the status as of 10 January 2006. The members who participate but, however, do not communicate – i.e. with their stakeholders on an

annual basis about the progress in implementing the Global Compact
principles – are listed online at http://www.unglobalcompact.org/
ParticipantsandStakeholders/noncommunicating.html
(08 March 2006) and amount to a total of 612 participants.

43 See: Global Compact & Office of the High Commissioner for Human
Rights (eds.), *The Global Compact and Human Rights: Understanding Sphere
of Influence and Complicity – an OHCHR Briefing Paper,* p. 4,
online at http://www.unglobalcompact.org/Issues/human_rights/gc_
and_human_rights.pdf (08 March 2006). Also see Paul Watchman,
Complicity: Charting a Path Through the Conceptual Minefield, The 2005
Business and Human Rights Seminar, 8 December 2205, London,
speech online at http://www.bhrseminar.org (08 March 2006).

44 Cf. Steven R. Ratner, *Corporations and Human Rights: A Theory of
Legal Responsibility,* in: Yale L.J. 2001, Vol. 111, pp. 443–545, p. 510.

45 See Klaus Leisinger, *Opportunities and Risks of the United Nations
Global Compact: The Novartis Case Study,* in: JCC 2003, Vol. 11, pp. 113–131,
p. 122, online at http://www.novartisfoundation.com/pdf/Corporate_
Citizenship_Journal_Art_KML_Septo 3.pdf (08 March 2006).

46 According to ILO Convention No. C138 from 1973, which has been
ratified by 142 countries, child labor is the full-time employment of
children that are – in general – under the age of 15 years, Article 2(3) ILO
Convention. Labor which, by its nature or the circumstances in which
it is carried out, is likely to jeopardise the health, safety or morals
of young persons shall not be conducted by workers under the age of 18,
Article 3(1) ILO Convention.

47 See comments to Principle 3 online at http://www.unglobalcompact.
org/AboutTheGC/TheTenPrinciples/principle3.html (08 March 2006).

48 See online at http://www.unep.org/dpdl/Law/PDF/Rio_Declaration.
pdf (08 March 2006).

49 See comments to Principle 10 online at
http://www.unglobalcompact.org/AboutTheGC/TheTenPrinciples/
principle10.html (08 March 2006).

50 Id.

51 See: McKinsey & Company (ed.), *Assessing the Global Compact's
Impact,* 11 May 2004, online at http://www.unglobalcompact.org/docs/
news_events/9.1_news_archives/2004_06_09/imp_ass.pdf
(08 March 2006).

52 Companies like Celestica, Cisco, Dell, Flextronics, HP, IBM, Jabil,

272

Lucent, Microsoft, Sanmina SCI, Seagate, Solectron and Sony have adopted and/or implemented these norms. This code is online at http://www.hp.com/hpinfo/globalcitizenship/environment/supcode.pdf (08 March 2006).

53 Similar codes of conduct have been created and implemented by companies such as LEGO, (online at http://www.lego.com/info/pdf/ LEGO_Company_code_of_conduct_eng_2005. pdf (08 March 2006)), Novartis (online at http://www.novartis.com/ downloads_new/cc/ Novartis_TP_Code.pdf (08 March 2006), and others.

54 Code of conduct online at http://www.yum.com/responsibility/ suppliercode.asp (08 March 2006).

55 See: U.S. Department of State (ed.), *Country Reports on Human Rights Practices (2001),* 4 March 2002, Section 6 (Workers Rights), online at http://www.state.gov/g/drl/rls/hrrpt/2001/af/8355.htm (08 March 2006). For a discussion on slavery in the chocolate industry in general, see Manuel Velasquez, *Business Ethics: Concepts and Cases,* 6th ed., New Jersey 2006, p. 51 et seq.

56 See Davuluri Venkateswarlu, *Seeds of Bondage: Female Child Bonded Labour in Hybrid Cottonseed Production in Andrah Pradesh,* study online at http://www.indianet.nl/sob.html (08 March 2006).

57 See Tuna GATT Case No. 72, online at http://www.american.edu/ TED/TUNA.htm (08 March 2006).

58 See report by Sergi Tudela, *Ecosystem Effects of Fishing in the Mediterranean: An Analysis of the Major Threats of Fishing Gear and Practices to Biodiversity and Marine Habits,* in: General Fisheries Commission for the Mediterranean Studies and Reviews No. 74, online at ftp://ftp.fao.org/ docrep/fao/007/y5594e/y5594e00.pdf (08 March 2006).

59 For further information see online at http://www.fluoridealert.org/ pesticides/effects.chem.weapon.precurs.htm (08 March 2006).

60 For a list of all states that have ratified the CISG, see http://www.uncitral.org/uncitral/en/uncitral_texts/sale_goods/ 1980CISG_status.html (08 March 2006).

61 However, in order to ensure uniform application, the term "validity" has to be interpreted autonomously. See Schlechtriem in: Schlechtriem/ Schwenzer (eds.), *Commentary on the UN Convention on the International Sale of Goods (CISG),* 2nd ed., Oxford 2005, Art. 4 para 7.

62 Cf. Hans Stoll/Georg Gruber in: Schlechtriem/Schwenzer (eds.), op. cit. (fn 61), Art. 79 para 37; Dietrich Maskow in: Enderlein/Maskow/

Strohbach (eds.), *Internationales Kaufrecht*, Berlin 1991, Art. 79 para 3.6. In a decision of the Bulgarian Chamber of Commerce and Industry Court of Arbitration, 24 April 1996, CISG-online 435, a Bulgarian buyer purchased coal from a Ukrainian seller. The seller relied on an export ban and a strike of miners. The Tribunal found that such circumstances could constitute impediments. However, in this case, the export ban as well as the strike was foreseeable at the time of the conclusion of the contract and the exemption was not granted.

63 The possibility of exemption under Article 79 CISG is primarily **274** one of distribution of risk. Cf. Peter Schlechtriem in: Schlechtriem/ Schwenzer (eds.), op. cit. (fn 61), Art. 8 para 8.

64 The examples of impediments given by the Commentary on the Draft Convention on Contracts for the International Sale of Goods prepared by the Secretariat ("Secretariat Commentary"), UN DOC. A/CONF. 97/5, are: wars, storms, fires, government embargoes and the closing of international waterways. See Secretariat Commentary, Art. 65 (now Art. 79) para 5, online at http://www.cisg-online.ch/cisg/materialscommentary. html#Article%2065 (08 March 2006).

65 Cf. Klaus Leisinger, *Are "Human Rights" the "Business of Business?,"* Comment to the Contribution of David Weissbrodt, in: zfwu 2005, pp. 298–303, p. 302.

66 However, they sometimes confederate in order to have more market power.

67 According to the prevailing view, at least some practice – i.e. a sequence of previous contracts – is necessary. Cf. Wolfgang Witz in: Witz/Salger/Lorenz (eds.), *International einheitliches Kaufrecht*, Heidelberg 2000, Art. 9 para 16; Martin Schmidt-Kessel in: Schlechtriem/ Schwenzer (eds.), op. cit. (fn 61), Art. 9 para 8.

68 See LG Frankenthal (Germany), 17 April 1997, CISG-online 479, online at http://www.cisg-online.ch/cisg/urteile/479.htm (08 March 2006), stating: "Eine Gepflogenheit im Sinne des Artikels 9 CISG setzt nämlich eine gewisse Häufigkeit und Dauer eines Verhaltens voraus, so daß es berechtigt erscheint, wenn eine Partei auf ein solches Verhalten als üblich vertraut".

69 For other examples of industry initiatives, see online at http://www1.umn.edu/humanrts/business/icgi.html (08 March 2006).

70 See International Council on Human Rights Policy (ed.), *Beyond Voluntarism: Human Rights and the Developing International Legal Obliga-*

tions of Companies, Vernier 2002, p. 70; Peter Muchlinski, *The Development of Human Rights Responsibilities for Multinational Enterprises,* in: Rory Sullivan (ed.), op. cit. (fn 2), p. 51.

71 Cf. Jan Heilmann, Mängelgewährleistung im UN-Kaufrecht, Berlin 1994, p. 179: *"Beschaffenheiten für die der Verkäufer wegen Wertbeeinträchtigung haftet, sind nur die wertbildenden Faktoren wie Herkunft, Zusammensetzung [...]"* (emphasis added).

72 Cf. OLG München, 13 November 2002, CISG-online 786, online at http://www.cisgonline.ch/cisg/urteile/786.pdf (08 March 2006). In this **275** case, the buyer purchased organically produced barley from the seller. The seller did not provide the buyer with the necessary documents that showed that the goods had been produced in the appropriate way. The court held that it is almost impossible to establish, with reasonable expense, whether the barley had, in fact, been produced organically. It further held that organically produced barley is more than twice as expensive as normal barley, i.e. DM 625 instead of DM 290 per ton. The court emphasized that it was not a question of missing documents, but one of non-conforming goods, because the documents had no independent meaning ("Das Begleitpapier hat hier keine eigenständige Bedeutung. Vielmehr macht sein Fehlen die Ware selbst vertragswidrig [...]").

73 Bundesgerichtshof (Germany), 3 April 1996, CISG-online 135, online at http://www.cisg-online.ch/cisg/urteile/135.htm (08 March 2006): "Selbst wenn man davon ausgehe, daß die Lieferung englischer Ware vereinbart worden sei und Kobaltsulfat in England tatsächlich hergestellt werde, stelle die in Südafrika produzierte Ware zwar ein aliud dar. Dieses sei nach UN-Kaufrecht jedoch wie eine Schlechtlieferung zu behandeln [...]."

74 Cf. John O. Honnold, *Uniform Law for International Sales,* 3rd ed., The Hague 1999, Art. 35 para 225; Ingeborg Schwenzer in: Schlechtriem/Schwenzer (eds.), op. cit. (fn 61), Art. 35 para 14; Hanns-Christian Salger in: Witz/Salger/Lorenz (eds.), op. cit. (fn 67), Art. 35 para 9. See also High Court of Auckland (New Zealand), 31 March 2003, CISGonline 833, online at http://cisgw3.law.pace.edu/cases/030331n6.html (08 March 2006).

75 But see Fritz Enderlein in: Enderlein/Maskow/Strohbach (eds.), op. cit. (fn 62), Art. 35 para 8, who agrees that goods are not fit for the ordinary purpose under Article 35(2)(a) CISG if their commercial value is reduced considerably because of the lack of conformity.

76 OLG München, 13 November 2002, CISG-online 786, online at http://

www.cisgonline.ch/cisg/urteile/786.pdf (08 March 2006).

77 Cf. Peter Schlechtriem in: Schlechtriem/Schwenzer (eds.), op. cit. (fn 61), Art. 25 para 9; CISG-AC Opinion No 5, *The Buyer's Right to Void the Contract in Case of Non-Conforming Goods or Documents*, 7 May 2005, Baden-weiler (Germany). Rapporteur: Professor Dr. Ingeborg Schwenzer, LL.M., Professor of Private Law, University of Basel, para 4.2, online at http://www.cisg-online.ch/cisg/docs/CISG-AC_Op_no_5.pdf (08 March 2006).

78 Cf. CISG-AC Opinion No 5, op. cit. (fn 77), para 4.1.

79 See Hans Stoll/Georg Gruber in: Schlechtriem/Schwenzer (eds.), op. cit. (fn 61), Art. 74 para 49.

80 In this regard, several aspects have to be taken into account. One is the very nature of the ethical standard. Another aspect is whether the breach is merely an anomaly, or occurs regularly.

81 For a study concerning the value of brands by Newsweek and Interbrand, see online at http://www.ourfishbowl.com/brand_val/best_brands_05/2005_rankings_dollars.pdf (08 March 2006).

82 See Hans Stoll/Georg Gruber in: Schlechtriem/Schwenzer (eds.), op. cit. (fn 61), Art. 74 para 21; Herbert Schönle in: Honsell (ed.), *Kommentar zum UN-Kaufrecht*, Berlin/Heidelberg/New York 1996, Art. 74 para 13; Christoph Brunner, *UN-Kaufrecht – CISG*, Bern 2004, Art. 74 para 8; Wolfgang Witz in: Witz/Salger/Lorenz (eds.), op. cit. (fn 67), Art. 74 para 12.

83 For Germany, see Reinhard Möller, *Das Präventionsprinzip des Schadensrechts*, Berlin 2006; Thomas Dreier, *Kompensation und Prävention*, Tübingen 2002, p. 500 et seq. For developments on a European level, see Ulrich Magnus, *Comparative Report on the Law of Damages*, in: Magnus (ed.), *Unification of Tort Law: Damages*, The Hague/London/Boston 2001, p. 185 para 8 et seq. See also Walter Van Gerven/Jeremy Lever/Pierre Larouche, *Cases, Materials and Text on National, Supranational and International Tort Law*, Oxford/Portland 2000, p. 25.

84 So-called "venire contra factum proprium."

85 Supra III: Incorporation of Ethical Standards in Sales Contracts.

86 According to Principle Two of the UN Global Compact, for example, businesses should make sure they are not complicit in human rights abuses.

87 See Narandran Jody Kollapen, *Human Rights and Business: The Apartheid Experience*, Speech given at the Novartis Symposium "Human Rights and the Private Sector," online at http://www.novartisfoundation.com/en/articles/human/symposium_human_rights/speeches/speech_

kollapen.htm (08 March 2006). For further information, see online at
http://www.business-humanrights.org/Categories/Miscellaneous/
Historical/Businessduringapartheid (08 March 2006).

88 See Hans Stoll/Georg Gruber in: Schlechtriem/Schwenzer (eds.), op.
cit. (fn 61), Art. 79 para 11. Impossibility, however, is not required as even
laws can be evaded. See John O. Honnold, op. cit. (fn 74), Art. 79 para 432.1.

89 See Hans Stoll/Georg Gruber in: Schlechtriem/Schwenzer (eds.),
op. cit. (fn 61), Commentary Art. 79 para 1.

90 Cf. Peter Schlechtriem in: Schlechtriem/Schwenzer (eds.), op. cit.
(fn 61), Art. 8 para 8; Hanns-Christian Salger in: Witz/Salger/Lorenz
(eds.), op. cit. (fn 67), Art. 79 para 5 et seq.

91 Under CISG this would be possible if, for example, goods from another
origin would be a 'commercially reasonable' substitute that satisfies the
purpose of the contract just as well as the original goods intended.
See Hans Stoll/Georg Gruber in: Schlechtriem/Schwenzer (eds.), op. cit.
(fn 61), Art. 79 para 23.

92 Art. 6.2.3. Unidroit Principles state that in case of hardship the disadvantaged party is entitled to request renegotiations. According to
the commentary, hardship consists in a fundamental alteration of the
equilibrium of the contract. The renegotiations should be conducted with
a view to adapting the contract to the new circumstances. See: Unidroit
(ed.), *Unidroit Principles of International Commercial Contracts 2004*,
Rome 2004, Art. 6.2.3., p. 188.

10 Human Rights – Best Practice in Mainstream Investment Decisions? — *Philippe Spicher*

1 Cp. Annex

2 SiRi Company, based in Fribourg, Switzerland, is a global provider of
ESG research and SRI solutions to investment professionals. SiRi research
is based on publicly available material (Annual Reports, CSR and Sustainability Reports when available, company Web Sites), direct contacts with
companies through various means as appropriate (feedback on initial
findings, email or letters requesting more information, phone interviews,
face-to-face meetings), extensive searches in the international, national
and local press and other independent sources (NGOs, trade unions,
international organizations, academics)

3 Integration of SRI into mainstream investment process is understood
here as the use of ESG factor across all assets usually, but not necessarily,

with an attempt to capture the materiality of such factors.

4 "Who Cares Wins – Connecting Financial Markets to a Changing World," December 2004.

5 There is no officially recognized definition of cluster munitions, but the one put forward by the International Committee of the Red Cross is useful "A container or dispenser with a large number of sub-munitions, also called bomblets, which is free falling and blankets large areas of territory with sub-munitions."

6 "2005 Report on Socially Responsible Investing Trends in the United States," Social Investment Forum, January 24, 2006.

7 In its "European SRI Study 2006," Eurosif defines simple screens as "an approach that excludes a single given sector from a fund such as arms manufacture, publication of pornography, tobacco, animal testing, etc. Simple screens also include simple human rights screens (such as excluding companies for activities in Sudan or Myanmar) and norms-based screening."

8 The AI CSRR is the Association for Independent Corporate Sustainability and Responsibility Research. This association developped, owns and manages the CSRR-QS 2.0, the Quality Standard for SRI Research.

9 Eurosif defines integration as "the explicit inclusion by asset managers of [corporate governance]/[social, environmental, ethical] risk into traditional financial analysis."

10 "2005 Report on Socially Responsible Investing Trends in the United States," Social Investment Forum, January 24, 2006.

11 "European SRI Study," Eurosif, 2006

11 Corporate Responsibility in the Global Market —
Fritz Brugger & Thomas Streiff

1 2006 annual conference of the Political Affairs Division IV of the Swiss Federal Department of Foreign Affairs, at: http://www.eda.admin.ch/eda/g/home/foreign/humsec/frpziv/jako.html

2 Classification based on "A Guide for Integrating Human Rights into Business Management"; at: http://www.blihr.org

3 cf. (for example) John Ruggie at: http://www.business-humanrights.org/Links/Repository/825101

4 Based on: Klaus M. Leisinger, On Corporate Responsibility for Human Rights, Basel 2006

5 Online assessment at: https://hrca.humanrightsbusiness.org

6 Details and scheduled events of the learning platform at:
http://www.unglobalcompact.ch/kmu

12 Actions Speak Louder than Words — *Danièle Gosteli Hauser*

1 See also point 5.4.2

2 The reports mentioned in the text can be found on the following websites: www.amnesty.org, www.amnesty.org.uk/business

3 Rendition is a covert operation whereby people have been arrested or abducted, transferred and held in secret or handed over to countries where they have faced torture and other ill-treatment.

4 The "Global Online Freedom Act" of 2006 is a proposed bill introduced by New Jersey Representative Chris Smith. It is designed to respond to and prevent censorship and abuse of freedom of expression on the Internet by placing restrictions on US Internet content-hosting companies operating in countries that censor, prosecute and/or persecute individuals based on the exercise of such freedoms.

13 Human Rights and Corporate Governance — *Katharina Pistor*

1 355 companies were de-listed in October and another 203 are about to be de-listed, because they were "inactive," i.e. did not comply with the GC's communication policy, which requires companies to file progress reports. Companies failing to file such a report for 2 consecutive years are considered "inactive." Note that the Global Compact's Web page currently lists 486 companies as "inactive." 756 companies are currently not communicating. For a list of inactive companies, see:
http://www.unglobalcompact.org/CommunicatingProgress/inactive_participants.html, last visited 12 January 2007

2 Laws of New York (1811) Thirty-Fourth Session, Chapter LXVII, pp. 15–153

3 C 208/00. Judgment of the European Court of Justice, 5 November 2002 (2002/C 323/13)

4 C 167/01. Judment of the European Court of Justice, 15 November 2003 (OJ C 275, 15.11.2003, p. 10)

5 In fact, the German Supreme Court has conceded as much in its decision, which implemented the ECJ's Ueberseering decision.
BGH, 13 March 2003, VII ZR 370/98

6 For an overview of the intellectual history of the enterprise model in the US see (Fligstein 1990).

7 "2005 Report on Socially Responsible Investing Trends in the United States," published by Social Investment Forum, January 24, 2006 at IV (foreword), available at http://www.socialinvest.org/areas/research/trends/SRI_Trends_Report_2005.pdf (Identifying US$ 2.29 trillion in total assets managed using one or more of three socially responsible investing strategies). For a comprehensive analysis of CSR actions, see Allison Snyder, "Non-Financial Disclosure" research paper, Columbia Law School (January 2007) on file with the author.

8 Dodge v. Ford Motor Co. 204 Mich. 459, 170 N.W. 668 (Mi. 1919)   **280**

9 See e.g. A.P. Smith Mfg. Col. V. Barlow, 13 N.J. 145, 98 A.2d 581 (June 25, 1953)

10 In re Caremark Intl, Inc. Derivative Litigation, 698 A.2d 959 (Del. Ch. 1996).

11 See their graph's reflecting the "stakeholder journey" at Cummins on page 233; at Motorola at p. 235; and at Shell at p. 238

12 A recent example is the award against Argentina granted by the arbitration tribunal of the International Center for the Settlement of Disputes (ICSID) in the case "CMS Gas Transmission Company c. República Argentina" (Case No. ARB/01/08). In this case the tribunal awarded CMS US$ 132.2 million plus interest on the basis that Argentina violated the principle of "fair and equitable treatment" enshrined in the US-Argentine BIT by failing to provide a fair and stable business environment. The key actions the Argentine government took were the emergency measures that effectively broke the currency peg of the Argentine Peso to the US dollar after the peg had become unsustainable. Notably, the tribunal did not hold that Argentina expropriated the foreign investor (which had expected the peg to hold and to provide a firm basis for his future returns). Nonetheless, the amount awarded was the equivalent of an expropriation. Argentina is currently seeking annulment of the award.

13 For a list of Bilateral Investment Treaties documenting this trend, see http://www.worldbank.org/icsid/treaties/i-1.htm

14 See, for example, the BIT between Argentina and the United States available at http://www.bilaterals.org/IMG/html/US-AR_BIT.html

15 For evidence in the context of the Asian growth experience, see (ADB 1997).

16 Rule of law in these studies typically refers to the ability of legal systems to settle the transfer of power and major disputes within the constraints of the law. See, for example, (Knack and Keefer 1994). This indicator correlates highly with other perception indices of institutional quality, wherefore some studies employ weighted averages. See, for example, (Kaufmann, Kraay, and Zoido-Lobaton 1999) and (Berkowitz, Pistor, and Richard 2003).

17 Data available at http://www.unctad.org/templates/webflyer.asp?doc id=6967&intItemID=1634&lang=1 (last visited 22 January 2007)

18 A remarkable case in this regard are the two parallel arbitration cases brought by Estée Lauder against the Czech Republic for an alleged expropriation (regulatory taking) of their stake in a Czech TV station. The two arbitration tribunals came to opposite results on the basis of the same facts. Nonetheless, the Czech Republic chose to comply with the ruling of the Stockholm arbitration tribunal, which held it liable for US\$ 353 million. See Luke Eric Peterson, "Czech Republic Hit with Massive Compensation Bill in Investment Treaty Dispute," in Investment Law and Policy Weekly New Bulletin, 21 March 2003 available at http://www. hartford-hwp.com/archives/63/487.html (last visited 22 January 2007)

19 The leading case is Filártiga v. Peña-Irala, 630 F.2d 876 (2d Cir. 1980). This case involved a claim filed by the father and sister of Joel Filártiga, a seventeen-year old Paraguayan kidnapped and tortured to death in Paraguay. The claim was successful, resulting in a US\$ 10.4 million award, which the plaintiffs have been unable to collect. Since the tortfeasor did not have assets in the U.S. and the plaintiffs have been unable to recover in Paraguay.

20 "The district courts shall have original jurisdiction of any civil action by an alien for a tort only if committed in violation of the law of nations or a treaty of the United States." 28 U.S.C. §1350. See (Donovan and Roberts 2006) for a discussion of the ATS role in creating universal jurisdiction for civil law matters.

21 For an excellent summary of the UNOCAL case, compare http:// www.globalpolicy.org/intljustice/atca/2005/09unocal.pdf

22 See supra fn. 1

23 Note, however, that recent studies suggest that the effect of creditor rights protection appears to be more pronounced for foreign banks than for domestic banks, suggesting that rights protection is not universally shared and/or that different players may have different governance mechanisms at their disposal (Haselmann, Pistor, and Vig 2006).

References

ADB. 1997. Emerging Asia, Changes and Challenges. Manila: The Asian
Development Bank.

Arsht, Samuel S. 1976. A History of Delaware Corporation Law. *Delaware Journal of Corporate Law* 1 (1):1–22.

Berkowitz, Daniel, Katharina Pistor, and Jean-Francois Richard. 2003. The Transplant Effect. *American Journal of Comparative Law* 51 (2):163–203.

Bjorklund, Andrea K. 2005. Reconciling State Sovereignty and Investor Protection in Denial of Justice Claims. *Virginia Journal of International Law* 45 (Summer):809–895.

Black, Bernard. 2000. The Core Institutions that Support Strong Securities Markets. *Business Lawyer* 55.

Black, Bernard S. 1990. Is Corporate Law Trivial? A Political and Economic Analysis. *Northwestern University Law Review* 84:542–597.

Cary, William L. 1974. Federalism and Corporate Law: Reflections upon Delaware. *Yale Law Journal* 83:663.

Coffee, John C. Jr. 1988. Shareholders Versus Managers: The Strain in the Corporate Web. In: Knights, Raiders and Targets, The Impact of the Hostile Takeover, edited by J. C. C. Jr., L. Lowenstein and S. R. Ackerman. Oxford: Oxford University Press.

Djankov, Simeon, Caralee McLiesh, and Andrei Shleifer. Decenmber 17, 2004. Private Credit in 129 Countries, unpublished mimeo, available at SSRN: http://ssrn.com/abstract=637301

Dolzer, Rudolf. 2005. The Impact of International Investment Treaties on Domestic Administrative Law.

Donovan, Donald Francis, and Anthea Roberts. 2006. The Emerging Recognition of Universal Civil Jurisdiction. *American Journal of International Law* 100:142–169.

Easterbrook, Frank H. 1997. International Corporate Differences: Markets or Law? *Journal of Applied Corporate Finance* 9 (4):23–29.

Easterbrook, Frank H., and Daniel R. Fischel. 1991. The Economic Structure of Corporate Law. Cambridge, Mass.: Harvard University Press.

Eisenberg, Melvin. 1999. Symposium: Corporate Law and Social Norms. *University of Pennsylvania Law Review*.

Elkins, Zachary, Andrew T. Guzman, and Beth Simmons. 2004. Competing for Capital: The Diffusion of Bilateral Investment Treaties: 1960–2000.

282

Fligstein, Neil. 1990. The Transformation of Corporate Control. Cambridge, Mass: Harvard University Press.

Hansmann, Henry. 1996. The Ownership of Enterprise. Cambridge, MA: The Belknap Press of Harvard University Press.

Hansmann, Henry, and Reinier Kraakman. 2000. The Essential Role of Organizational Law. *Yale Law Journal* 110:387–475.

Hansmann, Henry, and Reinier Kraakman. 2001. The End of History for Corporate Law. *Georgetown Law Journal* 89:439–471.

Haselmann, Rainer, Katharina Pistor, and Vikrant Vig. 2006. How Law **283** Affects Lending. *unpublished mimeo (available on ssrn.com)*.

Heal, Jeffrey. 2004. Corporate Social Responsibility – An Economic and Financial Framework.

Hellmann, Joel, Geraint Jones, and Dani Kaufmann. 2002. Far from Home: Do Foreign Investors Import Higher Standards of Governance in Transition Economies? *http://papers.ssrn.com/sol3/papers. cfm?abstract_id=386900*.

Jensen, Michael C., and William H. Meckling. 1976. Theory of the Firm: Managerial Behavior, Agency Costs and Ownership Structure. *Journal of Financial Economics 3* (October):305–360.

Jensen, Michael C., and William H. Meckling. 1979. Rights and Production Functions: An Application to Labor Managed Firms and Codetermination. *Journal of Business* 52 (4):469–506.

Kaufmann, Daniel, Aart Kraay, and Pablo Zoido-Lobaton. 1999. Aggregating Governance Indicators. Washington D.C.: The World Bank.

Kell, Georg, and David Levin. 2003. The Global Compact Network: An Historic Experiment in Learning and Action. *Business and Society Review* 108:151–181.

Knack, Stephen, and Philip Keefer. 1994. Institutions and Economic Performance: Cross-Country Tests Using Alternative Institutional Measures. *Economics and Politics* 7 (November):207–227.

Koehane, Robert O., Andrew Moravcsik, and Anne-Marie Slaughter. 2000. Legalized Dispute Resolution: Interstate and Transnational. *International Organization* 54 (3):457–488.

La Porta, Rafael, Florencio Lopez-de-Silanes, and Andrei Shleifer. 2006. What Works in Securities Laws? *Journal of Finance* LXI (1):1.

La Porta, Rafael, Florencio Lopez-de-Silanes, Andrei Shleifer, and Robert W. Vishny. 1997. Legal Determinants of External Finance. *Journal of Finance* LII (3):1131–1150.

La Porta, Rafael, Florencio Lopez-de-Silanes, Andrei Shleifer, and Robert
    W. Vishny. 1998. Law and Finance. *Journal of Political Economy*
    106 (6):1113–1155.
La Porta, Raphael, Florencio Lopez-de-Silanes, Andrei Shleifer,
    and Robert Vishny. 2000. Investor Protection and Corporate
    Governance. *Journal of Financial Economics* 58:3–57.
Levine, Ross. 1998. The Legal Environment, Banks, and Long-Run Eco-
    nomic Growth. *Journal of Money, Credit, and Banking* 30 (3):596–613.
Peterson, Luke Eric. 2004. The Global Governance of Foreign Direct   **284**
    Investors: Madly Off in All Directions: Friedrich Ebert Stiftung.
Pistor, Katharina. 1999. Codetermination in Germany: A Socio-Political
    Model with Governance Externalities. In: Employees and Corporate
    Governance, edited by M. Blair and M. Roe. Washington D.C.:
    Brookings Institute:163–193.
Pistor, Katharina, Yoram Keinan, Jan Kleinheisterkamp, and Mark
    West. 2002. The Evolution of Corporate Law. *University of Pennsyl-
    vania Journal of International Economic Law* 23 (4):791–871.
Post, James E., Lee E. Preston, and Sybille Sachs. 2002. Redefining the
    Corporation: Stakeholder Management and Organizational Wealth.
    Stanford: Stanford Business Books.
Romano, Roberta. 1993. The Genius of American Corporate Law.
    Washington D.C.: AEI.
Ruggie, John G. 2004. Reconstituting the Global Public Domain-Issues,
    Actors, and Practices. *European Journal of International Relations*
    10 (4):499–531.
Ruggie, John G. 2007. Business and Human Rights: Mapping Interna-
    tional Standards of Responsibility and Accountability for Corporate
    Acts. New York: United Nations.
Sagafi-Nejad, Tagi. 2005. Should Global Rules have Legal Teeth? Policing
    (WHO Framework Convention on Tobacco Control) vs. Good
    Citizenship (UN Global Compact). *International Journal of Business*
    10 (4):363–383.
Shleifer, Andrei, and Robert W. Vishny. 1997. A Survey of Corporate
    Governance. *The Journal of Finance* LII (2):737–783.
Swenson, Deborah. 2006. Why do Developing Countries Sign BITs?
    U.C. Davis Journal of International Law and Policy 12 (1):131–155.
Tobin, Jennifer, and Susan Rose-Ackerman. 2006. Foreign Direct
    Investment and the Business Environment in Developing Coun-

tries: The Impact of Bilateral Investment Treaties. In: *Yale Law and Economics Research Paper:* Yale Law School.

Winter, Ralph K. 1977. State Law, Shareholder Protection, and the Theory of the Corporation. *Journal of Legal Studies* 6:251–290.

15 Business and Human Rights: Mapping International ...
— *John G. Ruggie*

* Professor John G. Ruggie, the Special Representative of the UN Secretary-General on the issue of human rights and transnational corpora-   **285** tions and other business entreprises, presented this report http://www. ohchr.org/english/bodies/hrcouncil/docs/4session/A-HRC-4-35.doc on his 2-year mandate (2005–7) to the UN Human Rights Council on 28 March 2007.

1   John McMillan, Reinventing the Bazaar: A Natural History of Markets (Norton, 2002).

2   E/CN.4/2006/97, paragraphs 20–30.

3   Those produced by or at the request of the SRSG are posted on his home page on the Business and Human Rights Resource Centre's website at http://www.businesshumanrights. org/Gettingstarted/UNSpecial Representative.

4   The SRSG also received substantive written submissions from a number of organizations, including Allens Arthur Robinson; BankTrack; Business Leaders Initiative on Human Rights; EarthRights International; Global Witness; Halifax Initiative; Interfaith Center on Corporate Responsibility; International Commission of Jurists; International Council on Metals and Mining; International Network for Economic, Social & Cultural Rights; International Organization of Employers, International Chamber of Commerce, and Business and Industry Advisory Committee to the OECD; Lovells; Rights & Democracy, Canada; Tebtebba Foundation & Forest Peoples Programme.

5   Beyond the national territory, the duty's scope will vary depending on the state's degree of control. The UN human rights treaty bodies generally view states parties' obligations as applying to areas within their "power or effective control."

6   States also have duties to respect, promote and fulfill rights, but the most business-relevant is the duty to protect because it focuses on third party abuse. See Addendum 1. Where corporations perform public functions or are state-controlled, the secondary rules of state attribution

may also hold the state responsible for the abuse. See the International Law Commission's articles on "Responsibility of States for Internationally Wrongful Acts," adopted in November 2001. http://daccessdds.un.org/doc/UNDOC/GEN/No1/477/97/PDF/No147797.pdf?OpenElement.

7   Drawing on the language of subparagraph (b) of the mandate, this section uses "regulation" to refer to treaty body language recommending legislative or other measures designed to prevent or monitor abuse by business enterprises, and "adjudication" to refer to judicial or other measures to punish or remediate abuse.

8   HRC, General Comment 31, paragraph 8.

9   Some treaty bodies seem to be encouraging states to pay greater attention to preventing corporate violations abroad. For example, CESCR has suggested that states should take steps to "prevent their own citizens and companies" from violating rights in other countries. General Comment 15, paragraph 33.

10   Under the principle of "universal jurisdiction" states may be obliged to exercise jurisdiction over individuals within their territory who allegedly committed certain international crimes. It is unclear whether and how such obligations extend jurisdiction over juridical persons, including corporations. See Addendum 2.

11   Of course, the entire human rights regime may be seen to challenge the classical view of nonintervention. The debate here hinges on what is considered coercive. See Addendum 2 for details.

12   For an overview, see Andrew Clapham, Human Rights Obligations of Non-State Actors (Oxford: OUP, 2006), chap. 9; on Africa, see Nsongurua Udombana, "Between Promise and Performance: Revisiting States' Obligations under the African Human Rights Charter" (2004) 40 Stanford Journal of International Law 105.

13   See Addendum 3.

14   Perhaps uniquely, Norway manages the global portfolio of its government pension fund in accordance with ethical guidelines, which has led to disinvestments in two major transnational companies, one on human rights grounds. http://odin.dep.no/etikkradet/english/.

15   This section provides partial responses to subparagraphs (a) and (c) of the mandate.

16   International legal responsibility attaches to individuals for a wider range of acts than those covered by the ICC Statute.

17   Rosalyn Higgins, current President of the International Court of

Justice (ICJ), and Theodor Meron, former President of the International Criminal Tribunal for the former Yugoslavia (ICTY), both have used the term "participants." Already in 1949, the ICJ stated: "The subjects of law in any legal system are not necessarily identical in their nature or in the extent of their rights, and their nature depends on the needs of the community." Advisory Opinion on Reparations for Injuries suffered in the service of the United Nation, [1949] ICJ Rep 174 at 179.

18 "Common purpose" applies where an individual participates in a common design involving the perpetration of a crime, and shares an intention to commit the crime. The ICTY has also developed the doctrine of "joint criminal enterprise" which applies where a crime other than the intended one occurs, and where the individual foresaw the risk but continued to participate.

19 Doe v Unocal, 395 F.3d 932 (9th Cir, 2002). The case settled and the decision was vacated.

20 For a detailed survey of 16 countries from a cross-section of regions and legal systems, see Anita Ramasastry and Robert C. Thompson, Commerce, Crime and Conflict: Legal Remedies for Private Sector Liability for Grave Breaches of International Law – Executive Summary (2006) see at: www.fafo.no/liabilities. Of the 16, 11 were states parties to the ICC and 9 had fully incorporated the statute's three crimes; of these, 6 already provided for corporate criminal liability. Research has not been completed on all 104 countries that had ratified the Rome Statute as of November 2006.

21 The Fafo survey cites the examples of Japan, India, the United Sates, Indonesia, and Ukraine. The first three generally apply criminal laws to corporations.

22 Of the 16 countries in the Fafo survey, 11 provide for a nationality link, 5 rely on universal jurisdiction, and several do both; 9 of these provide for some form of corporate criminal liability in their domestic laws.

23 "Note on the work of the ICJ Expert Legal Panel on Corporate Complicity in International Crimes," 22 January 2007 (on file with SRSG).

24 See Australian Criminal Code Act 1995 (Cth), sections 12.3(2)(c) and (d).

25 The 2005 Federal Sentencing Guidelines permit judicial consideration of whether a corporation has an "organizational culture that encourages ethical conduct and a commitment to compliance with the law": §8B2.1(a).

26 See Connelly v RTZ Corporation plc [1998] AC 854, and Lubbe v Cape plc [2000] 4 All ER 268 (House of Lords, UK).

27 The Supreme Court's only decision under ATCA, Sosa v Alvarez-

Machain 542 US 692 (US, 2004), does not preclude such liability for corporations, and the weight of current US judicial opinion appears to support it – although there is disagreement among lower courts over its content and, in some cases, its existence.

28 Prosecutor v Furundžija, Judgment, No IT-95-17/1 (ICTY Trial Chamber, Dec 10, 1998) and Prosecutor v Akayesu, Judgment, No ICTR-96-4-T (ICTR Trial Chamber Sept 2, 1998). It is unknown whether the ICC will adopt this standard.

29 When applying the individual standard to corporations, the Court in Unocal did not adopt the element of "moral support."

30 This section responds to subparagraph (a) of the mandate.

31 For a study of 7 jurisdictions conducted for the SRSG, see Allens Arthur Robinson, Brief on Corporations and Human Rights in the Asia Pacific Region (August 2006), http://www.reports-andmaterials. org/ Legal-brief-on-Asia-Pacific-for-Ruggie-Aug-2006.pdf.

32 For one recent study, see Jennifer A. Zerk, Multinationals and Corporate Social Responsibility (Cambridge University Press, 2006); also see state survey in Addendum 3.

33 Adopted as General Assembly Resolution 217 (III), 10 December 1948.

34 Louis Henkin, "The Universal Declaration at 50 and the Challenge of Global Markets," Brooklyn Journal of International Law, 17 (April 1999), p. 25.

35 Common Article 5(1) of the ICCPR and ICESCR provides that the Covenants should not be interpreted as implying "for any state, group or person any right to engage in any activity or perform any act aimed at the destruction of any of the rights ... recognized herein". But it was not intended to establish substantive legal obligations on individuals or groups, nor have the treaty bodies interpreted it as such. Manfred Nowak, UN Covenant on Civil and Political Rights: CCPR Commentary (2nd rev ed, 2005): 111–119.

36 CESCR, General Comment 18, paragraph 52. For similar remarks see CESCR, General Comments 14 (paragraph 42) and 12 (paragraph 20). See also CRC, General Comment 5, paragraph 56, which says that the state duty to respect "extends in practice" to nonstate organizations.

37 HRC, General Comment 31, paragraph 8.

38 Additionally, UN Security Council panels that assess the effectiveness of sanctions have specifically considered the role of corporations in violations.

39 Juridical Condition and Rights of the Undocumented Migrants, Advisory Opinion OC-18, 17 eptember 2003, paragraph 146, http://www. corteidh.or.cr/docs/opiniones/seriea_18_ing.doc.

40 See Clapham, note 13 above.

41 Some soft law instruments may contain elements that already impose, or may come to impose, obligations on states under customary international law, which would give them binding effect independent of the soft law instrument itself.

42 This section responds to subparagraphs (a) and (e) of the mandate. **289**

43 Tripartite Declaration, para. 8.

44 OECD Guidelines, General Policies II.2. (Revised 2000) The commentary notes the Universal Declaration "and other human rights obligations."

45 Because many of the most serious corporate-related human rights violations take place in what the OECD describes as weak governance zones, the SRSG asked the world's largest representative business organizations to consult their membership and produce recommendations that could help close this governance gap. The International Organization of Employers and the International Chamber of Commerce collaborated with the Business and Industry Advisory Committee to the OECD on a set of proposals, including the following advice to companies that moves beyond the Guidelines' current requirement: "All companies have the same responsibility in weak governance zones as they do elsewhere. They are expected to obey the law, even if it is not enforced, and to respect the principles of relevant international instruments where national law is absent." IOE, ICC, BIAC, "Business and Human Rights: The Role of Business in Weak Governance Zones," December 2006, paragraph 15,available at http://www.business-humanrights.org/Gettingstarted/UNSpecialRepresentative.

46 One area where greater clarity is needed is indigenous peoples' rights. The current lack of consensus on the practical implications of "consent" – in the formula of "free, prior and informed consent" to largescale projects – is a major challenge for indigenous communities, business and governments alike.

47 Fundamental labor rights, the health and safety of surrounding communities, avoidance of involuntary resettlement, the rights of indigenous peoples, and protection of cultural heritage.

48 Although the IFC standards have been criticized for "not going far enough," they exceed the human rights requirements of the so-called Common Approaches among OECD member states' export credit agencies.

49 Critics charge that Equator banks themselves lack transparency in how they implement the principles.

50 For case studies and discussions of advantages and risks of these novel approaches to international regulation, see the symposium on "Global Governance and Global Administrative Law in the International Legal Order," European Journal of International Law, 17 (February 2006).

51 The VPs plenary is going through a difficult period persuading all companies that the credibility of the initiative depends on explicit participation criteria. Even the strictly voluntary Global Compact adopted such criteria; as a result several hundred companies have been "delisted."

290

52 Luka Binniyat, "NIETI Saves Nigeria US$ 1 Billion – Okogwu," Vanguard (Lagos), January 2, 2007.

53 Indications are that Colombia will become the first host country to join the VPs. The government has established a National Committee for the VPs, including companies. The government and companies have incorporated VP language into their agreements for public security forces protecting company operations. Both parties have established reporting systems for alleged abuses. And some companies use VP-related criteria in annual performance reviews of managers.

54 Drawing on the VPs precedent, the Swiss government and the International Committee of the Red Cross are leading an effort to elaborate recommendations and best practices for states with regard to private military and security forces. The pilot phase of The Colombia Guidelines, based on the VPs text, was just launched, aiming to extend the model to such non-extractive sectors as food and beverages.

55 The section responds to subparagraphs (a) and (e) of the mandate.

56 UNCTAD, World Investment Report, 2006, at: www.unctad.org/wir.

57 The FG500 survey is summarized in Addendum 3; the other three studies are reported in Addendum 4. Sampling and other methodological issues are discussed there.

58 Numeric differences in responses between the two samples are partially explained by the FG500 study relying on questionnaire responses, whereas the business recognition study examined actual company policies, but this does not account for order of magnitude differences.

59 See Addendum 4 for details.

60 The difference and its significance are described in a companion report, A/HRC/4/74.

61 Some estimates range as high as 3,000. "Trends in non-financial reporting," Global Public Policy Institute, Berlin, Research Paper Series No. 6, 2006, available at http://gppi.net/fileadmin/gppi/nonfinancial reporting01.pdf. But the trend appears to have levelled off, perhaps reaching a saturation point.

62 The United Kingdom adopted a new company law in November 2006, which will require large listed companies to include, as part of their directors' report, information on environmental matters, employees, social and community issues and "essential" business partners. Information must be provided "to the extent necessary for an understanding of the development, performance and position of the company's business." Section 417(5).

63 As of August 2006, data provided by GRI.

64 Association of Chartered Certified Accountants and CorporateRegister.com, "Toward Transparency: Progress on Global Sustainability Reporting, 2004"; and "KPMG International Survey of Corporate Responsibility Reporting, 2005" (both on file with SRSG).

65 International Auditing and Assurance Standards Board ISAE3000, and AccountAbility AA1000AS.

66 A test of this proposition is currently under way. The Business Social Compliance Initiative, a European network of retailers, industry and importing companies, has formed a strategic alliance with SA8000 and become an "organizational stakeholder" in GRI. That ought to generate credibility benefits. At the same time, the world's four largest supermarket chains, Wal-Mart, Tesco, Carrefour, and Metro are launching their own initiative with no external stakeholder involvement and, to date, no transparency. The proposition would predict difficulties ahead. During a recent US court case against Wal-Mart for alleged labor violations in overseas suppliers' factories, a company attorney stated that its supplier code of conduct "creates certain rights for Wal-Mart. It does not create certain rights and obligations on behalf of Wal-Mart." While the claim may be legally correct, it leaves unanswered the question of just what promises to workers and consumers the company's code is intended to convey, and how the public can be assured that the promise is being kept. (Josh Gerstein, "Novel Legal Challenge to Wal-Mart Appears to be Faltering on Coast," http://www.nysun.com/article/45009).

67 See note 6, above.

68 Iris Marion Young, "Responsibility and Global Labor Justice," Journal of Political Philosophy, 12 (No. 4, 2004).

Authors

Fritz Brugger holds a master's degree in Theology and specialized early in ethics as scientific collaborator at the Institute for Social Ethics of the University of Zurich; he also graduated in Association Management at the university of Fribourg.

Mr. Brugger currently works as consultant with BHP – Brugger and Partners Ltd in the areas of corporate responsibility, sustainable development, and development cooperation. Prior to this, he was an independent consultant and associated Partner of BHP for four years and was in charge of projects in the area of Public-Private Partnership (PPP), sustainable water management, strategy development and communication. His clients came from the public and private sectors as well as from NGOs. From 1996 to 2002, he was with Helvetas, a leading Swiss development NGO. His responsibility covered the domains "Development Policy" and "Communication" and during the last five years he was deputy director. During this assignment, Dr. Brugger specialized in options of collaboration with the private sector and issues of global water resources. Fritz Brugger is also the author of numerous publications and presentations in the fields of corporate responsibility, public-private partnerships, and water management.

Peter Buomberger is Group Head Government and Industry Affairs of Zurich Financial Services. He joined Zurich in October 2004.

Prior to joining Zurich, Dr. Peter Buomberger was the Managing Director of the CCRS Center for Corporate Responsibility and Sustainability, an associated Institute at the University of Zurich from 2003 to 2004. From 1986 to 2002 he was the Group Chief Economist and later Head Group Public Policy and Research at Union Bank of Switzerland (later: UBS AG). His previous professional activities include the position of Financial Counselor at the Embassy of Switzerland in Washington D.C. as well as research positions at the Swiss National Bank.

After studies at the Universities of Basel, Zurich and Berne he completed his academic education with a dissertation in economics in 1978 (Ph.D.). He pursued postdoctoral work as a visiting scholar at the University of Chicago.

Peter Buomberger is active in a number of professional and international organizations in Switzerland. These activities include: member of the Board of the CCRS Center for Corporate Responsibility and Sustainability, University of Zurich, Chairman of the Geneva Initiative Committee (mandate of the Swiss Foreign Minister Micheline Calmy-Rey) and from 1983 to 1998 member of the Swiss National Science Foundation.

Micheline Calmy-Rey, President of the Swiss Confederation, was born in Chermignon in Canton Valais on 8 July 1945. She is married with two children and has a degree in political science from the Graduate Institute of International Studies in Geneva.

For 20 years she ran a book distribution business. In 1979, she joined the Socialist Party of Geneva, which she later served as president for two terms. As a deputy in the Grand Conseil, or cantonal legislature, she took an interest in public finance, and when she became a member of the cantonal government in 1998, she took over as head of the Department of Finance. In four years, she achieved her goal through a thorough restructuring of the Department's services. She also successfully oversaw the restructuring of the Cantonal Bank of Geneva which was burdened by a large volume of non-performing loans.

Micheline Calmy-Rey was elected to the Swiss Federal Council on 4 December 2002 and was appointed as head of the Federal Department of Foreign Affairs (DFA). She pursues an active foreign policy marked by a commitment to promoting peace, respect for international law and human rights, and the fight against poverty. The aim of this policy is to ensure security and well-being for all Swiss citizens.

Carlo Donati, Swiss, born in 1946

Since 2005 Chairman & Chief Executive Officer,
Nestlé Waters, Executive Vice-President, Nestlé SA
2000 Region Head, Nestlé South Asia
1998 Market Head, Nestlé India
1996 Divisional Manager, Nestlé Italy
1993 Regional Assistant/Deputy,
Nestlé Africa – Middle East Zone
1987 Market Head, Nestlé Ivory Coast
1984 Market Head, Nestlé Cameroon
1983 Commercial Director, Nestlé Cameroon
1980 Country Manager, Nestlé Angola
1979 Product Manager, Nestlé Portugal
1976 Product Manager/Assistant to CEO, Nestlé India

Danièle Gosteli Hauser received an M.A. in political and social sciences in 1986 from the University of Lausanne, and a postgraduate degree in development and cooperation in 1987 from the EPFL and the "Institut Technologique d'Art, d'Architecture et d'Urbanisme" in Tunisia. From 1988–1992, she worked in the Population Studies and Labour Surveys Division of the Swiss Federal Statistical Office, where, among other things, she coordinated the development of new models for the population census.

Ms Gosteli Hauser has been working at the Swiss Section of Amnesty International since 1992. From 1992–1998 she was responsible for the coordination of international campaigns and actions. In 1996 she helped Amnesty International to set up the international Business and Economic Relations Network (BERN), which now includes more than 45 national sections. She was a member of the steering committee of the BERN network and has led the working group on economic relations and human rights of the Swiss Section of Amnesty International. Since 1998 she has been responsible for economic relations and human rights at the Swiss section, and has represented the organization at several symposiums and conferences, including the Global Reporting Initia-

tive, the Crans Montana Forum and the World Economic
Forum. She works with other NGOs to promote and
campaign for the integration of human rights within
company policies and in broader economic relations.

Thomas Greminger, Head of the Political Affairs Division IV, Human Security (Peace, Human Rights, Humanitarian Policy) since
2004. Ambassador Thomas Greminger joined the diplomatic service of the Swiss Federal Department of Foreign
Affairs in 1990 after completing his studies in history,
economics and political science at the University of
Zurich (PhD). He started his diplomatic career as an atta-
ché at the Swiss Embassy in Tel Aviv. In 1992 he became
diplomatic adviser for development policy at the Swiss
Agency for Development and Cooperation (SDC). He was
a co-author of the Federal Council's Guidelines North-
South and deputy-head of the division in charge of their
implementation in the SDC. In 1996, he was promoted
to head of the Development Policy and Research Division
of the SDC and Secretary of the Federal Council's Consultative Commission for International Cooperation.
From 1999 to 2001, he was chargé d'affaires of the Swiss
Embassy in Maputo and country-director of Swiss
Development Cooperation in Mozambique. On his return
to headquarters, he became deputy-head of the Political
Affairs Division IV, in charge of the Peace Policy and
Human Security Section.

Mads Holst Jensen is an adviser at the Human Rights & Business Department, Danish Institute for Human Rights. He is a referee of the Business and Society Review, member of the steering committee of the Asian Century Research School, co-editor of The China Newsletter, referee of the Research Council of Norway, and deputy member of the board of the Nordic Association for Chinese Studies (NACS). In addition to CSR and Human Rights & Business in China, the topics of Dr. Mads Holst Jensen's research and publications include social deviance, juvenile delinquency, public security, human rights and legal system reform in China. Mads Holst Jensen graduated from the University of Copenhagen and holds a Ph.D. degree in Modern Chinese Studies from the University of Aarhus.

296

Georg Kell is the Executive Director of the United Nations Global Compact, the world's largest voluntary corporate citizenship initiative with over 3200 business signatories and hundreds of other participating stakeholders from more than 100 countries.

Following assignments as a financial analyst in Africa and Asia, Mr. Kell started his UN career at the UN Conference on Trade and Development (UNCTAD) in Geneva in 1987. In 1990, he joined UNCTAD's New York office, which he headed from 1993 to 1997. In 1997, Mr. Kell became a senior officer in the Executive Office of the UN Secretary-General, responsible for fostering cooperation with the private sector. After the Global Compact was launched in 2000, Mr. Kell was appointed to head the initiative, a position he has held since.

A native of Germany, Mr. Kell holds advanced degrees in economics and engineering from the Technical University of Berlin.

Eberhard von Koerber chairs an international Investment and Asset Management company, Eberhard von Koerber AG, in Zurich, Switzerland. He also chairs a company which develops and holds infrastructure assets in Europe, the Middle East and Africa.

Dr. Eberhard von Koerber is Vice President of the Club of Rome, co-founder and Vice President of the Wittenberg Centre for Global Ethics and Immediate Past Chairman and Member of the Board of the World Scout Foundation. Moreover, Eberhard von Koerber is a member of the Board of Trustees of the Berlin Philharmonic Orchestra. He is member of the Clinton Global Initiative, New York, and Ambassador of the New Social Market Economy Initiative (INSM) in Germany.

Eberhard von Koerber is a member of the International Advisory Board of the Toyota Corporation, Japan, and of the Advisory Board of Hapag Lloyd AG, Hamburg as well as a member of the Board of Körber AG, Hamburg.

From 1988 until 1998 Dr. von Koerber was Vice President of the Group Executive Committee of ABB Ltd., Zurich. Before, he was serving as a member of the Group Management Board of BMW AG in Munich, Germany.

Benjamin K. Leisinger was born in Nairobi, Kenya. After finishing school in Germany, he studied law at the University of Basel, Switzerland. He graduated in December 2003 and started working as an academic assistant to Professor Ingeborg Schwenzer. In 2005, he made an internship at the Secretariat of the ICC's International Court of Arbitration in Paris. In December 2006, he received his doctorate at the University of Basel. Since October 2006, he works as a law clerk at Homburger Rechtsanwälte in Zurich.

Klaus Leisinger leads the Novartis Foundation for Sustainable Development as Chief Executive Officer and President of the Board of Trustees of the Foundation. The Foundation (www.novartisfoundation.com) has consultative status with the Social and Economic Council of the United Nations and is considered to be best practices by many multinational corporations.

In addition to his position at the Novartis Foundation, Klaus Leisinger is Professor of Sociology at the University of Basel where he teaches Business Ethics, Corporate Social Responsibility as well as Human Rights and Business. Klaus Leisinger served as invited lecturer or guest professor at several Swiss and German universities, as well as at the University of Notre Dame, the MIT Sloan School of Management (Cambridge), and at Harvard University. He is a member of the European Academy of Sciences and Arts.

Klaus Leisinger has held several advisory positions in a number of national and international organizations, such as the United Nations Global Compact, the United Nations Development Program (UNDP), the World Bank (CGIAR), the Asian Development Bank as well as the Economic Commission for Latin America (ECLA). Among others, he chairs the Board of Trustees of the German Network Business Ethics. Between September 2005 and December 2006, Klaus Leisinger served as "Special Advisor of the United Nations Secretary-General for the UN Global Compact" for Kofi Annan.

Katharina Pistor is Professor of Law at Columbia Law School, where she teaches Corporations, Lawyering in Multiple Legal Orders, Globalization in Comparative Perspective, and Law and Capitalism. She also serves as a member of the Committee on Global Thought at Columbia University. Pistor previously taught at the Kennedy School of Government and has held research positions at the Max Planck Institute for Comparative and International

Private Law in Hamburg and at the Harvard Institute
for International Development in Cambridge, MA.
Her research focuses on comparative law and institutional development with special emphasis on corporate
governance and financial market development. She has
conducted several studies on the legal framework for
the evolving corporate governance regime in transition
economies, including field research of privatized firms
and financial intermediaries in Russia. Pistor has
published widely on comparative legal developments.
Her book co-authored with Curtis Milhaupt "Law and
Capitalism: What Corporate Crises Reveal about Legal
Systems and Economic Development Around the World"
is forthcoming at Chicago University Press (2008).

Marc Probst studied economics and international relations both at the
University of St. Gallen (HSG) and the Chinese University
of Hong Kong (CUHK). He has been with the Political
Affairs Division IV (PD IV) of the Federal Department of
Foreign Affairs (DFA) since 2004, and is responsible for
human security and business (human rights and business, conflict and business).

John G. Ruggie is the Evron and Jeane Kirkpatrick Professor of International Affairs and Frank and Denie Weil Director
of the Sharmin and Bijan Mossavar Rahmani Center for
Business and Government. From 1997 to 2001 he was
Assistant Secretary-General and Chief Advisor for strategic planning to United Nations Secretary-General Kofi
Annan. He has been Dean of Columbia University's
School of International and Public Affairs, where he
taught for many years; he has also taught at the University of California's (UC) Berkeley and San Diego campuses
and directed the UC system-wide Institute on Global
Conflict and Cooperation. A fellow of the American Acad-
emy of Arts and Sciences, Ruggie is a recipient of the
International Studies Association's Distinguished Scholar
Award and the American Political Science Association's

Hubert H. Humphrey Award for outstanding public service by a political scientist. Ruggie has a BA in politics and history from McMaster University in Canada; a PhD in political science from the University of California, Berkeley; and a Doctor of Laws (honoris causa) from McMaster.

Ingeborg Schwenzer, Prof. Dr. iur., LL.M., studied law at the universities of Tübingen (Germany), Geneva (Switzerland), Freiburg (Germany) and U.C. Berkeley (United States). Since 1987 **300** she is a law professor, first in Mainz (Germany) and since 1989 in Basel (Switzerland). Among others she is specializing in international sales law. Numerous books and articles on contracts, torts, commercial law, comparative law and arbitration, for example Commentary on the International Sale of Goods (Oxford 2005), International Sales Law (London/New York 2007).

Philippe Spicher started his career in the SRI field in 1994 when he joined Centre Info as an ESG (Environmental, Social, Governance) Analyst. As Head of Research (1996–1999), he set up a formal system to assess corporate environmental and social performance and developed the relationships with international partner organizations. In 1999 he was appointed CEO of Centre Info SA and successfully developed the company by introducing new products and services and expanding the client base. He has been instrumental in the foundation of SiRi Group in 2000, a coalition of leading local SRI Rating agencies. Following the transformation of SiRi Group into a limited company (SiRi Company Ltd.), Centre Info SA (Switzerland) acquired a controlling stake (40%) in the new entity and Philippe Spicher has been appointed as Chairman of SiRi Company Ltd.

He holds a degree in economics from the School of HEC (University of Lausanne, Switzerland) and a master degree in environmental management from the Fondation Universitaire Luxembourgeoise (Belgium)

and the Swiss Federal Institute of Technology in
Lausanne.

Thomas Streiff joined BHP – Brugger and Partners Ltd. in August 2004.
His fields of expertise at BHP cover the strategic con-
sulting and coaching of multinational companies in shaping and integrating the principles of corporate responsibility. He advises clients of the public and private
sectors in implementing value reporting and in planning, **301**
managing and documenting complex multi-stakeholder
processes. He is program manager of The Sustainability
Forum Zurich, an internationally well-reputed organization that offers business leaders a platform to exchange
ideas and experiences with respect to sustainable
business models.

Prior to that, in the position of a senior manager,
he headed the Group Sustainability Management unit of
Swiss Re, a world wide leading reinsurance company
(1997–2004). From 1994–95 he was risk manager with the
same company. In total, Dr. Thomas Streiff was working
for five years for Swiss development and cooperation
agencies as technical advisor and project coordinator in
Kenya, Tanzania and India. During his assignment
as research assistant at the Institute of Food Science and
Nutrition of ETH Zurich, where he got his doctorate in
1989, he was teacher at a technical high school and
later lecturer at the Postgraduate Course for Developing
Countries.

Salil Tripathi is the senior policy adviser at International Alert,
a London-based conflict transformation organization,
where he works on business, economy, and conflict.
His current projects include piloting Alert's Conflict-Sensitive Business Practice: Guidance for the Extractive
Sector. Salil represents Alert on the steering committee of
the Voluntary Principles for Security and Human Rights,
and is part of the human rights working group at the

Global Compact. He is also on the International Advisory Network of the Business and Human Rights Resource Centre in London, as well as an advisor to the corporate complicity project at the International Commission of Jurists in Geneva.

From 1999 to early 2006, Salil was researcher, economic relations and human rights, at the international secretariat of Amnesty International. There, he helped develop Amnesty's work on business and human rights, **302** including engagement with the World Economic Forum, the Global Compact, the Voluntary Principles, and the Kimberley Process. He also co-wrote reports on Nigeria, Bosnia-Herzegovina, and Sudan, and prepared booklets on doing business in Saudi Arabia and the Russian Federation.

From 1990 to 1999 he was a foreign correspondent based in Singapore, from where he reported on business, economic and political developments in Southeast Asia, for the Far Eastern Economic Review, and he has written for the Wall Street Journal, the International Herald Tribune, the Guardian, the New Statesman, and the Independent, among others. Salil graduated with a Master's in Business Administration at Dartmouth College in the United States, and a Bachelor of Commerce from the University of Bombay in India.

www.ingramcontent.com/pod-product-compliance
Lightning Source LLC
Chambersburg PA
CBHW021945220326
41599CB00012BA/1182